Government
and Agriculture
in Zimbabwe

Government
and Agriculture
in Zimbabwe

William A. Masters

PRAEGER

Westport, Connecticut
London

Library of Congress Cataloging-in-Publication Data

Masters, William A.
    Government and agriculture in Zimbabwe / William A. Masters.
      p. cm.
    Includes bibliographical references and index.
    ISBN 0–275–94755–6 (alk. paper)
      1. Agriculture and state—Zimbabwe.   I. Title.
    HD2131.Z8M37   1994
    338.1′86891—dc20   93–38884

British Library Cataloguing in Publication Data is available.

Library of Congress Catalog Card Number: 93–38884
ISBN: 0–275–94755–6

First published in 1994

Praeger Publishers, 88 Post Road West, Westport, CT 06881
An imprint of Greenwood Publishing Group, Inc.

Printed in the United States of America

The paper used in this book complies with the
Permanent Paper Standard issued by the National
Information Standards Organization (Z39.48–1984).

10 9 8 7 6 5 4 3 2 1

Contents

Illustrations

TABLES

APPENDIX TABLES

APPENDIX MAPS

Acknowledgments

The research behind this book began in 1986; since that time I have benefited from the kind assistance of many people. For their early interest and support I would particularly like to thank Tobias Takavarasha of the Ministry of Lands, Agriculture and Water Development, Kay Muir-Leresche of the University of Zimbabwe, and Scott Pearson of Stanford University. They bear no responsibility for my conclusions, but I am grateful for their suggestions and inspiration at the outset of my research.

During 1988-1990, my work in Zimbabwe was hosted by the Department of Agricultural Economics and Extension of the University of Zimbabwe. I am grateful to Mandi Rukuni, Dean of the Faculty of Agriculture, and Godfrey Mudimu, Chairman of the Department of Agricultural Economics and Extension, for their generous assistance. The entire staff of the department were stimulating and supportive colleagues, and I am thankful for their help.

Fieldwork was carried out in collaboration with the Economics and Markets Branch, Ministry of Lands, Agriculture and Rural Resettlement, made possible by Tobias Takavarasha. Assistance was also received from Gordon Sithole, Andrew Rukovo, Ted Attwood, Nancy Gonese, Ephias Makaudze, Lovemore Mafurirano, Gladys Mutangadura, Tafirei Chamboko and many others. Special thanks are due to the ministry enumerators, particularly Lucky Maposa, Godfrey Msoveregwa and Jonathan Kurira, who served as superb hosts and interpreters in their survey areas, and to the 414 communal-area farm families who patiently responded to the survey throughout the 1988–1989 farming season.

The kind cooperation of many public and private sector officials is gratefully acknowledged. I received help particularly at Agritex, the Agricultural Marketing Authority (AMA), the Central Statistical Office (CSO), the Department of Research and Specialist Services (DR&SS), the Grain Marketing Board (GMB), and the Reserve Bank and in the private sector from the National Farmers Association of Zimbabwe (NFAZ), the Commercial Farmers Union

(CFU), and numerous input suppliers, agricultural consultancies, and transport companies.

Financial support for this research was received from the Rockefeller Foundation, a Fulbright Dissertation Research Grant, and a Stanford University Graduate Fellowship. I am particularly grateful to Malcolm Blackie of the Rockefeller Foundation, whose guidance and support made possible an extension of my work with the Ministry of Lands. I would also like to thank Bob Christiansen, Chris Delgado, Alex Duncan, Carl Eicher, Thom Jayne, Ulrich Koester, Edward Mazhangara, John Mellor, Ernst-August Nuppenau, David Rohrbach, and Alberto Valdes for assistance along the way, as well as Anthony Mwanaumo and the participants in Purdue's graduate seminar on Development in Africa for comments on the manuscript, and Jeri McIntyre and Tana Taylor for assistance in typesetting.

As always, my greatest debts are to Mia Lewis. This book is dedicated to her and to our children, Zoe and Beatrice.

Abbreviations

AMA	Agricultural Marketing Authority
CA	Communal Area
CFU	Commercial Farmers Union
CMB	Cotton Marketing Board
CSO	Central Statistical Office
DRC	Domestic Resource Cost
ESAP	Economic Structural Adjustment Program
FAO	Food and Agriculture Organization
GMB	Grain Marketing Board
GOZ	Government of Zimbabwe
LSC	Large-Scale Commercial
MCB	Maize Control Board
MLARR	Ministry of Lands, Agriculture and Rural Resettlement
MLAWD	Ministry of Lands, Agriculture and Water Development
PAM	Policy Analysis Matrix

PPP	Purchasing Power Parity
RA	Resettlement Area
RER	Real Exchange Rate
SSC	Small-Scale Commercial
UDI	Unilateral Declaration of Indepedence

Government
and Agriculture
in Zimbabwe

Introduction

Agriculture is the heart of the Zimbabwean economy. Farming employs over two-thirds of the workforce, and farm products account for about half of exports. Yet farmers receive under a sixth of the national income. Incomes are particularly low for the majority of smallholder farmers—indeed the majority of Zimbabweans—who live in relatively dry, low-productivity areas.

Why are smallholder farmers so poor? The analysis presented in this book finds that much of the value of what they produce is transferred to better-off groups through government intervention. Such transfers worsen income distribution and also dissuade farmers from taking full advantage of their production opportunities and investing in their farms to raise productivity. Fundamental reforms could thus improve both equity (by helping poorer farmers) and growth (by increasing national production).

This book focuses on Zimbabwe's most widely grown field crops: five grains (maize [corn], wheat, sorghum, and pearl and finger millet), three oilseeds (groundnuts [peanuts], soybeans, and sunflower), plus cotton (which produces both fiber and an oilseed). These nine crops form the core of the country's agricultural sector. They are produced over a wide geographical area using a variety of techniques and are consumed or exported for a wide variety of uses. Except for wheat, which is grown under irrigation in the winter, most farmers can shift among these crops relatively quickly. Numerous other crops and livestock are also important components of the agricultural sector, but they are more specialized products that will be discussed only briefly.

Land for crop production is segmented into legally separate land tenure areas, with very different farm sizes and agricultural techniques. The analysis focuses on the three largest groups of farmers: low-potential communal areas (CAs), high-potential CAs, and large-scale commercial (LSC) producers. There is considerable diversity within each group, but these three categories capture the main dimensions of variability in Zimbabwe's farming and marketing systems. Each of the three major systems is described at length, and selected data are given for two smaller land tenure categories, the resettlement areas (RAs) and small-scale commercial (SSC) areas.

Data for this study have been compiled from numerous published and unpublished sources. Information on smallholder farming comes primarily from the Communal Areas Farm Survey of the Ministry of Lands, Agriculture and Rural Resettlement (MLARR), supplemented by numerous other surveys and information from the extension and research services. For large-scale systems, data have been provided by the Commercial Farmers Union, private farm management consulting services, and input suppliers. At the national level, extensive use has been made of information from the Grain Marketing Board, Cotton Marketing Board, Central Statistical Office, and Reserve Bank. As in all empirical work, each individual data series may be subject to considerable error. But cross-referencing across multiple sources has produced one of the most accurate and consistent sets of data available on this topic.

The analysis presented in this book focuses on the 1980s, and the Policy Analysis Matrix results in Part IV focus on the 1989 harvest year. But as a Shona proverb warns, "The same year can never come again."[1] For many issues a longer-term perspective is needed. Historical data are presented wherever possible, and the origins of Zimbabwe's agricultural technology and institutions are highlighted throughout the book.

GOVERNMENT POLICY AND AGRICULTURE: AN HISTORICAL PERSPECTIVE

The study identifies three principal areas of opportunity for the promotion of equitable growth. In Part I, it is found that economy-wide constraints influenced by trade and exchange rate policy put strong pressure against agriculture, transferring income from farmers to other groups. In Part II, constraints on resource use influenced by land tenure policy are found to penalize farmers in communal areas and assist farmers in large-scale commercial areas. And in Part III, constraints influenced by the marketing system are found to transfer incomes from more remote, resource-poor farmers to better-endowed farmers nearer market centers. Taken together, the economy-wide, sectoral and marketing constraints sharply reduce real incomes for the majority of Zimbabweans, who are smallholder farmers in remote, low-rainfall areas.

The policy changes required to address these constraints would reverse long-standing traditions in the country. None of the key policies identified in this study originated after 1980. The trade restrictions originated in the mid-1960s, while discrimination within agriculture originated with white settlement in the 1890s. But after the achievement of majority rule these policies were not targeted for reform, and they continued to undermine the popularly elected government's efforts to achieve its social and economic goals. The evolution of each individual policy is detailed later in the study, but it may be helpful to begin with a general perspective on government policy towards the agricultural sector.[2]

Before independence in 1980, support for whites—if necessary at the expense of blacks—was the explicit foundation of government. Minority power was firmly established in the first quarter of this century, when all of Rhodesia was administered by a private, profit-oriented monopoly: the British South Africa Company (BSAC). The BSAC was the first central government to gain control over all of what is now Zimbabwe, with help from its private army, the British South Africa Police (BSAP), as well as British Imperial forces. The BSAC alienated much of the country's land to its soldiers and to other white settlers, demarcating some other areas as "native reserves." Company rule lasted from 1890 to 1923, with only limited oversight from Great Britain and from a Legislative Council elected by a highly restricted voters roll.

Between 1923 and 1965, when Rhodesia was a self-governing colony of Britain, the colony's governments became somewhat more representative of the white population. Since the hoped-for mining potential of the region had failed to materialize, agriculture was the country's dominant enterprise and principal export earner. White settler farmers controlled much of this key sector and enjoyed a correspondingly dominant political importance. Throughout this period government appears to have been largely of, by, and for settler farmers. Settler farmers were a large proportion of the white electorate and were well organized both inside of government and in the private sector.

After World War II, immigration increased Rhodesia's white urban population, weakening farmers' relative political influence. This shift may have contributed to the government's willingness, in 1965, to make a Unilateral Declaration of Independence (UDI) from Britain. The move provoked trade sanctions, forcing import substitution into nonagricultural activities at the expense of farm export earnings. A further closing-off of trade was self-inflicted; the Rhodesian government itself imposed strict foreign exchange controls in an attempt to block capital flight and provide more political control over the economy. After an initial two years of real income decline, the UDI "hot-house" regime yielded a decade of rapid urban growth in which the Rhodesian government appeared to be holding the world—as well as their own African population—at bay. But this situation was not sustainable. During the late 1970s a rapid decline in real income erased all the early gains, because of the escalating guerilla war as well as the increasing inefficiency and corruption that is a common feature of import-substitution regimes. Eventually the Rhodesian government surrendered power, in exchange for British-guaranteed military, financial, and legal protections under the Lancaster House Agreement of 1979.

The economic objectives of the country's first popularly elected government were set out in *Growth with Equity* (GOZ 1981). This document combined the languages of militant socialism and economic efficiency, opening with: "The

Government is determined to pursue and implement policies based on socialist, egalitarian and democratic principles in conditions of rapid economic growth, full employment, price stability, dynamic efficiency in resource allocation and an equitable distribution of the resulting benefits" (p. 1). A similarly optimistic tone was maintained in the subsequent National Development Plans (GOZ 1982, 1986a).

The hope that state control could be used to improve both equity and efficiency remained a constant theme of policy-making throughout the 1980s. After opening the voters' rolls to all citizens and ending other forms of overt racial segregation, the government took measures to strengthen womens' legal rights, expand health services, and make other profound changes. But in many cases, the new regime simply opened the doors of the old regime's house, without changing its colonial structure. For example, primary and secondary schooling was quickly extended throughout the country, but the academically oriented British "O" and "A" level examination system was maintained. Similarly, more and better-quality housing was built for urban workers, but these were still in isolated dormitory townships far from the city center and work sites.

Major changes were also made in economic policy. The government imposed a high minimum wage, offered high farm prices, expanded the civil service, and borrowed foreign currency to pay for imports. These and other factors, including two years of exceptionally good rains, contributed to rapid catch-up growth in 1980 and 1981. But foreign borrowing could not be sustained, and rapidly growing domestic demand caused the foreign exchange shortage to worsen. Private investment failed to materialize, and bottlenecks in the economy led to sluggish, stop-go growth. After the independence boom, there was a deep recession in 1982–1984, recovery in 1985, recession in 1986–1987, and recovery again in 1988–1990. These cycles were triggered primarily by rainfall levels, with good agricultural years raising domestic demand, inflationary pressure, and demand for imports. But production bottlenecks made it impossible to sustain that growth, with particularly severe effects on nonfarm employment levels: virtually no new jobs were created, and open unemployment grew rapidly.

In 1989 and 1990, the government began to implement a series of fundamental economic reforms. The initial objective was trade liberalization, but this was not accompanied by sufficient exchange rate devaluation or reduction in inflationary pressures and therefore resulted in a surge of imports and little growth in exports or employments. In 1991, with the support of World Bank and IMF loans, a standard "economic structural adjustment program" (ESAP) was announced, combining liberalization with devaluation and reduction in government spending to combat inflation. A major (40%) devaluation and various export promotion schemes were implemented to initiate the program, but as of the time of writing it is still not clear whether there will be enough reduction in the government deficit and inflationary pressures to make the reforms successful.

The slow pace of public sector reform under ESAP is partly due to the effects of a calamitous two-year drought that hit the 1991 and 1992 harvests and led to massive imports in 1992 and 1993. The high cost of imported maize was then magnified by government subsidies to maintain real retail prices at pre-drought levels. The resulting government deficits make it likely that inflationary pressure will continue to negate the effects of devaluation and limit economic growth. Without a rapid and sustained recovery from the drought, there will be continued popular skepticism about the value of reform: It is widely felt that ESAP stands for "Extended Suffering of the African People," "Endless Starvation And Poverty," and similar expressions of popular frustration. The public's distrust of reform makes the direction of future policy change not yet clear. But whatever the outcome of ESAP in the 1990s, the fundamental issues at the core of the study are likely to remain topics of lively debate in Zimbabwe and elsewhere for many years to come.

STRUCTURE OF THE PRESENTATION

The book is divided into four main parts. Part I evaluates the impact on farmers of the government's economy-wide policies, focusing particularly on employment regulations and restrictions on international trade. Part II looks within the agricultural sector, at how policies towards land, credit, and other inputs affect different types of farmers. Part III examines markets for the main agricultural products, to show how prices and marketing arrangements are sometimes favorable to but often undermine farm production. Part IV integrates the analyses presented in Parts I, II, and III through the Policy Analysis Matrix (PAM), in which the combined impact of economy-wide, sectoral, and commodity-specific policies can be assessed at the farm level. Some conclusions are then summarized in a brief final chapter.

It is intended that each section of the book potentially stand alone, for readers interested only in those specific topics. But the material, proceeding from the general to the more specific, is cumulative. Many of the economy-wide and sectoral issues discussed in Parts I and II arise again in their influence on individual markets discussed in Part III and the PAM results of Part IV. Taken as a whole, the book is intended to survey the most important ways in which government policy affects agricultural performance. Not all topics are addressed, but it is hoped that the book captures at least some of the rich complexity of Zimbabwean agriculture and agricultural policy.

The book focuses entirely on Zimbabwe and is primarily intended to contribute toward a better understanding of the Zimbabwean situation. But Zimbabwe is not alone in its agricultural policy dilemmas. The country's experience has important implications elsewhere as well, particularly in places that share some of Zimbabwe's unique history, institutions, physical environment, and economic conditions—most notably South Africa, Zambia, Botswana, Malawi, and Kenya but also elsewhere in Africa, Asia, and Latin America. Some general features of Zimbabwe's experience may also be of universal relevance, wherever farmers seek opportunities for faster and more equitable agricultural growth.

NOTES

1. *Gore harizi rakaze rimwe,* cited in Beach (1984), p. 39.

2. This section is a synthesis of many sources on the economic history of Zimbabwean agriculture and agricultural policy, including Johnson (1964), Yudelman (1964), Dunlop (1971), Weinmann (1973, 1975), Weinrich (1975), Mosley (1983), Hodder-Williams (1983), and Moyana (1984). A chronology of selected legislative and political events drawn from these sources is provided in the appendix.

Part I

Economy-wide Conditions and Policies

In the 1980s the Zimbabwean economy was characterized by increasing unemployment and a worsening scarcity of foreign exchange. Vehicles stood idle for want of essential spare parts or tires, and many consumer goods were periodically unavailable. Such shortages imply missed opportunities and divergences between market prices and economic values that could be sustained only by extensive government intervention. These interventions weighed heavily against agriculture.

This chapter analyzes the effects of intervention in the use of three economy-wide resources: labor, foreign exchange, and capital. In each case, availability is restricted by rules that block resource mobility, typically preventing smallholder farmers from taking advantage of opportunities elsewhere in the economy and reducing their contribution to national productivity growth. Employment opportunities have been restricted by conditions in the formal labor market, international trade opportunities have been restricted by exchange rate policy, and credit opportunities have been restricted by government borrowing and interest rate policy. These restrictions constrain the entire economy, with particularly adverse effects for agriculture.

EMPLOYMENT AND WAGES

The economy's most fundamental resource is its people. Wages in formal employment account for about 60 percent of measured national income (CSO 1989), but as shown in Table I.1, under a third of all workers have a formal job. Over two-thirds are unemployed, work informally, or are smallholder farmers in communal areas.[1]

Table I.1
Labor Force Participation and Employment, 1989

	Number (millions)	Percentage of:	
		Population	Labor Force
Total Population	9.12	100	
Estimated labor force	3.35	37	100
Informal employment			
Miscellaneous & unemployed	1.20	14	37
Communal farmers	1.13	12	33
Formal employment			
Non-agricultural	0.80	9	24
Agricultural	0.20	2	6

Source: Author's calculations, from data in CSO (1989).

The small number of formal jobs forces many communal-area farmers and children of farmers to choose between informal work, such as petty trading or craft industries, and staying on the farm. Urban unemployment, which in practice typically means dependence on working relatives or friends, may be increasingly common—but inevitably the absence of nonfarm jobs raises the number of farmers. This reduces the amount of land and other resources available per farm and thereby reduces farmers' income and productivity. Improved farming techniques and more favorable agricultural policies can certainly improve farmers' welfare, but in the long run the single most important determinant of farm incomes may be farmers' off-farm opportunities. Thus, our study begins here.

Wages and Employment in the Formal Sector

Opportunities to find off-farm work are adversely affected by a number of government policies.[2] Some of these restrict employment directly, while others promote the use of machinery instead of workers. Direct policy constraints on employment began well before independence, when harsh rules were applied to African employees to reduce their options and keep wages low.[3] After independence, an opposite set of restrictions were imposed on employers, to force them into raising wages. Before 1980 the restrictions benefited employers, while afterwards they benefited employees—but both sets had the effect of reducing total employment, which penalized all except those fortunate enough to enjoy formal-sector employment.

The twin pillars of 1980s labor policy were minimum wages and strict antidismissal rules.[4] The antidismissal rules, requiring formal permission from the Minister of Labor for any retrenchment, were important in helping government to enforce the minimum wage. But they also had a force of their own, discouraging new hirings by making most employees permanent irrespective of their productivity. Since very few dismissals were approved, voluntary retrenchment became common, in exchange for payments of several months' wages (World Bank 1987). In 1988, employers cited this requirement as a more significant constraint on new hirings than the minimum wage (Hawkins et al. 1988).

Policies that encourage substitution of machinery and other inputs for labor include both low interest rates (which reduces the cost of capital, including seasonal loans) and real exchange rate appreciation (which reduces the purchase cost of imported machinery and inputs relative to labor). In LSC farming, for example, these two effects combine to provide a significant subsidy on the use of machinery, chemicals, and fertilizers in substitution for labor, as detailed in Part IV of this book. Similar substitutions have occurred in the nonfarm sector; for example, Zimbabwe has an extremely capital-intensive textile industry, with some of the most technically advanced equipment in the world.

The effects of government policies on real wages an employment in the formal sector can be seen in Figure I.1. The farm jobs shown are almost entirely in the LSC sector and apply only to permanent employees. Many daily or piecework employees are not included here, and any wage labor in the smallholder sector is also unrecorded.

The formal (LSC) farm sector had already seen five years of decline in employment by 1980, but the minimum wage rules—along with other changes such as the government's acquisition of some farms for resettlement—seem to have accelerated that decline dramatically. Employment in the nonfarm sector rose along with average wages in the first three years of independence, under the influence of increased demand for nonfarm products. As a result, there was a sharp fall in the proportion of formal employment on farms: this ratio peaked at over 40 percent in 1964, fell to a level of around 35 percent in the 1970s, and then dropped sharply to around 26 percent in the 1980s.

Between 1954 and 1980, real wages in the nonfarm sector rose steadily, but real LSC farm wages were virtually unchanged. The divergence between them is evidence of an almost complete segregation of the two labor markets. The isolation of farmworkers is due in part to their history of state-sponsored recruitment from very low-income areas in neighboring Malawi and Mozambique. Immigration slowed in the 1970s, but even today LSC farmworkers enjoy almost no mobility within Zimbabwe and their wages bear little relation to wages elsewhere. Most farmworkers have no rural home with

Figure I.1
Employment and Real Wages in the Formal Sector, 1954–1985

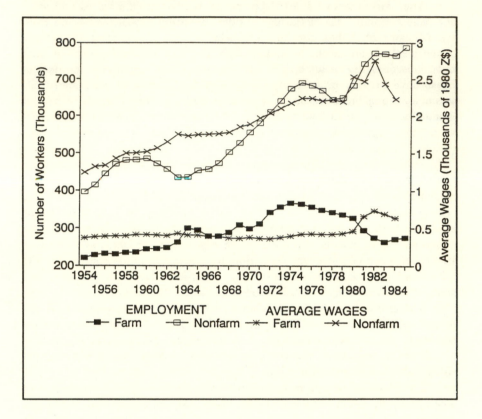

Source: Author's calculations from data in CSO, *Quarterly Digest of Statistics* (various years).

farming rights, as do most other black Zimbabweans, and would probably find it difficult even to move from one LSC farm to another. Their mobility off the farm is also restricted by their relative lack of education, which is limited to whatever the farm-owner chooses to provide.[5]

    After 1980, minimum wages and antidismissal rules helped raise average real farm wages by almost 60 percent over two years. Nonfarm wages rose sharply as well (26 percent over three years) but then fell back to below trend levels as inflation outpaced statutory wage increases. Farm wages also fell back somewhat, but in 1984, the last year of available data, they were still well above historical levels. Some of this increase could be false reporting of wages, and some could be a monetization of benefits previously given in kind. In any case, despite these increases LSC farmworkers remain among the poorest people in Zimbabwe, with among the worst health and nutritional status (Mason 1990).

Overall, national-average real wages were raised well above their historical trends after independence, but by the mid-1980s faster inflation had reduced real wages back to trend levels. Thus the high-wage policy of the early 1980s seeems not to have brought lasting benefits to employed workers, while it does seem to have reduced employment opportunities for others. Those deprived of access to formal jobs were forced to work in the informal sector and as communal farmers, so the policy actually lowered wages for those activities in which a majority of Zimbabweans are employed.

Returns to Labor and Employment in the Informal and Communal-farming Sector

Most workers not in a formal wage-paying job are self-employed farmers in the communal areas. Estimates of what typical workers can earn by sharing in their own family's communal-area farm are presented in the budgets for CA farming in Part IV, with details on labor allocations and returns. These data show average 1989 earnings of about Z$0.32/hr among family workers and about Z$0.35/hr for the relatively fewer hired workers.[6] This was about half the average wage for full-time LSC farmworkers, although differences in nonwage conditions make it difficult to compare the two types of employment.

Opportunities for informal employment outside of the family farm are relatively limited in Zimbabwe. There is a small urban informal sector, but the enforcement of land-use planning rules limits its growth.[7] In rural areas there is some nonfarm employment (Helmsing 1987), but as in much of Africa this appears to be less than Asian and Latin American levels of rural nonfarm work (Haggblade, Hazell, and Brown 1987). There are some landless farmworkers in the communal areas, and it is sometimes said that their number is increasing. But they are relatively few, at least compared to the number of landless rural workers in Asia or Latin America.

The amount of wage labor on communal area farms is limited partly because of low population densities, but probably also because land access in the communal sector is relatively uniform, in comparison with the distribution of cattle and equipment.[8] Thus there is much more active trade in plowing services, to match cattle and plows with land and labor, than there is supply or demand for wage workers since labor and land are already well matched. Also, some of the functions of wage labor are being filled by labor sharing arrangements among farmers, primarily in the form of work parties (*nhimbe*) motivated by beer and sometimes food. These are typically reciprocal, aimed at reducing the loneliness of field work and compressing the duration of field operations. Work parties can provide some net labor flows between households, but normally almost all agricultural labor in the CAs is self-employed. In this context farmers' welfare is largely determined by whole-farm profits.

Population Growth and Structural Transformation

Population growth brings a steady reduction in the land available to each farmer; unless agricultural productivity rises, the only alternative to a steady decline in real farm incomes and in economy-wide real wages is an increase in nonfarm employment: the "structural transformation" of the economy, from relatively low-wage agriculture to employment in higher-wage urban industry and services. Zimbabwe's nonagricultural sector is already substantial, earning about 85 percent of national income (CSO 1990). But there has been little structural transformation in terms of employment, as nonagriculture employs barely a quarter of workers (Table I.1).

The links between population growth and structural transformation begin with the location of the workforce. This should more or less reflect the employment patterns shown in Table I.1, but since employment shown in that table is self-declared, the actual farm labor force is probably understated. Looking at actual population by location, as in Table I.2, gives a more accurate view and also allows for the breakdown of the farm sector into its four subsectors.

Population growth causes the workforce to expand continuously, but this occurs at different rates for different groups of workers. To bring the figures in

Table I.2
Population Location at 1982 Census

	Number (millions)	Percentage of:	
		Total Population	Rural Population
Total Population	7.55	100	
Urban Areas (>2500 persons)	1.94	26	
Rural Areas	5.60	74	100
Communal areas (CAs)	4.23	56	76
LSC farming areas	1.07	14	19
SSC farming areas	0.18	2	3
Resettlement areas (RAs)	0.13	2	2

Source: Author's calculations, from data in CSO (1984).

Table I.2 up to 1989, a rough guess would begin with the intercensus (1969–1982) growth rates for each category. These growth rates were 5.7 percent for urban areas and 3.0 percent for communal areas. Applying these rates puts the 1989 urban population at 2.86 million and the 1989 communal-area population at 5.21 million.[9] In this period the resettlement areas probably absorbed no more than 150,000 communal residents, while the urban areas absorbed perhaps four times that many people.[10] The population in another land tenure area, the small-scale commercial (SSC) farms, was little changed. It is likely, therefore, that during the 1980s neither resettlement nor urbanization could keep pace with communal-area population growth; about half of the natural increase in the communal area population remained within the communal areas. This change over time lowers labor productivity and real wages, in agriculture and throughout the economy.

Growth in formal or nonfarm employment can partially offset growth in the total labor force. But since the absolute size of formal or nonfarm employment is relatively small, it would need to grow at an impossibly fast rate to absorb all of the new workers entering the labor force. This can most easily be seen mathematically. Separating the total number of workers (L_t) into agricultural workers (L_a) and those in nonfarm employment (L_n), the percentage rate of growth in the farm labor force ($\% \Delta L_a$) is determined by the following identity (Johnston and Kilby 1975):[11]

$$\% \Delta L_a \equiv \% \Delta L_t / (L_a / L_t) - \% \Delta L_n / (L_a / L_n)$$

This simple but powerful "arithmetic of structural transformation" implies that the number of communal area farmers will continue to rise despite the creation of new jobs elsewhere. Before 1975, as growth in formal jobs was faster than population growth, communal area farming declined as a proportion of total employment. Thus even though the number of communal area farmers continued to increase, the structural transformation from agriculture to industry was gradually progressing. But since 1975, formal employment has grown more slowly than population, and communal area farming has increased as a proportion of the labor force. In terms of employment—from the job-seekers' point of view—the country has been deindustrializing for over fifteen years, even as increasing numbers of farm children have been educated into the expectation of nonfarm employment. The share of the population in formal employment peaked at over 17 percent in 1975 and stood at about 11 percent in 1989 (for details see Hawkins et al. 1988).

Two scenarios of future change are illustrated in Figure I.3, based on 1982 census data. In the current-trend case, nonfarm jobs grow at the 1980–1985 level of 2.3 percent annually; in the optimistic case, nonfarm jobs grow at 4 percent annually. The number of farmworkers is then calculated from the preceding equation, using the CSO's median estimates of total labor force

Figure I.2
Projected Structural Transformation in Zimbabwe, 1990–2100

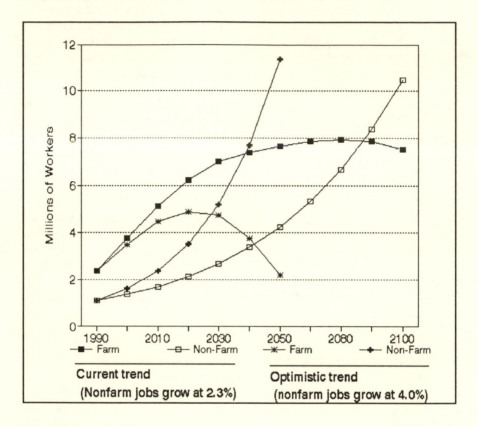

Source: Author's calculations, from data in CSO (1985) and CSO (1986).

growth (sources and calculations are detailed in appendix Table A.3). The structural transformation turning point, when the absolute number of farmers (or farmworkers) begins to fall, is shown to occur around 90 years from now at almost 8 million farmworkers in the current-growth case, and around 30 years from now at almost 5 million workers in the optimistic-growth case.

Future growth could be very different from the predictions of this simple model, particularly given the calamitous proportions of the current AIDS epidemic.[12] But it is nonetheless clear that the number of farmers is virtually certain to rise before it falls. How the increased number of workers in agriculture will be employed depends on the land tenure system and the labor market. Currently, most are given a share of their own family's land in communal areas, a practice that results in falling average farm sizes. Eventually this system may change, and a significant group of landless farmworkers may emerge. In either case, a central feature of the rural economy is decreasing land per worker, which would tend to reduce the marginal productivity of labor and hence rural incomes. An offsetting factor will be investment in labor-using technologies, including better crop varieties, new agronomic techniques such as tied ridges, and more labor-intensive livestock herding practices such as rotational grazing. The balance between these two factors—the number of workers and their productivity—will determine any net change in real wages and the opportunity cost of labor. Government policies have a major influence on that balance, through growth in the nonfarm sector and though agricultural research.

INTERNATIONAL TRADE AND EXCHANGE RATES

In the 1980s, Zimbabwe's international trade and exchange rate policies hurt most farmers. To show how, this section begins with a brief historical review of trade policy in general, followed by more detailed discussions of the exchange rate, the allocation of foreign exchange, and domestic-currency trade incentives. Foreign exchange is a "resource" used to buy foreign as opposed to domestic goods. Thus its price—the exchange rate—reflects the value of all domestic factors (land, labor, and capital) in exchange for foreign goods. Foreign trade is influenced not only by changes in the exchange rate, but also by the allocation of foreign currency to buy imports and by domestic-currency taxes and subsidies.

Trade Policy

For most of the twentieth century, Zimbabwe's borders have been relatively open, and trade has been central to the country's growth. But in 1965, following Rhodesia's Unilateral Declaration of Independence (UDI) from Great Britain, the United Nations imposed severe sanctions on the country. Trade was not halted, but import costs rose, export prices fell, and volumes of both were decisively cut back.

To protect established importers and block capital flight, the UDI government imposed strict licensing requirements on all trade and currency transactions. Export licenses were used to force the surrender of foreign exchange earnings, while import licenses allocated those earnings to specified firms for particular goods, generally in terms of pre-UDI market shares.

At independence in 1980 the international sanctions were lifted, but the national foreign-exchange controls remained. The system inherited from UDI

Figure I.3
The Trade Balance and Total Trade, 1964–1987

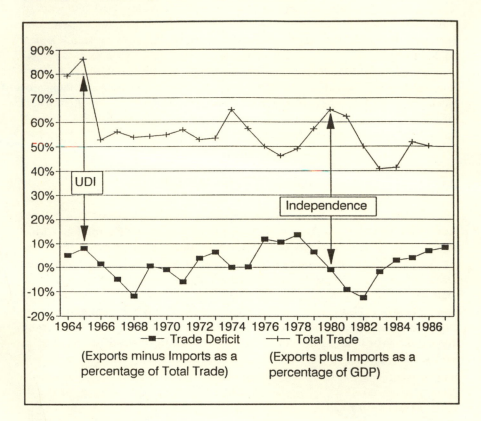

Source: Author's calculations from data in CSO, *Quarterly Digest of Statistics* (various years).

was and remains extremely secretive (the Reserve Bank's "Green Book," which details the full rules, is not a public document) and unusually well-enforced.

The effects of the UN sanctions and UDI import restrictions are visible in Figure I.3. Just after 1965, the trade balance plunged and the share of trade in the economy as a whole dropped sharply. The UDI restrictions then brought the trade balance back into surplus, but at a much lower share of GDP. After a worsening of the trade balance in the late 1970s and early 1980s, imports were again restricted, using the UDI import licensing system, to restore a trade surplus. This left the economy as a whole even more closed, with trade a smaller share of GDP than it had been under sanctions.

After independence the government generally opposed freer trade, but some efforts were made toward regional market integration. The primary forum has been the sixteen-member Eastern and Southern Africa Preferential Trade Area (PTA) founded in 1982.[13] The official goal of the PTA is a regional common market, and some mutual tariff reductions have already been achieved. But almost all PTA members have nonconvertible currencies, which effectively put quotas on all imports. To reduce the need for convertibility, the PTA has developed an innovative currency Clearing House to finance intra-PTA trade, but this has enjoyed only a partial success.[14]

In the 1980s other efforts at facilitating trade, though not liberalizing trade policy, proceeded within the Southern African Development Coordination Conference (SADCC)—now renamed the Southern African Development Community (SADC). This ten-member grouping was created to help build the regional infrastructure necessary to delink its members from economic dependence on South Africa and was remarkably successful in this mission. Donor support was mobilized for numerous major railway, seaport, and communications projects, which undoubtedly helped to lower transport costs for both regional and external trade.

Despite the efforts of both the PTA and SADC, however, intraregional trade remains small. The only exception is trade within the South African Customs Union (SACU): as each SACU member's currency is convertible in other SACU countries, intra-SACU trade is not controlled by import licensing. Figure I.4 illustrates the complex overlapping structure of regional integration efforts through the PTA, SADC, and SACU. There has been some discussion of a merger between the PTA and SADC, without success. Although such a merger could simplify intraregional trade negotiations, the resulting lower tariff rates or easier border controls will have little effect on the amount of trade, unless individual countries take the measures needed to achieve currency convertibility and an end to import licensing.

Outside of the region, independence brought Zimbabwe into the European Community's Lome Convention, under which it receives privileged access to the European market for beef and sugar.[15] In the mid-1980s, considerable effort went into encouraging barter and countertrade, primarily with Eastern Europe.[16] By the end of the decade, however, the only major barter activity remaining was triangular food aid, mostly U.S. and Australian wheat shipped to Zimbabwe in exchange for maize shipped to Mozambique and Malawi.[17]

At the end of the 1980s, a broad import liberalization program was initiated by the Ministry of Finance, Economic Planning and Development (GOZ 1989, 1990). In 1991 and 1992 the government announced further reforms under a five-year Economic Structural Adjustment Program (ESAP) and accepted World Bank and IMF loans to finance increased imports. These programs acknowledged that the import controls inherited from UDI had reduced economic growth, by giving monopoly powers to those fortunate enough to receive

Figure I.4
Regional Economic Groupings in Southern Africa, 1990

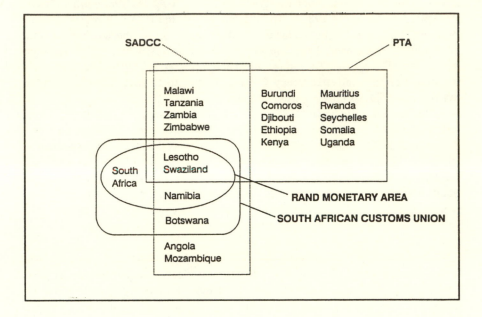

import licenses. Broad trade liberalization would give more Zimbabweans access
to trade opportunities. But unless domestic inflationary pressures are reduced,
trade liberalization will be unsustainable, as growth in import demand will continue to outpace growth in export supply. Thus the prospects for ESAP, and
trade liberalization more generally, remain uncertain.

The Exchange Rate Level

The need for import licenses and other trade restrictions depends crucially
on the exchange rate: at a sufficiently depreciated exchange rate there would be
no excess demand for imports and no need for import licenses. The exchange
rate determines the degree of scarcity, while the licensing system determines
how the scarce foreign currency will be distributed among goods and importers.

A stylized partial equilibrium diagram of the relationship between the
exchange rate and trade is shown in Figure I.5. Under the UDI system, which
remained in place after independence, foreign exchange for imports is restricted
to the level of official exports at a fixed official exchange rate. At this restricted
level, excess demand for imports produces a black-market demand for foreign

Figure I.5
The Exchange Rate and Trade in Partial Equilibrium

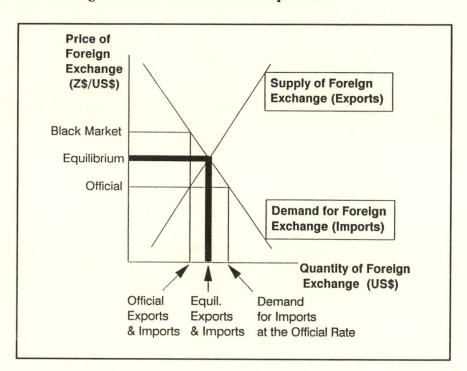

exchange that is well above the equilibrium exchange rate, and trade is balanced at smaller quantities than in equilibrium. In 1989, black market rates were roughly twice the official exchange rate.[18]

The equilibrium rate depends on the location and slopes of the export supply and import demand curves. These "fundamental" exchange rate determinants include foreign prices of tradables (the terms of trade), transport and handling costs (marketing margins), local production costs (technology and factor prices), and product demand (income and preferences). Several other more transient policy-influenced factors may also affect the observed supply and demand for foreign exchange, particularly the government's import restrictions and export subsidies (trade policy) and excess credit creation or other domestic inflationary pressures (monetary policy).

As drawn in Figure I.5, the equilibrium rate is where imports and exports are equal, because there is no other source of foreign exchange.[19] But sustained capital flows would allow a sustained trade imbalance, so the equilibrium exchange rate should accommodate a feasible and desirable level of foreign

borrowing (or lending). The desired level of capital flows (and of trade
imbalance) depends on government's relative rate of time preference between
present and future income, based on expectations of the future profitability and
risk of investments, government budget deficits, and other factors.

The model shown in Figure I.6 is analytically simple, but empirically so
difficult to estimate that relatively few studies in developing countries attempt
to use it directly (a recent exception is the series of country studies summarized
in Krueger, Schiff, and Valdes 1988). More commonly, researchers construct
indexes of exchange rate changes over time and target some historical rate as a
desired equilibrium. Informal adjustments to that rate might then be made, to
account for changes over time in the underlying fundamentals (capital flows, the
external terms of trade, domestic technology, and domestic factor prices).[20]

The recent history of Zimbabwe's official exchange rate is shown in
Figure I.6, using a trade-weighted effective index averaging across Zimbabwe's

Figure I.6
Nominal Effective Exchange Rate Index, 1966–1988

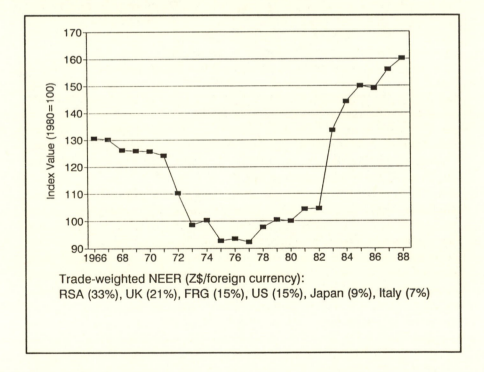

Trade-weighted NEER (Z$/foreign currency):
RSA (33%), UK (21%), FRG (15%), US (15%), Japan (9%), Italy (7%)

Source: Masters (1991).

six major trading partners.[21] This Nominal Effective Exchange Rate (NEER) index, defined as

$$NEER_t = \Sigma_i(w_i * NER_{it})$$

shows that in the early 1970s there was a sharp nominal revaluation of the Zimbabwe dollar, caused primarily by a devaluation of the South African rand. This caused a relative appreciation of Zimbabwe's nominal effective exchange rate, increasing demand and reducing supply of tradable goods and foreign exchange (as in Figure I.5); by 1982 the country faced a severe trade deficit (see Figure I.3) and balance-of-payments crisis, and in December of that year a one-time 20 percent devaluation was undertaken. There were further mini-devaluations throughout the 1980s, and by 1988 the nominal effective exchange rate was substantially devalued relative to its mid-1960s level.

If other relative prices had remained unchanged, the nominal devaluations of the 1980s would have substantially reduced the shortage of foreign exchange. But inflationary pressures were substantially higher in Zimbabwe than in its trading partners, so real relative prices did not change. Thus the devaluations were not effective, and no real depreciation occurred. This can be seen in nominal exchange rates corrected for international differences in inflation, measuring the relative values of the two currencies. Such differential-inflation measures are known as Purchasing Power Parity (PPP) exchange rate indexes.[22]

Two different PPP exchange rate indexes for Zimbabwe are shown in Figure I.7. They are constructed similarly to the NEER index, but each bilateral exchange rate is adjusted for the effects of differential inflation. In PPP1 each country's GDP deflator is used:

$$PPP1_t = \Sigma_i(w_i * NER_{it} * GDPdefl_{it}/GDPdefl_{zt})$$

The PPP1 index shows a clear decline in the late 1980s, but over the full twenty-two-year period there is a slight rise in the index. This suggests that the Zimbabwean devaluations have more than offset differential inflation, causing a slight fall in the overall purchasing power of the Zimbabwe dollar compared with foreign currencies.

From Zimbabwe's point of view, foreign GDP deflators include items such as foreign housing and wage costs, which are not as important in determining Zimbabwe's equilibrium exchange rate as the prices of foreign tradable goods. For this reason many international comparisons are made with an index such as PPP2, which uses foreign wholesale price indexes (WPIs) to measure foreign inflation:

$$PPP2_t = \Sigma_i(w_i * NER_{it} * WPI_{it}/GDPdefl_{zt})$$

Figure I.7
PPP Exchange Rate Indexes, 1966–1988

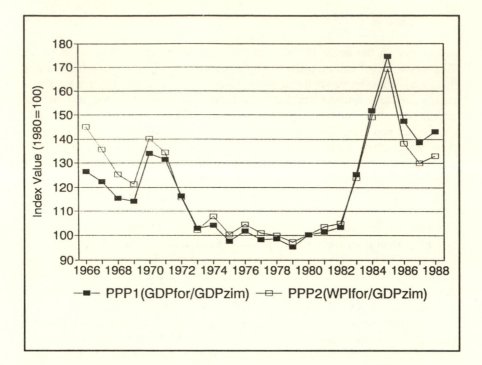

Source: Masters (1991).

This modified PPP index falls below PPP1, to a late 1980s level slightly below
that of 1966 and equal to 1967 (Figure I.7), suggesting no significant change in
the purchasing power of the Zimbabwean dollar relative to foreign wholesale
goods over the whole period.

International price comparisons such as the NEER and PPP exchange rate
indexes are only approximations to the actual domestic incentives for trade,
which would be the relative price of tradables to nontradables (Pt/Pnt) inside the
country (the real exchange rate, RER). This domestic relative price would give
a more accurate "price of foreign exchange" for Figure I.5 than the international
relative prices shown in Figures I.6 and I.7. However, true RER indexes, fully
separating tradables from nontradables, are difficult to construct. In the principal
recent textbook on the subject, Edwards (1989, p.7) notes that, given the particularly severe data constraint encountered in the majority of developing

countries, measured RER indexes "invariably" take the form of international price comparisons such as PPP indexes.[23] Thus the standard methodology for estimating real exchange rates is with PPP indexes; a few researchers use an index like PPP1 (e.g., Woods 1988), but most use an index like PPP2 (Edwards 1989; Schafer 1989).

The formal relationship between the internal RER and the differential-inflation PPP indexes is derived below, for the case in which the domestic and foreign inflation indexes (P and P^*) are geometric averages of subindexes of tradables (Pt and Pt^*) and nontradables (Pnt and Pnt^*), using weights (α, β) on nontradables that are between zero and one.

(1) $P \equiv Pnt^{\alpha}Pt^{(1-\alpha)}$; $P^* \equiv Pnt^{*\beta}Pt^{*(1-\beta)}$

The PPP is defined generally to include any type of international differential-inflation comparison, where E is the nominal exchange rate:

(2) $PPP \equiv EP^*/P$

Combining (1) and (2), in logarithmic form, yields:

(2') $\ln PPP \equiv \ln E + \beta \ln Pnt^* + (1-\beta)\ln Pt^* - \alpha \ln Pnt - (1-\alpha)\ln Pt$

Foreign tradables prices (Pt^*) are assumed to be transmitted to domestic tradables (Pt) through trade at the nominal exchange rate (E), but modified by the tariff-equivalent of commercial policy and the ad-valorem margin required for transport and marketing $(1+t+m)$.

(3) $Pt = E(1+t+m)Pt^*$

(3') $\ln Pt = \ln E + \ln(1+t+m) + \ln Pt^*$

Substituting (3') into (2') yields:

(4') $\ln PPP = \alpha(\ln Pt - \ln Pnt) - \beta(\ln Pt^* - \ln Pnt^*) - \ln(1+t+m)$

Taking antilogs and substituting into the definition of RER and RER^* ($RER \equiv Pt/Pnt$ and $RER^* \equiv Pt^*/Pnt^*$):

(5) $PPP = [1/(1+t+m)]RER^{\alpha}/RER^{*\beta}$

This derivation highlights the following limitations of PPP exchange rates as proxy indexes for the RER:

(a)   PPP indexes assume that equation (3) holds exactly, thus assuming immediate and full effectiveness of nominal devaluations. In fact, imperfect markets, imperfect substitution, and traders' expectations of future changes could all cause the actual RER response to be delayed and either magnified or dampened in the short run.

(b)   PPP indexes understate the true RER (showing too much appreciation or too little depreciation) when marketing margins (m) rise or trade policy (t) becomes more restrictive. Conversely, when (m) and (t) decline, as might be expected for example during periods of trade liberalization, the PPP indexes show too much depreciation.

(c)   PPP indexes always understate the RER by the exponent α. For example, if the domestic price index were a CPI with a nontradables content of 50 percent (such as house rent and services), the PPP shows the square root of the actual RER level. At the margin in this case, percentage changes in the PPP would be half the percentage changes in the RER.

(d)   PPP indexes always understate the RER by the factor of $RER^{-\beta}$. Conversely, the PPP overstates the RER (showing too much depreciation or too little appreciation) during foreign appreciation. This can be expected to occur consistently as productivity or real wages rise among the major trading nations, as shown by Balassa (1964) and more recently by Wood (1988). In the Zimbabwean case, for example, the effect of foreign appreciation accounts for the large difference between PPP1 and PPP2, as foreign GDP deflators (in PPP1) rise faster than foreign WPIs (in PPP2).

Limitations (a) and (b) can be expected to cause mismeasurement mostly in the short run only, but (c) and (d) can be expected to cause large and sustained mismeasurements. Since α is relatively constant, limitation (c) can be expected to distort the magnitude but not the direction of RER changes; it makes the PPP a relatively insensitive measure, but not biased in one direction or another. In contrast, limitation (d) is likely to distort consistently the direction of change, usually suggesting that countries' real exchange rates are more depreciated than they in fact are.

Many researchers are aware that the international PPP measures are different from the domestic RER, and some may recognize that there is a systematic relation between them. But the consistency and importance of both the dampening effect (c) and the bias effect (d) is not apparent in the standard literature.[24] The ingredients for an internal RER index are not obvious, are not available from standard sources, and may not be available at all. For this study, RER indexes are built using the unit values of actually traded goods for Pt and either the prices of building materials (representing nontradable goods) or the average wage (representing nontradable services) for Pnt; both indexes were constructed from raw figures in the CSO's *Quarterly Digest of Statistics*.

The index used for Pt is a trade unit value (TUV) index, constructed as the average of the import and export unit value indexes published by the CSO. This measure of Pt uses border rather than internal prices, thus showing the effect of exchange rate policy independently of commercial (commodity-specific) trade policies, which are discussed separately later on. Relative to other possible tradable-good price indexes, the TUV has the virtues of both precision, including only items actually traded by Zimbabwe, and broad coverage, including all traded items for which quantities are known. Like all price indexes, however, the TUV will overstate price rises when average quality improves.[25]

For nontradables (Pnt), there is greater difficulty. Most nontradables are services; often, quantities are not clearly defined so a price index cannot be calculated. Two kinds of nontradables do, however, have readily available price indexes. The first is building materials, for which a price index is published by the CSO. The items in building materials price index, primarily bricks, sand, cement, and timber, are rarely traded internationally, so their prices are determined by domestic supply and demand. A second nontradable price index is the nominal average wage, since labor is the principal component of most services.

Figure I.8 presents the two resulting RER indexes, following the formula

$$RER_t = Pt_t/Pnt_t$$

Several important conclusions can be drawn from Figure I.8. First, the two RER indexes are very similar to one another, conforming with a model that posits common determinants for all nontradables relative to tradables. Second, the RER indexes follow nominal exchange rate changes much less than the PPP indexes, conforming with differences (a) and (b) noted above. And third, over time the RER indexes show much more appreciation than the PPP indexes, conforming with differences (c) and (d).

Over the entire period, the RER indexes show no trend during the UDI period: An initial decline was reversed by the first oil price shock of 1973, and a further fall was again reversed by the second oil price shock of 1978-1979. The average throughout the UDI period was only slightly below the 1964 level. But after 1979 the RER indexes dropped sharply, with an initial decline of about 30 percent over two years. This was partially reversed by the nominal devaluations of December 1982 and 1983, but after 1984 devaluations failed to keep up with inflation in nontradables, and the index continued to fall, to a level roughly two-thirds of its pre-UDI level.

Such a decline in the index shows incentives turning against trade, leading to increased demand for and reduced supply of foreign exchange. This would be sustainable if it were matched by a lasting increase in Zimbabwean productivity, improvement in the terms of trade, or capital inflows, each of which would provide additional foreign exchange to offset worsened trade incentives. To some extent, these did occur as a result of the end of the war and the lifting of international sanctions, but this primarily served to restore the pre-UDI situation.

No average-wage data are available beyond 1984, and no TUV data beyond 1987. But if the results of Figure I.8 can be taken as roughly indicative

Figure I.8
Real Exchange Rate Indexes, 1964–1987

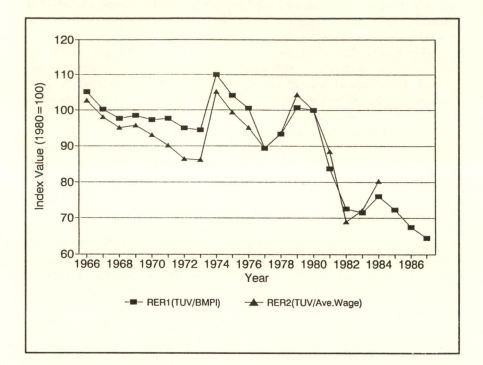

Source: Masters (1991).

of the 1989 situation, the RER index was then about two-thirds of its 1960s and 1970s average and 62 percent of its pre-UDI (1964-1965) level. Thus the prices of traded goods would have to increase by a factor of 1/0.62 or roughly 60 percent above current levels to restore pre-UDI levels or 1/0.66 or roughly 50 percent to restore the UDI-period average. To allow for some improvement in the target equilibrium rate from increased productivity and increased capital flows, the smaller 50 percent foreign exchange premium is used in Part IV.

Because farmers produce tradable crops using mostly nontradable land and labor, they are almost always hurt by such exchange rate overvaluation. Through RER appreciation the government's policies worsen farmers' relative terms of trade with the rest of the economy, transfering income from them to urban people and others who are net producers of nontradables and consumers of tradables. The farm-level importance of Zimbabwe's large (roughly 50 percent) exchange rate premium in the late 1980s is measured through the PAM in Part IV.

Given the exchange rate level, the specific incidence of trade policy on individual commodities is set by commercial policy, including such measures as foreign exchange allocations, customs duties and export subsidies payable in foreign currency, and local-currency taxes and subsidies. These are detailed below.

Foreign Exchange Allocations

To appreciate the importance of the allocation system we must examine the pattern of allocations in some detail. In Zimbabwe foreign exchange is granted by the Reserve Bank, which issues import licenses and releases foreign exchange. Most licenses are given under "basic allocations," issued in biannual quota periods on the recommendation of the Ministry of Industry and Commerce.[26] Commodity guidelines are set by the Ministerial Economic Coordinating Committee (MECC), using overall balance-of-payments estimates provided by each economic ministry.

Licenses are issued to individual firms as well as for particular goods, so they serve to protect recipients from domestic as well as foreign competition. Furthermore, historical import shares are used to guide basic allocations, which gives a strong conservative bias to trade policy. Indeed, a major function of exchange controls was to cushion pre-1965 foreign exchange users from the austerity of UDI and sanctions.

In the mid-1980s, two new foreign exchange allocation programs were introduced to help break the conservative tendencies of the UDI system. The first, initiated in 1983 to help nontraditional manufactured exports, was the Export Revolving Fund (ERF). This program allowed firms to fill the import content (up to 60 percent) of confirmed export orders. A separate ERF Bonus Scheme rewarded incremental exports, through licenses to import anything up to the value of 25 percent of the previous year-to-year increases. Although the ERF applied only to goods of a "value-added" nature, excluding primary production such as agriculture or mining, a few large agro-industrial firms do qualify for the Bonus Scheme.

The second new allocation method, begun in 1987 to help agriculture and mining, was the Export Promotion Program (EPP).[27] Under the EPP, the MLARR and the Ministry of Mines are allowed to allocate foreign exchange to both producers and input supply firms, on the basis of historical and likely future exports. The idea is to rebuild the productive base for these traditional exports, which earn the bulk of foreign exchange but had been largely neglected in the post-independence period.

Table I.3 presents the approximate total allocations given to the agricultural sector under the programs operating in 1988 and 1989, showing that those

Table I.3
Foreign Exchange Allocations to Agriculture, 1987-1988

	1987	1988
Total Allocations	113	141
Basic	79	82
Chemicals (crop and veterinary)	28	30
Machinery and spares	22	27
Fertilizer	17	15
Packaging	12	8
Stockfeed	1	2
Export Promotion Program	24	55
Machinery and spares	6	17
Crops (fertilizer and chemicals)	11	9
Livestock (veterinary and feeds)	4	8
Horticultural	1	5
Transport		6
Packaging		3
Miscellaneous	2	7
ERF Bonus Scheme	10	4
Sugar	6	
Grains	2	..
Wood	1	1
Meats	..	1
Inputs		1
Other	2	1

Source: MLARR estimates, based on Reserve Bank and MLARR data.

programs benefited primarily the input-intensive large-farm sector. Almost a third of basic and EPP allocations were for machinery and spares, virtually all used on large farms. Over half were for fertilizers and chemicals, of which about 80 percent and 99 percent respectively are used on large farms. Even the indirect inputs, for packaging and transport, were of more help to farmers who marketed a larger share of their product.

In 1990, two new initiatives were announced as part of the government's trade liberalization efforts, to increase imports for agriculture beyond the allocations shown in Table I.3. The first was a small increase in the number of items on open general import license (OGIL). The second was to introduce an export-retention scheme (ERS), in which import licenses for up to 5–7 percent of export earnings, depending on the sector, would be given to final exporters. The maximum portion of foreign exchange that may be retained has since been raised to 50 percent, but such a system remains of little help to smallholders who are not themselves the final exporters and hence do not receive the ERS allocations.

As will be shown in Part IV, the use of imported inputs helps significantly to offset the effect of exchange rate policy on large farmers. In a few cases, some farmers may even find themselves net beneficiaries of the exchange control system. But among smallholders, despite the considerable efforts of government to target these programs toward their needs, there is little effective demand for imported inputs. As a result, foreign exchange allocations can do little to offset the impact of real exchange rate appreciation.

Local-currency Taxes, Subsidies and Price Controls

In addition to the exchange control system just discussed, trade incentives are also affected by local-currency import taxes, export subsidies, and price controls. For imports, the principal instruments are customs duties (ranging from zero to 40 percent), an import surtax (20 percent on most items), and price controls fixing proportional markups. The impact of these on particular farm inputs is detailed in Part IV. On average, taxes took just under 30 percent of import values during the late 1980s, providing 15 percent of government revenue. But as these taxes did not absorb all the excess demand for imports experienced at current exchange rates, import licenses remain scarce for all categories. Price controls, which are relatively well-enforced at the wholesale and urban retail levels, are used to limit markups, leaving excess demand and periodic physical shortages for many retail items.

On the export side, under the Export Incentive Scheme (EIS), a 9 percent subsidy is given on foreign exchange earnings from certain exports. This does not apply to agricultural products, but does to farm inputs exported to the region. For these goods, principally seeds and fertilizer, price controls are fixed at absolute levels, and trade is a very small portion of the total market. Thus price transmission from exports to the local market is limited and the EIS has little effect on local-market prices.

To conclude, the fundamental shortage of foreign exchange caused by real exchange rate appreciation can only be remedied by a reversal of that appreciation. Such real depreciation would require a combination of devaluation and reduction in inflationary pressure, to turn the domestic terms of trade back in favor of small farmers.

CREDIT AND INTEREST RATES

After labor and foreign exchange, the third most important macroeconomic resource for agriculture is capital. In Zimbabwe, formal-sector nominal interest rates are controlled, at levels about equal to inflation (around 14 percent) in the late 1980s. Despite these low rates, Zimbabwe's relatively extensive banking system maintained a high degree of liquidity. Formal sector savings rates were high and the demand for private investment low, as physical shortages and administrative rationing for many inputs prevented firms from building new capacity. In consequence, farm credit remained widely available at the low official rates, from the parastatal Agricultural Finance Corporation (AFC) or from private commercial banks. AFC lending to CA farmers is detailed in Part III, as a determinant of the production of individual crops.

During the 1980s both CA and LSC farmers took advantage of the funds available at low rates, and farm indebtedness rose quickly. This was particularly true in the large-farm sector. For smallholders, credit has been a much smaller proportion of total sales, partly because of their lesser underlying demand for capital (due to lower relative labor costs and hence lower capital intensities), their higher rainfall risks (which make fixed-term seasonal debt less attractive), and their generally lower agroeconomic potential (which makes input use less profitable). In sum, smallholders farmers have received little benefit from easy credit, while large farmers have been much helped.

The net effect of the credit situation at the farm level is shown in the Policy Analysis Matrixes of Part IV. For large-scale farmers with easy access to formal credit markets, the opportunity cost of capital is taken to be equal to the average return on shareholder equity as shown in Table I.4: a real cost of capital of 8 percent per year, for a nominal cost of about 23 percent after inflation at about 14 percent per year. This rate is near the bottom of the 7–10 percent cost of capital scale conventionally applied to lower-middle income countries such as Zimbabwe.

For communal-area farmers, a somewhat higher cost of 10 percent in real terms (25 percent in nominal terms) is used, because lending to communal farmers is more costly than lending to large-scale farmers. There are two central reasons for this. First, smaller farmers can be expected to present a higher credit risk, because they can offer the lender less collateral, information about them is less easily available, and they face higher production risks. Second, smaller farmers present higher proportional transactions costs, because they borrow in smaller quantities and are more remote from central banking offices.

Although most attention to the role of Zimbabwe's capital markets in the farm sector is focused on direct lending for inputs, much larger total borrowing is undertaken by the marketing boards to finance their product purchases. Some of these funds are borrowed overseas, by the Agricultural Marketing Authority (AMA), against the exports made by its constituent marketing boards. The

Table I.4
Return to Shareholder Equity in 48 Non-financial Companies Listed on the Zimbabwe Stock Exchange, 1980–1987

(percentages)	Average 1980–1987	1980	1981	1982	1983	1984	1985	1986	1987
Nominal return	22.6	26.8	30.7	28.2	21.4	11.3	18.3	21.7	22.5
Inflation (CPI)	13.5	5.3	13.2	10.6	23.1	20.2	8.5	14.3	12.5
Real rate of return	8.0	20.4	15.5	15.9	-1.4	-7.4	9.0	6.5	8.9

Sources: Rate of return data from Dailami and Walton (1989); inflation from CSO (1990).

remainder is borrowed locally, through bond issues (known in Zimbabwe as "government stocks") in the same way as other government debt. The AMA's overall demand for capital to pay farmers is a major component of the national capital market, especially after good years when farm sales are high.

Among small farmers, informal lending does exist, but primarily through rotating credit societies rather than through moneylenders. Credit societies, to which each household contributes regularly and withdraws in turn, are found throughout Zimbabwe and are used primarily to finance household and farm implements. This informal institution helps fulfill rural needs for month-to-month credit, while seasonal credit needs are either self-financed or filled through the AFC. The type of credit most lacking for Zimbabwean smallholders is year-to-year credit, for both medium and long-run farm investments and for consumption.

CONCLUSIONS

Macroeconomic conditions in Zimbabwe discriminate strongly against farmers, particularly smallholders. In the labor market, low rates of nonfarm employment growth increase the number of workers in farming, thus reducing the land available per farmer. In trade, a reduced (appreciated) real exchange rate reduces returns to production of tradable farm products relative to land and labor inputs. These two biases reduce the income of all farmers. Other macro-economic factors discriminate more directly within the farm sector, in favor of LSC farmers. These forces include the special export-promotion programs that reach primarily larger mechanized farmers and low real interest rates for credit that benefit primarily larger borrowers. Smallholders reap little benefit from either imported inputs or formal credit. They could be helped mainly through an improvement of overall relative prices, reversing the real exchange rate appreciation of the 1980s.

NOTES

1. The figure of 1.13 million "communal farmers" is much lower than the actual number of farmers in communal areas. Many people who work on communal farms were counted as outside the labor force or as un- or underemployed in a preferred occupation.

2. A few of the other major forces limiting formal employment include communication problems from the use of a foreign language (English), the difficulty of acquiring and signaling practical skills under an academically-oriented educational system (based on British "O" and "A"-levels), shortages of urban housing and transport (particularly due to the siting of workers' townships

far from workplaces), and racial prejudice in a polarized society. All these constraints reduce productivity and raise labor costs, but only some of them could be alleviated by the government.

3. Colonial rules included limits on African workers' physical movements ("pass laws," under the 1936 Native Registration Act and its successors), labor organizations (such as the 1934 Industrial Conciliation Act and successors), and housing in urban areas (such as the country's various planning acts). By independence, only the last group remained, with periodic evictions of squatters and unregistered enterprises used to keep the urban landscape free of shanty-towns and informal activities.

4. These and other post-independence labor laws were substantially modified in 1989 and 1990 as part of the government's structural adjustment efforts, but their residual effects remain.

5. Further evidence of the relative immobility of black LSC farmworkers is given by the fact that the difference between farm and nonfarm wages in the formal sector is almost entirely confined to blacks. Black farmworkers' wages were 75 percent of black nonfarm employees' wages in 1954 and fell steadily to under 40 percent by 1977. Among nonblacks (mostly European whites), on the other hand, farm employment paid roughly the same as nonfarm employment between 1954 and 1959, somewhat more between 1959 and 1968, and somewhat less between 1968 and 1977. (Race-segregated employment statistics were ended in 1977.) In terms of numbers of jobs, the proportion of blacks and whites employed in agriculture stayed roughly constant during this period, at around 40 percent for blacks and 5 percent for whites, although there was a small rise, to 45 percent and 6 percent, during the agricultural boom years of the 1960s (CSO, *Quarterly Digest of Statistics*, various years).

6. Farm labor earnings are very difficult to measure. It is particularly difficult to separate returns to labor from returns to land in a family system with little hired labor. These estimates are survey-wide totals from MLARR (1990), at a rate which is just high enough to capture almost all farm income except returns to land of Z$10 per hectare in the low-potential areas and Z$150 per hectare in the high-potential areas. It would also be possible, of course, to consider that returns to labor vary while returns to land are constant. This makes little difference to the results of Part IV, where land and labor are always added together. Measuring returns to labor more precisely would be very difficult in part because it would vary greatly by location and situation. Without much flexibility in land markets (as discussed in Part II), it is difficult for farmers to move from low- to high-productivity locations and equalize their marginal product across the country.

7. Rural-urban migration to join the informal sector has been particularly restricted: a 1983 survey (Moyo et al. 1984) showed that only 16 percent of a sample of urban informal workers had come from working in rural areas, while

13 percent had come from urban unemployment; over two-thirds had come to the sector after losing a formal-sector job.

8. The CSO's Agriculture and Livestock Survey found, for the 1984–1985 and 1985–1986 seasons, that only 24 percent of communal-area households farmed less than one hectare. Cattle ownership, on the other hand, is relatively unequal; the same survey showed 44 percent of households owning no cattle at all (CSO 1986). A similar result was found by the MLARR's 1989 Communal-Area Farm Survey, in which inequality indexes (Gini coefficients) by adult resident were measured at 0.40 for area planted, 0.49 for livestock, and 0.56 for farm equipment (MLARR 1990).

9. Seasonal migration probably caused the urban population to be undercounted in 1969 and overcounted in 1982, resulting in some overestimation of intercensal urbanization. The 1969 census was undertaken during the harvest season of an exceptionally good year, at which time many city-dwellers were temporarily in the countryside. Exactly the opposite occurred in 1982, when the census was carried out after the harvest of a below-average year (CSO 1984). It is not clear, however, how much if any correction should be made to offset these errors.

10. Unpublished MLARR censuses of the resettlement areas show that their population roughly tripled between 1982 and 1989 and that most of the resettled people came from communal areas. But the total increase was only about 220,000 people, of whom perhaps 190,000 were immigrants and at least a third came from the previously LSC areas.

11. This can be derived as follows, beginning with absolute changes in the number of workers (ΔL_t):

$$\Delta L_t \equiv \Delta L_a + \Delta L_n$$
$$\Delta L_a \equiv \Delta L_t - \Delta L_n$$
$$L_a(\Delta L_a/L_a) \equiv L_t(\Delta L_t/L_t) - L_n(\Delta L_n/L_n)$$
$$L_a(\% \Delta L_a) \equiv L_t(\% \Delta L_t) - L_n(\% \Delta L_n)$$
$$\% \Delta L_a \equiv \% \Delta L_t(L_t/L_a) - \% \Delta L_n(L_n/L_a)$$

12. In early 1991, for example, the Minister of Health announced that late-1990 surveys found "an HIV incidence rate of 28.5 percent in the country's labor force" ("Chilling Aids Figures Disclosed," *Financial Gazette* [Harare] 15 February 1991). As most of these people were infected relatively recently, AIDS has not yet had a major impact on mortality and the size of the labor force. But even if the HIV incidence were to remain at roughly 30 percent, mortality among infected adults would have to rise to only about 10 percent per year for AIDS-related deaths to bring labor force growth to zero.

13. Regional market integration had been important long before independence. The country was a member of the South African Customs Union from 1903 to 1930; and an attempt at regional integration without South Africa, the Federation of Rhodesia and Nyasaland, was founded in 1953 and enjoyed a common market between 1956 and 1962.

For the origins and early progress of the PTA, see Chr. Michelsen Institute (1986) and Hall (1987). For regional agricultural trade in particular, see Koester (1986), Rusike (1989), and Kingsbury (1989).

14. The Clearing House is managed by the Reserve Bank of Zimbabwe. It gives member countries interest-free trade credits, with hard-currency settlement of net balances only every 60 days. This facility accounted for over 35 percent of intra-PTA trade by August 1989, with only about half of Clearing House-financed trade being settled in hard currency ("PTA Clearing House Total Over $1 Billion," *Financial Gazette* [Harare] 4 August 1989). Although the Clearing House has probably reduced trading costs, it may not actually have increased regional trade, either through diversion of existing trade or expansion of the total, because most member countries still use the same hard-currency import controls for intra-PTA as for other trade. Another PTA initiative, regional travellers checks, has faced the same problem.

15. For beef, Zimbabwe, along with Botswana, Kenya, Madagascar, and Swaziland, is entitled to a 90 percent abatement of the CAP levy, for up to 8,100 metric tons. This quota, granted in 1982, was first used in 1986 after a successful EC inspection of Zimbabwe's abattoir system.   Average export realization more than tripled between 1985 and 1986. In 1988, Zimbabwe supplied an additional 1,000 mt from others' unfilled quotas, but in 1989 exports were temporarily suspended due to EC veterinary restrictions after an outbreak of hoof and mouth disease (Eurostat 1989).

For sugar, Zimbabwe enjoys a 100 percent abatement on 30,204 mt annually; this quota has been filled every year since 1980. Sugar exports were also assisted by duty-free access to the U.S. market for up to 10,630 mt in 1988 and 12,636 mt in 1989.

16. Barter trade rose from Z$53 million over the three-year 1984-86 period, to Z$320 million (almost 9 percent of total trade) in 1987, before falling back to Z$199 million in 1988 (Eurostat 1990). The composition of barter trade had over 80 percent of exports being tobacco and the remainder being asbestos, ferrochrome, maize, and milk powder and barter imports being primarily intermediate industrial and capital goods. In 1988 and 1989, barter trade declined because of dissatisfaction with the quality and value of the imported items and a preference for more flexible hard currency earnings on open markets.

17. The Zimbabwean arrangement is only the second major triangular food aid operation, after the arrangements begun in 1979 to supply Kampuchean refugees with Thai and Burmese rice (Clay and Benson 1990). Begun in 1983, triangular exchanges accounted for most Zimbabwean maize exports in the 1980s.

18. This can be seen in occasional newspaper reports on the issue, such as "Expats in Big Forex Racket: Claim" (*The Chronicle* [Bulawayo], 8 November 1989, p. 7), and "Business Booming over Visas to South Africa" (*Sunday Mail* [Harare], 22 July 1990, p. 1).

19. Indeed, this corresponds to Zimbabwe's medium-term average position since UDI, as shown in Figure I.5.

20. If sufficient data were available, a formal model of exchange rate determination could be estimated econometrically. Typically the exchange rate index is shown to be a function of a few "fundamental" determinants (such as capital flows, the terms of trade and technological change), plus some "disequilibrium" variables (chiefly import restrictions and excess credit creation). The estimated model is then used to simulate the equilibrium rate that would hold in the absence of the disequilibrium factors. This is the approach used in, for example, Edwards (1989) and Schafer (1989).

21. The weights are 1980–1988 average shares of exports plus imports for the top six partners: South Africa (0.33), UK (0.21), West Germany (0.15), U.S. (0.15), Japan (0.09), and Italy (0.07). Together these six partners accounted for 56 percent of 1980–1988 trade. See Masters (1991) for details and individual country data.

22. There is a very long tradition of PPP indexes, surveyed in Officer (1976) and Frenkel (1978). The earliest PPP indexes (in the 1920s) measured the purchasing power of each currency over all types of goods, as in PPP1; later, particularly after Balassa (1964), some PPP indexes have been made focusing on tradable goods only, as in PPP2.

23. The standard sources are the IMF *International Financial Statistics* and the World Bank *World Tables*. The IMF and World Bank data are widely available, generally reliable, and can be obtained on computer tapes. This last concern is particularly important for large cross-country studies.

24. The relationship between the PPP and RER is discussed by Edwards (1989), Coes (1989), and Wood (1988), but none produces the results of equation (5) and the specific limitations highlighted here.

25. A further disadvantage of the Zimbabwean TUV is that, although export prices are measured correctly as ex-Zimbabwe ("fob") prices, import prices are measured at the port of origin, instead of into-Zimbabwe ("cif") prices. Thus changes in the transport cost component of import prices would be omitted from the TUV.

26. Basic allocations are further divided into capital goods, allocated by the Industrial Import Control section, and intermediate and finished items, allocated by the Commercial Import Control section. These were previously handled separately, by the Ministry of Industry and Technology and the Ministry of Trade and Commerce, until the two ministries merged in 1990.

27. The EPP should not be confused with the Zimbabwe Export Promotion Program (ZEPP), an EC-funded project established in September 1987 to provide technical services to potential exporters within Zimbabwe and in Europe. This program is widely credited with increasing export skills in industry but has had little impact on agriculture.

Part II

The Agricultural Sector

Zimbabwe's agricultural sector is rich and varied.[1] To analyze the effects of policies within the sector, this chapter proceeds from the general to the specific. The chapter begins with land tenure and farming systems, then covers long-term investments in irrigation, research, extension, and transport, and concludes with purchased inputs such as fertilizer, seeds and crop chemicals. Marketing conditions and other commodity-specific issues are discussed in Part III.

LAND TENURE AND FARMING SYSTEMS

Zimbabwe has unusually sharp divisions between farming areas. In the countryside, it is not uncommon to see fences tracing clear lines across the plains. On one side will be a single farm, with a few well-tilled rectangular fields, little erosion, abundant grazing areas and many trees. The other side will be a patchwork of many farms, with small irregular plots, a high degree of erosion, sparse grazing, and few trees.

Such lines are the boundaries between "commercial" farms and their "communal" neighbors. Many countries have similar distinctions between rich and poor farming areas, but in Zimbabwe land distribution is both extremely unequal and almost uniquely enshrined in law. Four distinct farm subsectors operate under different land tenure rules, and each has a characteristic farming system. Legislation restricts transactions within each category as well as labor and product movements between categories.

Just over half of all agricultural land is on the communal side of the fence. This is unsurveyed land, originally set aside by the colonial authorities for African occupation.[2] The BSAC and later Rhodesian governments then forcibly moved Africans from elsewhere into those areas. The boundaries of the communal areas were generally fixed by local Native Commissioners, almost always including only lands not previously claimed by settlers: the most remote and driest lands, with the shallowest soils.[3] Land tenure rules in the CAs are similar to those in many other parts of Africa: unrestricted access to grazing areas and individual control over plowed areas.[4] But all CA land is nominally owned by the state and so cannot be formally bought, sold, or rented.[5]

The other half of agricultural land is classified as Commercial. Most Commercial land was alienated to white settlers beginning in 1890, forming what are now the Large Scale Commercial (LSC) farming areas. Beginning in 1925, a small amount of unassigned land was leased or sold at concessional rates to selected African farmers, forming what are now the Small Scale Commercial (SSC) farming areas. In both LSC and SSC areas, all land is individually owned and titles may be registered. They are therefore sometimes called "freehold" areas, although since subdivision rights are restricted there is a market only for whole farms and not for land itself.

After 1980, a much larger area than the SSCs has been purchased for the new Resettlement Areas (RAs), where tenure is broadly similar to that of the Communal system, with open-access grazing areas and individually held arable plots.[6] In the RAs, land allocations are made administratively, at standard rates of five arable hectares per household and variable amounts of grazing land. This is substantially larger than average farm sizes in the communal areas, and resettlement areas are sometimes known in Shona as "the large fields" (*minda mirefu*).

Selected indicators of land use for all four farming areas are shown in Table II.1 (boundaries are shown on Map 2 in Appendix E). Since the CA and LSC areas are much larger than the other two, most of the analysis in this study focuses on them.

Table II.1 shows extreme differences in land use across areas: population density and cropping intensity is about three times as high in the CAs as in the other subsectors. As shown in Table II.2, this is despite far lower average land quality in the CAs.

The present highly unequal distribution of land and people is more the result of deliberate colonial policy than voluntary settlement patterns. The grand-parents and, in some cases, parents of many communal area residents were forcibly moved from what are now the LSC areas and crowded into what are now the CAs.[7] The result was to provide white settlers with large tracts of high-quality, low-cost land and large numbers of low-wage workers.

Forced movements reduced the implicit price of land and wages paid to African labor, thus increasing settler incomes. But that transfer almost certainly reduced total agricultural productivity by reducing the intensity of use of lands allocated to the LSC sector, in terms of both crops and livestock, while increasing the intensity of land use in the CAs. This history is still very much in evidence today, as shown in Table II.1.

Table II.1
Land Use by Farming Area, 1989 Estimates

	CA	LSC	RA	SSC
Totals				
Total area (million ha)	16.4	11.2	3.3	1.4
Population (1989 est., millions)	6	1.2	0.4	0.2
Number of farms (thousands)	900	4.5	50	11
Averages				
Area per farm (ha/hh)	18	2,500	66	125
of which: area planted (ha)	2	103	3	7
Cropping intensity (%)	11	4	5	6
Livestock density (head/km^2)	27	16	4	na
Population density (pers/km^2)	33	11	11	15

Notes: An additional 6.3 million hectares (16% of the total) is set aside for national parks, forest, and game reserves; and 0.2 million hectares are urban lands. Livestock density is for 1987; goats are included as cattle equivalents by a conversion factor of 0.2.
Source: Author's calculations, from CSO and MLARR data.

Table II.2
Distribution of Land by Tenure Classification, 1989

Nat. Reg.	Average Rainfall	CA	LSC	RA	SSC
		Percent			
I	Over 900 mm/yr	1	2	4	1
II	750-1000 mm/yr	8	33	18	17
III	650-800 mm/yr	17	22	38	38
IV	450-650 mm/yr	45	22	25	36
V	Under 450 mm/yr	29	22	19	7
Total area (million ha)		16.4	11.0	3.3	1.4

Source: Author's calculations, from CSO and MLARR data. Natural Regions are defined as in Vincent and Thomas (1961).

One way to analyze the influence of tenure arrangements on land-use intensity and input use would be through curves showing how crop yields vary when cropping intensity (the proportion of total land that is planted) or input use is changed. On the left half of Figure II.1, the yield per hectare that is planted is shown to decline as the proportion of land that is planted rises. Declining yields are due to both reduced fallow time in crop rotations and the lower quality of land being planted. The model shown here assumes that farmers plant their best lands first and use the longest possible fallows, increasing their plantings only as they are driven to do so by an increasing scarcity of land relative to farm output. At the margin farmers will plant only up to the point where the marginal revenue from cropping just equals the relative value of land in terms of output (Pland/Po).[8] Any remaining land will be kept fallow and used in crop rotations, grazing or forestry.

Currently, LSC farmers plant only about 4 percent of their land (Table II.1). If land that is currently kept fallow to protect tobacco from nematode buildup is considered fully cropped, this percentage would rise to 5 or 6 percent. In contrast, CA farmers plant twice as much of their arable land every year (11 percent of total land area).[9] Land prices and marginal productivity levels corresponding to these rates of land use are not directly observable, but evidence

Figure II.1
Land Use and Input Intensity in LSC and Communal Areas

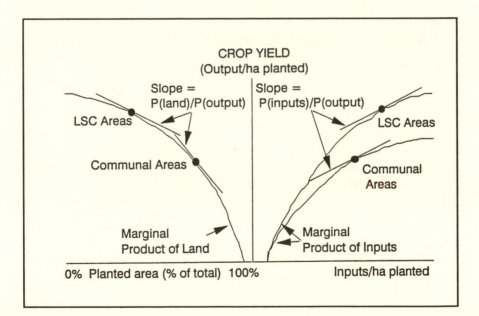

presented in Part IV suggests average returns to land in high-potential natural regions of around Z$150/ha in CAs and Z$90/ha in LSC areas, using 1989 prices, crop budgets, and cropping patterns.[10]

The right half of Figure II.1 shows the intensity of input use which corresponds to each land price and yield level. Land in the higher-valued area has lower marginal productivity, meaning less input-responsiveness: a lower marginal product of inputs curve. Thus, under the same input and output prices (slope Pi/Po), farmers will give this land a lower level of input use than in the other farming area.

This simple model shows the effects of different land tenure rules and land prices alone; many other factors also affect farming systems and productivity. But still the simple model sketched out in Figure II.1 explains much of Zimbabwe's pattern of land and input use. In the CAs, farmers use little fallow but also few inputs, while in LSC areas farmers plant only a small proportion of their land but apply high rates of inputs.

Advocates of large-scale farming often claim that high levels of yields and input use in the LSC areas are the result of economies of scale. The model shown here provides an alternative explanation. Economies of scale, if they existed, would lead LSC farmers to plant a *larger* proportion of their land than do CA farmers. There are clearly increasing returns to the sizes of some farm inputs, notably plowing and irrigation equipment, and perhaps also in the pro-cessing and marketing tasks for tobacco and horticultural crops.[11] But these cases of increasing returns are not sufficient to completely offset decreasing returns in other inputs, so LSC farmers use their land less intensively than CA farmers.

The discrepancy in land values and land-use patterns between the subsec-tors leaves room for substantial increases in agricultural productivity, by revers-ing the earlier forced migration. The Rhodesian government made some effort in this direction by establishing the African Purchase Areas, now known as the SSC areas. But the farm sizes allotted under the program were very high, so land use rates on SSC farms are not much better than in LSC areas (Table II.1).

After independence, a much greater effort was made through the resettle-ment program.[12] In the six years between 1981 and 1986 over 300,000 blacks were placed on almost 3 million hectares of previously white-owned land. In contrast, resettlement in Kenya took over twice as long to settle roughly the same number of people, on a much smaller area of land (Hazlewood, 1985). But because a relatively large area has been given per settler, there has been no sig-nificant increase in population density compared with the remaining LSC areas (Table II.1). There has been a net decrease in livestock density and only a small increase in cropping intensity compared to the LSC areas. Land use intensity remains far below the CAs, despite better average land quality.

Zimbabwe's resettlement program has been a remarkable success by histor-ical standards but has clearly not ended the disparity in land use and productivity between the CAs and the rest of the country. Partly this is due to the relatively large area given per settler. But it is also due to the high cost and limited availability of government resources for planning and infrastructural development, which makes it more difficult for resettlement areas to be used as intensively as farmer-owned land.[13] Centrally planned resettlement areas are administered using blanket rules, which leaves little room for farm-level variation to take advantage of local opportunities.

Much of the early resettlement was facilitated by low-cost acquisition of lands abandoned during the war and rapid selection of settlers, including many who were already living as squatters on or near those farms. But by the late 1980s, it became more difficult to find suitable low-cost land, and the selection of settlers became a more contentious political issue. The program slowed to a few thousand families annually.

In the government's 1990 reelection campaigns, some officials publicized their intention to acquire an additional half or more of the remaining LSC area for resettlement. At the same time, the 1980 Lancaster House agreement lapsed, and the constitution was amended to allow forced sales at government-set prices. Land acquisition was then passed, and some farms have been "designated" for forced purchase, but these farms have not yet actually been taken over, and it is still not clear what direction future land policy will take.

Further efforts at planned resettlement could be successful, but only if they achieve a much higher density of population, crops, and livestock than the old schemes. But whether or not the formal resettlement program expands, other kinds of policy change could contribute to more equitable and efficient land use. These opportunities are reviewed below, first for the commercial (LSC and SSC) areas, then for the CAs.

Land Tenure Policy in Commercial Areas

The greatest promise for improved resource allocation lies in moving toward more equal marginal land productivities between communal and commercial areas. This almost certainly involves breaking down many LSC farms into smaller operational units, to raise the relative marginal value of land and thereby increase the intensity of land use. The fact that land in larger farm units has lower value has been aptly summarized by one of the country's leading private-sector farm valuation practitioners, who wrote of LSC land values that, for a given location and quality, "the larger the property, the less it is worth per unit area" (Mullett 1983, p. 13). The loss of productivity caused by concentrating land ownership in a few large farms while other farmers cultivate very small plots is an inevitable result of diseconomies of farm size and is a major constraint on agricultural growth in many countries (Johnston and Tomich 1985).

As suggested by Figure II.1, although LSC farms are very large (averaging 2,500 hectares), they are almost always managed with a strong internal dualism: Equipment and labor are focused on a relatively small cropped area, while the remainder of the farm is left to low-input uses.[14] Within the plowed area, the economic efficiency of LSC farming is comparable to that of smallholders (as shown in Part IV), so breaking up established LSC cropping systems is unlikely to increase productivity. But it would not be productive to extend LSC systems across a greater area, because their high degree of input use is profitable only on the most convenient and best soils: to use large, low-cost tractors, plowed areas must be relatively large and accessible, and to apply high levels of fertilizer, soils must be relatively deep and well-watered. Thus neither expanding nor reducing cropped area under large-scale farming methods would be very profitable.

From the point of view of both equity and efficiency, one solution to the "land question" would lie in the use of currently unplanted LSC lands, which are typically used for low-input grazing. Smallholders would gladly increase the productivity of these areas, by simultaneously increasing the intensity of grazing (through replacing free-range movements with managed herding) and the intensity of cropping (by using ox-plows in pockets of arable soils too remote, rocky, dry, or shallow to justify mechanized cultivation). Between 1908 and 1930 such mixed farming was allowed and became common, as LSC farmers rented or sharecropped some or all of their land to large numbers of African tenants. This practice acquired the derogatory name of "kaffir farming" and was halted in the 1930s to enforce race segregation under the Land Apportionment Act (Moyana 1984, p. 70).

The voluntary subdivision of commercial farms is now governed by the Town and Country Planning Act, last amended in 1976. The intention of the act is to ensure that subdivided farms are "economically viable," meaning that the farm must allow the proprietor to reach target incomes in the range of other farms in its land tenure category. Subdividing farms to create smallholdings is illegal, and even the routine adjustment of boundaries among large farms has been difficult. In the late 1980s there were few applications, and many were refused: fewer than 50 were approved each year (Department of Physical Planning 1986, 1987, 1988).

One common justification for the Town and Country Planning Act is to prevent soil erosion and land degradation. This is an important objective, but it is currently being achieved at an extremely high cost. Large areas of LSC land are left fallow (or in low-input grazing and forestry), while in the land-scarce CAs farmers cannot afford so much fallow; to feed themselves they must plant as much land as possible every year, causing rapid erosion (Whitlow 1988). National soil conservation objectives would be better served by more equal intensity of land use between sectors, rather than the current situation of extreme conservation in LSC areas and rapid degradation in the CAs.

Another common justification for the act is to prevent land speculation. It is feared that land would attract financial speculation that, in the context of inflationary pressures coupled with foreign exchange controls, would be subject to speculative runs. This could push the price of land well above its agricultural productivity at least temporarily, causing inequality and inefficiency in land use. Again, this is a legitimate concern, but the almost complete prohibition on subdivision raises the prices of those few small farms that do come on the market, while lowering the per-hectare price and productivity of land in larger farms. In this case, the cure is worse than the disease.

Voluntary subdivision would result in a wide range of farm sizes, depending on location, available technology, and household characteristics. Some subdivisions would consist of several hundred hectares, while others might be as small as three or four hectares. The size of the smallest farms would be dictated in part by the availability of draft power for plowing; where farmers can hire teams of oxen or tractors and do not need to maintain their own herds and grazing areas, farms as small as one or two hectares planted to high-value crops such as tobacco could yield higher incomes than are currently achieved on larger, lower-quality farms in the communal areas.

The increase in production from voluntary subdivision would come primarily in the form of crops, as smallholders would plant the areas currently used in low-input grazing. This would probably result in a decline in beef marketing from the high-potential regions, where most of Zimbabwe's commercial beef herd is currently located. Some of the beef herd would be displaced to lower-potential areas less suitable for crops, while there might also be an increase in pen-fattening of animals. There would still be a substantial role for livestock in the higher-potential regions, but under smallholder management cattle often have a higher value as an input into crop farming than as for sale as beef. Grazing for beef production would continue only where it was in fact more profitable than crop production, under the full potential range of farm sizes and techniques.

The near-prohibition of voluntary subdivision means that all resettlement in commercial areas is done by the formal resettlement program. This program conceivably could achieve efficient land use, but doing so would require a massive planning effort to identify optimal plot sizes and boundary locations for each farm in each area. Because administrative resources are limited, there have been relatively small improvements in land use as shown in Table II.1. Although it may appear equitable to give settlers as much land as possible, giving them more than enough to equalize conditions in the resettlement and communal areas is hardly equitable from the communal farmers' point of view, and it is certainly not efficient.

In national terms, efficiency and equity would both be served by allowing voluntary subdivision of commercial farms, allowing settlers to buy or lease just as much land as they can profitably use. Such a voluntary resettlement process could complement the planned resettlement, without necessarily replacing it.

Also, a voluntary, decentralized resettlement process need not be limited to the LSC areas; as Table II.1 suggests, there is also a relatively low intensity of land use in SSC areas, although the total area involved is much smaller. In all commercial areas, a more flexible land allocation system could allow increased intensity in land use, higher land productivity, and lower production costs.

To help motivate land sales, a progressive land tax increasing with larger farm size could be used. Allowances could be made for quality and location, with tax levels set for example as a proportion of average gross revenue per hectare in each district or farming area. Thus tax rates might be set, for example, at zero for the first hundred hectares, then 1 percent of average gross revenue per hectare for next hundred, 2 percent for the next group, and so forth. The exact system matters less than the general idea of motivating the subdivision of underused land. Some landowners might attempt to reduce their tax burden by subdividing farms among family members or friends, without actually reducing the operational unit of the farm. Some degree of tax evasion is inevitable, but the problem could be reduced through a provision requiring that the names of buyers and sellers be published or more stringently through a requirement that subdivisions be sold or leased on some kind of open market such as a public auction.

At the same time, to help facilitate purchases, a land bank offering credit or lease guarantees could be used—as was done to attract white settlers to Rhodesia in the first place. The interest rate need not be subsidized, since land productivity would be sufficient to pay for credit at market rates. But the government (or a foreign aid donor) could use a credit subsidy to accelerate the land transfer process. The benefits of such a subsidy would go primarily to land sellers, because the supply of land is much more inelastic that demand, but it could still be desirable if it accelerates the rate of sales.

Although changes of ownership are desirable, some economic gains could be achieved through leases as well as sales. Leases would allow those with little capital to begin farming, on a share or a cash-rent basis. Farmers could be allowed to evolve their own arrangements, or standard contracts could be issued by government. The most economically efficient contracts allow tenants and landowners to share costs, profits, and risks, thus bringing both sides' resources to the farm. But less than perfect arrangements would still allow improvements in resource allocation, moving towards the general goal of opening up currently underused land, bringing more labor and other inputs onto the land to increase its productivity and value.

An important institutional aspect of voluntary resettlement would be the provision of public services such as education, health, and infrastructure to the new smallholders in commercial areas. Local government in LSC areas has traditionally been implemented through Rural Councils, elected by landowners and not residents. In contrast, after independence local government in the CAs was established on the basis of District Councils, elected by all residents. In keeping with their different constituencies, Rural Councils generally provide far less education and health care to their residents than District Councils. In LSC areas such services, if provided at all, have been the responsibility of the individual landowner, whose own family's education and health services have typically been obtained elsewhere, often in the private sector. To ensure the provision of public services, smallholders would have to be included in the constituency of local government. Smallholders could then help guide the provision of their own services, as is currently done in the CAs unlike in the RAs, where services are centrally planned.

The opening of commercial land to a larger number of farmers will be a complex problem, involving many changes. One perhaps unexpected requirement, for example, would be a rapid increase in the number of licensed surveyors: currently only a few firms are practicing in the entire country, partly because there is so little farm subdivision business. As such changes cannot all be predicted, so appropriate land policy would have to evolve as new problems and opportunities arose.

Proposals for "part-farm" resettlement have been made before, particularly by Sam Moyo of the Zimbabwe Institute of Development Studies (Moyo et al. 1989, as cited in Gasper 1990). But this analysis, in the context of an explicit model of land and input use (Figure II.1) with data for both LSC and communal areas (Table II.1 and the PAM results of Part IV), highlights the ability of a voluntary, decentralized process to achieve the full efficiency and equity advantages of widespread land ownership. Under a decentralized allocation mechanism, government officials would have to give up control over who moved onto which land. That element of control was widely seen as necessary in the immediate postwar period, but since the initial phase of planned resettlement has now been completed, voluntary subdivision may be a desirable new direction for government policy.

Land Tenure Policy in Communal Areas

Land allocation within the communal areas is not as inequitable and inefficient as between the communal and commercial sectors, but there may still be opportunities for improvement. The central idea, again, would be to move toward more equal productivity for farmers in different areas. There is now wide variation in land and labor productivity, both between and within regions. Changes in CA land tenure rules could reduce these inequities, while improving farm productivity and lowering production costs.

Historically, some population movements toward higher-potential areas have occurred, leaving the lower-rainfall areas with lower population densities and larger cropped areas and livestock herds per household.[15] But this movement has not been enough to offset lower land productivity in the drier areas, where incomes remain very much lower than in the higher-productivity areas.[16] Further migration from lower to higher productivity areas would help to reduce some of these disparities. But although CA residents enjoy full individual use rights over housing and arable lands, these rights cannot now be formally sold or rented. Thus residents may not capitalize on the value of their land to finance out-migration, and in-migration is similarly restricted by the difficulty of acquiring use rights.[17]

Not only does the communal-area tenure system restrict migration between regions, it also restricts adjustments between households within local areas. Households cannot easily change their arable landholdings to match their holdings of livestock, labor, or equipment. Because households cannot buy arable land, it is difficult for households to expand their cropped area, and those wishing to invest in agriculture usually expand their livestock herds instead, taking advantage of open-access grazing wherever possible. Conversely, because households cannot sell land, those wishing to migrate or invest elsewhere have no incentive to give up their arable land to others.

The land sales issue is particularly serious for urban migrants, who typically leave most or all of their family behind at their rural home in order not to give up their use-rights, even if they see their best income and investment opportunities off the farm. Such partial migration fragments the family, selectively removes young men from the farm labor force, and often paralyzes farm decision-making. From each individual migrant's point of view, however, such fragmentation may be preferable to the alternatives of either giving up their communal-area home or not migrating at all.

To a certain extent, the communal-area tenure system does provide a safety net for the poor, in the form of unalienable rights to "free" land. Unfortunately, because many poor households lack the resources needed to make their land productive (livestock, implements, or even seed and labor), for them land rights are of more spiritual and social value than of practical use. Such nonmaterial values are important, but many of the rural poor might prefer the material benefits of capitalizing on their land values, by either borrowing against or selling some of their inheritance. Making this option available through voluntary title registration would help to promote more efficient and probably also more equitable land use patterns.

Farm Technology, Cropping Patterns, and Yields

Largely as a result of the dual land tenure system, Zimbabwean agriculture is divided into two completely different farming systems. LSC agriculture, with an abundance of land and capital, is highly mechanized. As will be noted, there is widespread use of irrigation (usually by electrically pumped overhead sprinklers), crop chemicals sprayed both aerially and from tractors, and combine harvesters. Yields are typically among the highest in the world, with high levels of input use.

Among smallholders production is based on a mixed system in which livestock provide tillage, transport, manure, milk, meat, some cash income, and a store of wealth, while cropping provides most of the household food plus some cash income.[18] Almost all plots are prepared for planting with an ox-plow, some are weeded with an ox-drawn cultivator, and transport is often done by ox-cart. All other operations (seeding, most weeding, harvesting, and threshing) are typically done by hand. Some small-scale commercial (SSC) farmers, and a very small proportion of CA and RA farmers, own or can hire tractors and other mechanical equipment. Several donor-funded tractor-hire schemes are in operation, but they require large subsidies because long distances between fields, small field sizes, and high capital and maintenance costs typically make tractor plowing much more expensive than ox-drawn plowing (Rusike 1988).

For smallholders, traditional cropping patterns were based on a wide variety of products (for a comprehensive listing, see Gomez 1988). Before white settlement, a seventeenth century traveler wrote: "Provisions are not wanting in the land, for it abounds with them, namely millet, some rice, many vegetables, large and small cattle, and many hens" (Antonio Bocarro, quoted in Mudenge 1988, p. 162). The dominant grain undoubtedly varied across the country. "The principal crop of the Shona must have been finger millet and that of the Matabele, bulrush [pearl] millet" (Johnson 1964, p. 175). Rice was also probably of considerable local importance.[19]

Today, the national farming system is dominated by maize. Maize was probably first brought to Zimbabwe by the Portuguese several hundred years ago (Miracle 1966), but it does not seem to have spread significantly into Zimbabwean farming systems until the arrival of white settlers in 1890. As suggested by Sawer, some expansion of maize had already occurred by 1909, but there was undoubtedly much greater expansion of maize beginning in the 1920s with the spread of mechanical hammermills (Johnson 1964).

Statistics on African farming systems begin with the estimates of local Native Commissioners, starting in 1902. These suggest that in the forty years between white settlement and World War II, smallholder average grain yields fell by half, from over 710 to 360 kg/ha. Area planted more than tripled, but still production per capita fell sharply (Weinmann 1975). Average land quality was undoubtedly worsening, because of both forced migration and area expansion, causing the cultivation of less productive lands. Ox-plows and maize grinding mills were spreading during this period, which allowed an increase in area and a reduction in processing time, but few new technologies to improve yields were available.

The first nationwide surveys were undertaken in the 1949 and 1960 harvest years (Table II.3). These surveys framed the decade of the 1950s, when smallholders decisively switched from millets to maize.

Table II.3
Cropping Patterns and Yields in African Areas, 1949–1960

Harvest Year	African Farmers	Cultivated Area (ha/hh)	Percentage of Area			Average Yields (kg/ha)	
			Maize	Millets	Other	Maize	Millets
1949	273,000	3.3	30%	48%	22%	450	225
1960	323,000	2.9	50%	41%	9%	1125	450

Source: LeRoux (1969).

The growth of maize area and the increasing yield gap between maize and millets was largely due to improvements in maize varieties. Although these new maize varieties were intended for the higher-rainfall areas, they were preferable to unimproved millet in many dry regions as well. Between the 1949 and 1960 surveys, in areas receiving under 500 mm of effective rainfall the proportion of cultivated acreage under maize doubled from 19 to 38 percent (LeRoux 1969, p. 84).

Rapid technical change continued after the 1960 survey. In the 1960s came the release of a very high-potential maize hybrid (SR52), along with the development of more effective pesticides for cotton. In the 1970s, the R200 series of short-season/short-stature maize hybrids was released, bringing higher yields to even the driest areas. The initial impact of these innovations was muted by the reduction in area planted caused by the war, but after 1980 the new maize and cotton technologies allowed production to increase rapidly, in the context of a return to rural peace, the rapid expansion of marketing services, and relatively favorable pricing.

Today, among smallholders, maize and cotton are the dominant cash crops, although area planted to the small grains (millets and sorghum) and oilseeds (groundnuts and sunflowers) is also high. The large-scale commercial sector is somewhat more diversified in the aggregate, although individual farms are typically more specialized.

Table II.4 illustrates the national-average cropping pattern over the past few years, in terms of the major field crops. (Other crops also have significant value but take much smaller areas, such as sugar, horticultural products, coffee and tea for exports; bambara nuts, cowpeas, and many vegetables for subsistence; and forage crops for livestock.)

As shown in Table II.5, national production for most of the listed crops is dominated by the communal areas, because of their larger size and greater cropping intensity. The listed crops dominated by the LSC sector are yellow maize, which is grown as a livestock feed and is therefore not very attractive as a food crop for smallholders; Virginia tobacco, for which processing and marketing remains highly capital- and management-intensive; wheat, which must be grown under irrigation in winter; and soybean, commonly grown in rotation with wheat. In a typical year, about half of smallholder production is devoted to home consumption, so that the LSC sector dominates most formal marketings of the listed crops.

Average yields, shown in Table II.6, are similar in the three smallholder subsectors but about two to three times higher in the LSC subsector. Smallholder and national-average yields are typically somewhat below the FAO estimates for Africa as a whole and substantially below FAO estimates for all developing countries and the world. LSC yields, on the other hand, are above global averages and often above European or North American averages as well.

Table II.4
Cropping Patterns by Farming Area, 1987–1989 Harvests

	CA	LSC	RA	SSC	Zimbabwe
			Percent		
Maize (white)	52	26	68	48	49
Maize (yellow)	..	7	..	..	1
Sorghum	9	1	4	4	8
Pearl Millet	10	..	2	2	8
Finger Millet	6	..	4	5	5
Cotton	8	18	-10	17	10
Groundnuts	10	2	7	15	8
Soybeans	..	17	..	..	3
Sunflower	5	2	4	9	4
Virginia Tobacco		17			2
Wheat (winter)		12			2
Total ('000 ha)	1,868	359	169	77	2,474

Note: Totals may not add to 100 because of rounding.
Source: Author's calculations, from CSO data.

These data on land use dramatize the extent to which Zimbabwean agriculture is marked by extreme dualism. LSC areas have high yields but only plant a small proportion of the available area; smallholder areas have lower yields but plant a much larger share. This dualism is caused largely by historical events but maintained in part by current land tenure policies, particularly the restrictions on farm subdivision. Changes in these policies could alter the national pattern of land distribution, improving both equity and agricultural productivity.

INVESTMENT IN AGRICULTURE

Land itself is not very valuable. What makes farmland productive is farmers' investment of labor, purchased inputs, and capital needed to raise yields. Both private and public investment in agriculture is needed if productivity is to be raised and production costs lowered over time. In this section three major types of investment in agriculture are discussed: irrigation, research and extension, and transport infrastructure. In each case attracting sufficient private investment also requires government spending, because these investments have

Table II.5
Production Shares by Farming Area, 1987–1989 Harvests

	CA	LSC	RA	SSC	Zimbabwe
			Percent		
Maize (white)	62	26	8	3	1,618
Maize (yellow)	..	100	..	..	142
Sorghum	84	11	3	2	103
Pearl Millet	98	..	1	..	112
Finger Millet	91	..	6	3	62
Cotton	41	49	7	3	278
Groundnuts	74	16	4	5	105
Soybeans	2	97	..	..	114
Sunflower	75	11	7	7	50
Virginia Tobacco		100			126
Wheat (winter)		100			234

Source: Author's calculations, from CSO data.

large spillover effects among farmers or between farmers and consumers. Historically the government has been generous in providing such public goods within the white settler LSC areas; since independence, providing them to the much larger CA farm community has been difficult.

Irrigation

With low and uncertain rainfall levels, one key area of agricultural investment is irrigation. Irrigation raises productivity in the short term as each crop grows and in the long run by deepening the soils and building up organic matter. Irrigation covers 36 percent (178,500 ha) of cropped area in the LSC sector, but under a quarter of 1 percent (4,600 ha) in the CA sector (FAO/Harare 1990).[20] Within the LSC sector, the proportion irrigated varies widely by crop (Table II.7).

The dominant method of irrigation is the use of dams to capture surface water, with canals and electrical pumping into overhead sprinklers to distribute it. As a result, agricultural use of electricity is a significant proportion (about 8 percent) of national electrical consumption (ZESA 1988), although it is not a large part of average farm-level production cost (see Part IV). Flood irrigation

Table II.6
Average Yields by Farming Area, 1987–1989 Harvests

(mt/ha)	CA	LSC	RA	SSC	National	Africa	LDCs	World
Maize (white)	1.03	4.67	1.15	1.33	1.33	1.54	2.26	3.45
Maize (yellow)		5.50			5.50			
Sorghum	0.47	2.86	0.41	0.66	0.53	0.89	1.11	1.40
Pearl Millet	0.54	0.51	0.41	0.35	0.54	0.68	0.74	0.79
Finger Millet	0.48	0.42	0.46	0.56	0.48			
Cotton	0.75	2.14	1.05	0.72	1.13	1.00	1.35	1.57
Groundnuts	0.43	3.10	0.42	0.47	0.51	1.13	1.08	1.13
Soybeans	0.68	1.84	0.55	0.66	1.75	1.09	1.60	1.83
Sunflower	0.44	0.97	0.53	0.51	0.47			
Virginia Tobacco		2.10			2.10	1.03	1.35	1.46
Wheat (winter)		5.75			5.75	1.57	2.18	2.31

Note: Figures are simple averages of yields across years.
Source: Author's calculations, from CSO data. Africa, LDCs, and World estimates are from FAO Production Yearbook, 1989.

Table II.7
Irrigated Proportion of LSC Area, 1989 Harvest (percentages of each crop)

Maize (white)	8
Maize (yellow)	16
Cotton	41
Groundnuts	86
Soybeans	31
Wheat	100
Tobacco	15
All Crops Average	36

Source: CSO Crop Forecasting Committee, April 1989. All crops average is calculated from FAO/Harare (1990).

is used on less than a quarter of all irrigated area, mostly on heavier soils at lower altitudes (FAO/Harare 1990).

The bulk of irrigation facilities have been privately developed and are privately owned, by individual LSC farmers or a partnership of neighbors. But longstanding government credit subsidies for irrigation have accelerated the rate of investment, and in some areas LSC farmers get public water at low rates from government irrigation projects. After independence, both credit subsidies and government projects have been directed at expanding irrigation in communal areas, but with limited success. The demand for irrigation credit in communal areas has been limited, and government-backed irrigation schemes have not grown rapidly. Constraining factors include the availability of surface water, the lack of electricity where pumping would be needed, and the geographic dispersion of individual farms around dam sites (FAO/Harare 1990).

Small irrigated gardens can be found throughout the CAs, but their total area is unknown and does not appear in Table II.7. For such gardens water is drawn from surface streams, wells, and occasionally government-drilled boreholes and is usually applied by hand with buckets. Garden produce is often a major element of the diet and also a major source of cash income. Group garden irrigation schemes under government or donor administration have been constructed in several areas, but management and coordination problems have limited their growth.

In total, Zimbabwe has only marginally more cropped and irrigated area than the African average and considerably less than the developing countries or world as a whole (Table II.8). This is partly due to the fact that Zimbabwe, like much of Africa, has less water available than the rest of the world, with national average precipitation of 674 mm/yr compared to a world average of 860 mm

Table II.8
FAO Estimates of Land Use and Irrigation, 1988

	World	LDCs	Africa	Zimbabwe
Land Area (million ha)	13,069	7,587	2,964	39
Of which:				
Cropped and fallow	11%	11%	6%	7%
Permanent pasture	25%	26%	27%	13%
Irrigated	1.7%	2.2%	0.4%	0.6%
Memo item:				
Irrigated (% of				
cropped and fallow)	15.5%	20.6%	6.0%	7.7%

Source: FAO *Production Yearbook*, 1989.

(Wells 1988), but it is also partly due to historical under-investment in communal area irrigation facilities.

The relative productivity of further irrigation development has recently been investigated in FAO/Harare (1990). Their results suggest that most new irrigation investment appears to be financially unprofitable for private investors, but economically profitable from the national point of view. Using FAO/Harare data on a sample of twenty-four dam proposals (each of four dam types in both CA and LSC areas across three natural regions), it can be calculated that private profits would be positive for only two cases in the LSC areas and none in the CAs, while national profits would be positive for nine cases in the LSC areas and five in the CAs.[21] These results offer evidence of the need for public irrigation investment in general, while cautioning that the costs and returns of particular projects can vary widely.

Research and Extension

After irrigation, a second major determinant of farm productivity is crop research and extension. Zimbabwe's efforts in this area are among the oldest and most successful in Africa—the country's first experiment station was founded in 1903—but they have been closely targeted to large-scale farms and LSC environments.[22]

Before independence, the research system operated as a generally close partnership between government and settler farmers. Farmer associations participated directly in the funding and oversight of government research service covering most crops, while government grants helped support the private

Tobacco Research Board. This system was highly successful for maize and tobacco, whose area planted and yields expanded dramatically from the late 1940s. In the early 1960s the system also produced successful varieties of winter wheat. The use of hybrid maize (along with chemical fertilizers) required neither mechanization nor irrigation and was adopted by CA as well as LSC farmers. But because the early varieties were tall and slow-maturing their expansion was limited to areas with relatively long rainy seasons. Tobacco and wheat, on the other hand, were successful only on LSC farms, perhaps because there appear to be substantial economies of scale in curing tobacco and irrigating wheat.

After UDI, both government and private support for non-tobacco research was intensified in an effort to overcome the loss of tobacco exports under sanctions. Between 1967 and 1970 research spending more than doubled in real terms, rising from 0.5 percent to 1.5 percent of agricultural GDP. This level of spending was sustained during the 1970s with strong private support, as the Rhodesian National Farmers' Union (now the CFU) directly contributed around 13 percent of the government research budget, using revenue from levies on members' marketings.

In this period there were two major breakthroughs—the improvement of pest control techniques for cotton in the mid-1960s and the release of early-maturing, short-stature maize hybrids (principally R200, R201, and R215) in the 1970s. Both innovations were intended to assist former tobacco farmers in diversifying, but in suiting the relatively dry, sandy environments favored by tobacco they also suited many smallholder areas. After 1980 both technologies were rapidly adopted by smallholders.

With independence and majority rule, government research objectives were largely redirected toward the concerns of African farmers. This thrust was almost immediately handicapped by reductions in real spending. In 1983 the farmers' associations, representing LSC grains and oilseeds producers, formed their own private Agricultural Research Trust (ART) and withdrew their support for government research, which never again reached the peak levels of real spending achieved in 1981 and 1982.

In the 1980s private research expanded rapidly, particularly on maize. The ART Farm focused on agronomy and field trials, while the privately owned Seed Coop—the sole distributor of government-bred varieties and hybrids—undertook its own crop-breeding efforts. A local affiliate of the multinational Pioneer Seed Company also began local research. These efforts were rapidly successful: By the late 1980s, among the more promising newly released white maize hybrids in government trials were the Seed Coop's SC501 and Pioneer's PNR473, although neither surpassed the performance of R201 and R215 (Crop Breeding Institute file data).

Figures II.2 and II.3 summarize government spending in the agricultural sector; figures in terms of current dollars are also presented in appendix Table

Figure II.2
Real Government Expenditure on Agriculture, 1967–1989

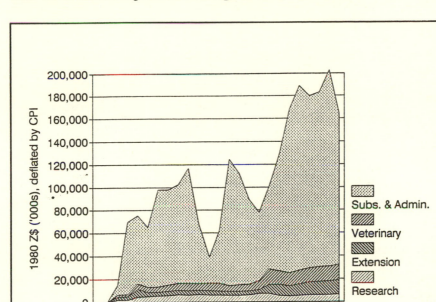

Source: Table C.7, calculated from CSO and MLARR data.

C.7. These data include all revenue sources, including private contributions, and represent actual expenditure rather than budget allocations.

Figure II.2 shows that the initial growth of research spending in the late 1960s was accompanied by similar increases for all the other government activities in the agricultural sector: extension and veterinary services as well as subsidies and administration.[23] Then, in the 1970s, the research, extension, and veterinary services had roughly constant real budgets, while subsidies and other costs fluctuated widely.[24] But after 1981, spending patterns diverged sharply: When research expenditure fell as CFU funds were withdrawn, extension and veterinary services continued to expand. Subsidies and other costs rose past their 1970s peaks in 1983 and 1984, then continued to rise until 1989.

Figure II.3
Agricultural Expenditure as a Percentage of GDP, 1967–1988

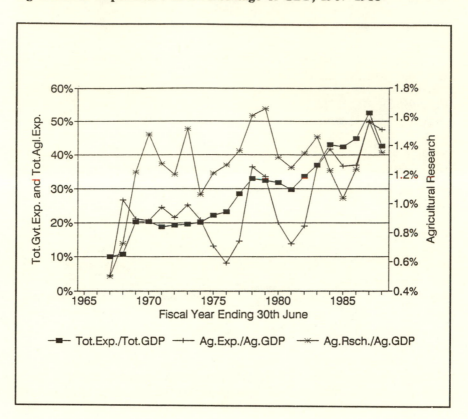

Source: Table C.7, calculated from CSO and MLARR data.

Total agricultural spending as a proportion of agricultural GDP has generally risen at a similar rate to total government expenditure as a proportion of total GDP: Government's share of both agricultural and total GDP rose from 10 percent or under in 1967, to over 30 percent before independence, and then to a peak of 50 percent in 1988 (Figure II.3, left axis). But the growth of research spending as a proportion of agricultural GDP has been quite different: it tripled, from 0.5 percent to 1.5 percent, between 1967 and 1970 and has been roughly constant since then (Figure II.3, right axis).

Zimbabwe's agricultural research expenditures as a proportion of agricultural GDP are among the highest in Africa; in 1980, only three other African countries (Mali, Senegal, and Kenya) spent more than 1 percent of agricultural

GDP on agricultural research (Eicher 1984). But the decline of research relative to other government activities is striking. The largest recent review of studies measuring rates of return to research (Echevarria 1990) finds consistently high profitability, and it appears likely that renewed research investment in Zimbabwe would have similarly high payoffs.

Research is particularly important in combination with extension. Among African farmers the Rhodesian government had a long tradition of extension without research, using extension to enforce government rules and teach general managerial skills rather than introduce new technology. Overall spending patterns after 1982 (Figure II.2) indicate a return to this pattern; this is also suggested by an increasing use of the extension service for the management of irrigation and grazing schemes, for land-use planning in resettlement and communal areas, and for the enforcement of conservation rules. Such efforts are typically less productive than using extension to introduce new techologies, which can only be produced by research.

Extension efforts for Africans began in 1926, with the appointment of an American former missionary, E. D. Alvord, to constitute the Department of Native Agriculture in the Ministry of Native Affairs. The focus of early extension efforts was on crop separation, crop rotation, and manure use, through demonstration plots and the training of master farmers. But these technologies were of limited value: Despite a considerable extension effort (at his retirement in 1946, Alvord had a staff of 373), over his twenty years of work Alvord found no positive trend in yields either on demonstration plots or on farmer fields (Kennan 1980).

In the 1950s and 1960s, when productive new technologies first became available, relations between African farmers and government extension agents were decisively soured by the implementation of the 1951 Native Land Husbandry Act. The act imposed harsh restrictions on farmers, aiming "to provide for the control of the utilization and allocation of land occupied by natives to ensure its efficient use for agricultural purposes" and "to require natives to perform labor for conserving natural resources and for promoting good husbandry." The act's major provisions—freehold tenure, compulsory destocking, and forced labor on soil conservation projects—were extremely unpopular, totally unsuccessful, and abandoned in 1961.

After the abandonment of the Native Land Husbandry Act, extension efforts were transferred from the Ministry of Native Affairs to the Ministry of Agriculture, which helped to restore professionalism to the extension service. But the African and European services remained separate until independence, when the current Department of Agricultural, Technical and Extension Services (Agritex) was formed, out of the old African service (the Department of Agricultural Development, DEVAG) and that for European farmers (the Department of Conservation and Extension, CONEX). Services to the LSC sector were taken over by private-sector consultants.

As of 1989, Agritex had a staff of 2,500 of whom 1,600 were extension agents; the Agritex presence in the countryside is substantial, enough to ensure fairly widespread dissemination of whatever technologies are produced by the research establishment. But Agritex's success, like Alvord's, is constrained by the quality of the technical innovations it has to offer farmers. The historical bias of research programs favoring the crops, techniques, and environments of settler farmers in the LSC areas has limited the domain of many varietal and technical breakthroughs. The exceptions, however, have been rapidly adopted by CA farmers. In a favorable context, particularly where profitable innovations from local research are available, investments in extension seem to be profitable. It is much more difficult to measure returns to extension than returns to research, but a thorough recent review concluded that "the few studies which were undertaken demonstrate very high rates of return in both developing and developed countries" (Birkhaeuser, Evenson, and Feder 1989, p. 46). Extension could be extremely valuable in Zimbabwe as well, to the extent that productive new techniques are being generated by the research service.

Transport Infrastructure

A final category of public investment that fundamentally affects farm costs is transport infrastructure. In Zimbabwe, product and input movements between farm and market (or marketing board depot) can easily cost farmers a fifth or more of their revenues. Delays from transport bottlenecks can also retard plantings and increase post-harvest losses. Better transport is needed, but in most areas the problem is vehicles, not roads.

Historically, Zimbabwe's rural roads, like most other government investments, were designed to serve white settlers. Over time an extensive network was built, the quality of which was much improved in the 1970s when many unpaved roads were tarred to protect vehicles from the guerillas' land mines. By the end of the war, road density per capita within the LSC areas rivalled that of the United States, and in the CAs was among the best in Africa. Compared with Asia, Zimbabwe's CA road density is low in terms of area, but relatively high in per-capita terms.

Despite Zimbabwe's relatively good roads, after every harvest in the late 1980s there have been frequent news reports of farmers awaiting transport, occasionally for several months until the onset of the next season's rain.[25] Both farmers and the transport industry almost always blame a shortage of vehicles and spare parts,[26] rather than road quality.[27] Some evidence in favor of this hypothesis is provided by the regional pattern of transport costs paid by farmers: the 1989 MLARR Communal Areas farm survey found transport payments per ton-kilometer to be unrelated to road quality, but strongly correlated with farm profits. Higher farm profits were associated with higher transport prices,

Table II.9
Road Density in Zimbabwe and Selected Countries

		Road Density		Memo Item:
		(km/km²)	(km/ 1000 pers.)	GNP/CAP. (US $)
Zimbabwe	LSC Areas	0.20	20.3	
	Communal Areas	0.12	4.9	
	National Average	0.14	7.7	600
Africa	Zambia	0.05	5.4	300
	Kenya	0.09	2.5	300
	Senegal	0.07	2.0	420
	Nigeria	0.11	1.0	640
	Botswana	0.02	11.1	840
Asia	Bangladesh	0.35	0.5	160
	India	0.41	1.7	290
Other	United States	0.67	26.0	17,480

Source: Road length data are for 1976–1978 from Ahmed and Rustagi (1987), except Zimbabwe, which are for 1983, from Heidhues and Thalheimer (1986). Population and income data are for 1986, from World Bank, *World Development Report* (1988).

suggesting that transporters were setting prices on a willingness-to-pay basis in a noncompetitive market, because a shortage of vehicles blocked the entry of potential competitors who would otherwise have reduced prices in areas with better roads.

Vehicles and spares are a major import-substitution industry, highly protected by restricted foreign currency allocations. But the domestic industry has not kept up with demand, which can be seen in vehicle ages: in mid-1990, an estimated 67 percent of the country's goods vehicle fleet was more than seven years old (TOA 1990). The small truck fleet, which is particularly important for serving smallholder areas, was found to be even older: an estimated 75 percent of vehicles dated from 1983 or earlier. The age of the fleet raises fuel, lubricant, and spare part costs. Spares are subject to almost as severe a shortage as new vehicles, and an estimated 27 percent of the goods fleet was off the road in June 1990, awaiting parts, tires, or both.

International transport is also very costly for Zimbabwe, particularly for agriculture. Traditionally most of Zimbabwe's external trade passed eastward to the Indian Ocean, first along the Mutare-Beira rail line completed in 1897 and later on the longer but faster Limpopo rail line to the deeper port of Maputo (then Lourenço Marques). This historical pattern was interrupted after UDI in 1965, when Rhodesian trade was diverted through the friendly government in South Africa to escape UN-mandated sanctions. Later, in 1975, the newly independent government in Mozambique completely closed both eastern routes, forcing all trade to pass through South Africa to Durban and Port Elizabeth.

Upon Zimbabwe's own independence, Mozambique reopened the eastern routes, but South Africa was able to maintain their earlier monopoly because guerillas promptly sabotaged the Mozambican rail lines.[28] In the early 1980s bombings reduced traffic significantly along the Beira line and closed the Limpopo line to Maputo. This forced almost all of Zimbabwe's trade through the much longer and costlier routes southward to South Africa, which gave the South African authorities political leverage over Zimbabwe and earned them revenue (Lewis 1987).

By 1987, donor-funded reconstruction, Zimbabwean army protection, and a Mozambican devaluation combined to make the Beira route viable again, and in 1988 almost 30 percent of Zimbabwean trade passed through Mozambique. Transport rates for 1989 are given in Table II.10. For the budgets in Part IV of this study, actual 1989 Beira transport costs are used. These could fall if a durable peace were reached in Mozambique, but no such change can yet be predicted.

PURCHASED INPUTS

After factor costs, production technology, and long-term investments, perhaps the most important determinant of farm productivity is the cost of variable

Table II.10
Distance and Cost for Grain Trade by Rail, 1989

Between Harare and:	Distance (km)	Cost (Z $/mt)
Beira (Mozambique)	700	32.91
Durban (South Africa)	2100	85.23

Note: Costs given are for wheat imports; other products would have slightly different rates.
Source: Cargill Technical Services (1989).

inputs. These are briefly surveyed here; prices and quantities for specific items are presented in the notes to the crop budgets in Part IV.

Fertilizer

Zimbabwe's domestic fertilizer industry is old and large. It dates from 1924, when a small phosphatic fertilizer plant was built. Mixing of compound fertilizers began in 1947, and synthesis of nitrogenous fertilizers began in the 1960s, when low-cost electricity from Kariba Dam became available (World Bank 1987). Currently the average import content of wholesale fertilizers is estimated at 26 percent (GOZ 1986); a small amount (about 15,000 mt/yr, or 3 percent of total production) was exported to neighboring countries in 1988 and 1989.

The industry consists of four very large firms. One produces nitrogenous fertilizer in the form of ammonium nitrate (AN), using ammonia locally produced by electrolysis and some additional imported ammonia. Another firm produces phosphatic fertilizer in the form of single and triple super-phosphate (SSP and TSP), using domestically mined phosphate rock and pyrites, supplemented by imported sulphur. Two downstream firms blend, package, and distribute these products, plus some imported ingredients, as straight or compound fertilizers.

The current production process is generally considered to be efficient, in both technical and economic terms (World Bank 1987). The profitability of local fertilizer production depends critically on the relative values of nitrogen imports versus local electricity for electrolysis. Local production of ammonium nitrate is estimated to have benefitted from a nominal protection rate of 16 percent in 1989, as detailed in Part IV of this study. But as long as nitrogen can be produced using nontradable hydroelectric power, this degree of nominal protection is probably more than offset by the foreign exchange premium of 50 percent (see Part I). Thus domestic production is probably efficient from an economic point of view.[29]

Fertilizer use patterns are very different in the LSC and smallholder sectors. LSC fertilizer use rates are very high, carrying on from the early settlers' practice of using green manures to maintain nearly continuous cropping of maize fields (Dunlop 1971, Collinson 1986). Smallholder use of fertilizer is much lower, perhaps because it is less profitable (because of higher transport and credit costs in obtaining fertilizer and lower fertilizer productivity under lower levels of rainfall, irrigation, and soil organic matter) and also riskier (because of a higher variance of rainfall and lower use of irrigation).[30]

Interesting evidence regarding the interaction between average productivity and risk in fertilizer use can be derived from data provided by Rohrbach (1988), who estimated yield-response functions for 241 farmers in Mangwende, a relatively high-rainfall/low-risk CA, and 127 farmers in Chibi, a low-rainfall/ high-risk CA. From his regression results it can be calculated that in Mangwende, the marginal value product of nitrogenous fertilizer was about $1.20 per dollar of additional fertilizer use at the mean (180 kg/ha), whereas at Chibi CA, it was $7.80 at a much lower mean (5 kg/ha). These results indicate that fertilizer use in drier areas is reduced both by lower average productivity (which lowers the point at which marginal value product equals one and by greater yield risk (which raises the marginal value product "premium" required to compensate for that risk).[31]

    The history of fertilizer use in the LSC sector (Figure II.4 and Appendix Table C.8) shows continuous rapid growth between 1956 and 1975, as both

Figure II.4
Crop Area and Fertilizer Use in LSC Areas, 1956–1988

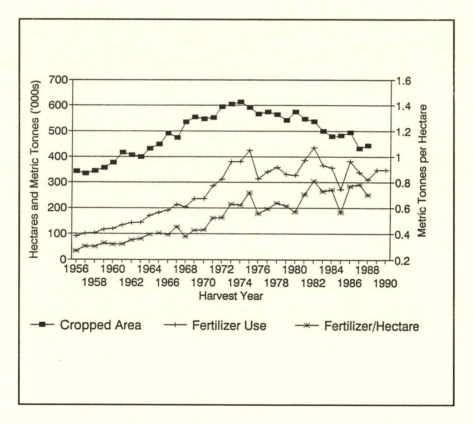

Source: Author's calculations, from CSO and ZFC data (Table C.8).

application rates and area planted rose sharply. After 1975, as LSC farmers have cut back on area planted, application rates have risen only slightly and total use has declined.

In the CA sector (Figure II.5), area planted also fell during the late 1970s, but unlike the LSC sector the CA sector expanded again after the war. This included a virtual explosion in estimated fertilizer sales in the one year after independence, when the smallholder sector as a whole (including the SSC sector) is estimated to have tripled its fertilizer purchases.[32] Underlying increased small-holder fertilizer sales were several factors, including exceptionally good weather

Figure II.5
Estimated CA Crop Area, and Smallholder Fertilizer and Maize Seed Purchases, 1965-1990

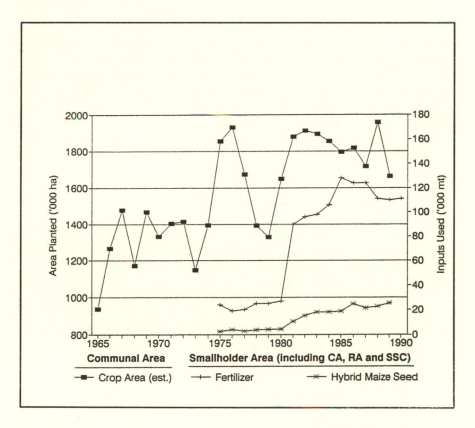

Source: Author's calculations, from CSO, ZFC, and Seed Coop data (Table C.8).

in 1981, a return to rural peace, and favorable pricing, as the fertilizer/maize price ratio was temporarily lowered to around 1.5 in the 1980-1985 period, from the more typical level of around 2.0 (Appendix Table C.9).

An additional factor supporting post-independence fertilizer sales was that the credit with which to buy it was being aggressively extended by the parastatal Agricultural Finance Corporation, at low real interest rates and with repayment based on stop-orders against marketing board receipts rather than cash. Less than half of the initial 1981 burst of fertilizer purchases was bought with AFC credit, but this proportion rose quickly as farmers became aware of the opportunity to borrow on relatively favorable terms (Appendix Table C.9). Farmers do appear to have alternative sources of seasonal capital, however: in 1988, when new AFC lending was cut back by Z$15 million (20 percent) because of high arrears, fertilizer purchases declined by only Z$1 million (2 percent).

The weak transport sector is probably more important than tight credit in limiting fertilizer use, particularly when crop transport delays are compounded by delays in payment for the crop after delivery, which occasionally forces farmers to postpone fertilizer purchases for the next crop. But even without transport, payment, and credit constraints, experimental evidence suggests that the financially most profitable levels of fertilizer use in most smallholder areas are half or less of the levels officially recommended by Agritex (see, for example, Bratton and Truscott 1985 and annual reports of the DR&SS Agronomy Institute). Reaching these levels could still involve some further increase in fertilizer use, although any potential profits would be somewhat offset by increased risk.

Seeds and Crop Chemicals

After fertilizer, the most important inputs are seeds and crop chemicals. As shown in the crop budgets of Part IV, these represent relatively small proportions of total costs; as seeds and pesticides also have relatively little substitutability with other inputs, they can be expected to show relatively little price responsiveness.[33] Their critical attributes are technical, as the embodiment of research on new varieties and techniques.

In the LSC sector, seeds are typically purchased for almost all crops; in the smallholder sector, seeds are typically purchased for maize and cotton, while seeds for all other crops are retained. Some neighbor-to-neighbor sales of retained seeds are made, but most farmers keep their own. Some inoculant may be purchased and used with groundnut seed, but this is not common.

Zimbabwe's seed industry is dominated by the Seed Coop, a privately owned company that enjoys a statutory monopoly over the distribution of varieties developed by the national research service. In the case of hybrid maize, this firm has been able to maintain relatively low prices, high quality, and wide distribution, but seeds for other crops have been less successfully produced and distributed. This largely reflects the low returns on investment in developing and marketing seeds for open-pollinated varieties, which unlike hybrid seeds need not be purchased every year. (For details of the Zimbabwean seed market, see Friis-Hansen 1990.)

Agricultural chemicals, in comparison with Zimbabwe's other industries, are produced under a high degree of competitive pressure. There are a total of fifteen members of the Agro-Chemical Industry Association, although a few of these specialize in veterinary products. The industry blends and packages imported materials, with a local value added generally under 20 percent. Virtually all sales (over 98 percent) are to the LSC sector (Chivinga 1984).

CONCLUSIONS

The most important policy issue identified in this analysis is the land tenure system. Rules against farm subdivision and other restrictions inherited from the colonial era serve to isolate groups of farmers on their land, with little hope of resource mobility. As a result, Zimbabwe's strongly dualistic agricultural sector has, simultaneously, among the most and the least input-intensive farming systems in Africa.

The LSC sector is composed of extremely large farms in favorable areas, which now may not be subdivided into smallholdings. As a result the marginal value of land is low, and LSC farmers find it profitable to plant only their most productive fields, on which they reach among the highest yields in the world with great concentrations of inputs and capital. The CA subsector, on the other hand, contains most of the country's population, in isolated dry areas with few prospects for either intra-rural or rural-urban migration. In this environment land is scarce, so fallow periods are brief, erosion is severe, purchased inputs have low productivity, and yields of many crops are well below African averages. The same forces that have shaped input intensity have guided long-term investments in infrastructure and research. High potential regions enjoy good roads and a substantial shelf of productive techniques, while low potential areas have neither, which has compounded the underlying differences in land tenure rules, land values, and land productivity.

If there were no prospects for land and labor mobility between the CA and LSC subsectors, future input allocations would continue to face the same stark choice between a low-productivity, resource-depleting form of development in the CAs and a high-productivity, conservation-oriented LSC subsector. But Zimbabwe has the opportunity to allow internal resource migration—to subdivide LSC farms and spread out the country's labor, purchased inputs, and capital over a broader land area, yielding potentially large gains in total factor productivity.

The capacity of Zimbabwe's smallholder farmers to expand production rapidly when opportunity strikes was shown in the early 1980s, when a combination of fortuitous events simultaneously relaxed previously tight constraints in crop marketing, production technology, and input availability. The last bottleneck, much harder to open, is access to LSC land. If the Zimbabwean government continues to attempt centrally planned resettlement, it seems likely the experience of the 1980s' resettlement schemes will be repeated, and land use may not be much more equitable or efficient in the RAs than under LSC tenure. But if flexible and decentralized institutional mechanisms can be devised to mobilize LSC land resources to meet the excess demand from smallholder farmers, the country could achieve a second great agricultural success story. From a more equitable and efficient land distribution would follow a more equitable and efficient distribution of inputs and investment, leading to higher levels of productivity.

NOTES

1. For a general introduction to Zimbabwean agriculture, one of the best sources remains Chavunduka (1982). LSC farming is described in the CFU's *Annual Commercial Agriculture in Zimbabwe*, while marketing statistics are compiled in the AMA's annual *Economic Review of the Agricultural Industry*.

2. Particularly useful historical sources on land tenure include Johnson (1964), Bannerman (1982), and Moyana (1984).

3. The CAs were actually created in two groups: as Native Reserves between 1894 and 1914 and then as additional Special Native Areas between 1948 and 1950. The earlier group are generally poorer, with less agricultural potential and often a denser population, than the later group.

4. Customary-law property rights over arable lands include indefinite use and inheritance (typically by division among male heirs) and a well-defined system of claims against the owners of livestock causing damage to crops. In grazing areas access is generally unrestricted, although in a few locations, limited-access "grazing schemes" designed to raise fodder yields through rotation are being implemented (see Cousins 1987, 1989). For both grazing and arable areas disputes are typically resolved by traditional courts under hereditary leadership, although the nominal authority is the elected District Council.

5. Land allocations are controlled by local District Councils under the Communal Lands Act of 1982. Private sales are occasionally attempted, but are highly controversial. See "Disappointment after 'sale' of communal land," (*Herald* [Harare], 4 January 1989), and "Chief warns on land selling," (*Herald* [Harare], 20 October 1990). In contrast informal land rentals are quite common, although they are often among relatives and are usually in exchange for plowing or labor services rather than products or cash.

6. Most resettlement areas are subdivided into individual plots (model A), but a small proportion (accounting for about 10% of resettlement land and well under 10% of resettled people) are organized as whole large-scale farms under collective management (model B). The collective schemes have not been very successful and are not heavily promoted by government (Gasper 1990).

In the model A schemes, tenure is in the form of annual permits to reside, to plant crops, and to depasture stock. These are given free of charge by the MLARR, but in return settlers must pledge to hold no other job, to give up their communal-area homes, and to follow any cropping directives issued by the local Resettlement Officer. Because these conditions do not appear to be frequently enforced, however, RA tenure seems to be relatively secure.

7. White settlement was not entirely a zero-sum conflict at first, in that the settlers moved initially to the heavier, more loamy red and black soils that they could cultivate with ox-drawn plows, while the African population was settled more densely on the lighter, sandier soils that could more easily be cultivated with traditional hand-hoes (Johnson 1964, p. 167). This complementarity disappeared as soon as Africans, too, could buy iron plows.

8. The results of this model are driven by the price of land relative to farm outputs (left diagram) and variable inputs (right diagram). One could therefore derive the same result holding the scarcity (and price) of land constant, while the other two prices change. This would be the familiar explanation of agricultural intensification over time: population growth raises the demand for crops and the supply of labor relative to land, thus increasing the proportion of land planted and decreasing marginal land productivity, which leads to the application of more yield-increasing substitutes for land such as fertilizer. Here the traditional model has been reversed to highlight that, in a segmented land tenure system such as Zimbabwe's, it is land scarcity (and price) that differs across areas, while wages and crop prices are roughly equalized.

9. These figures are national averages; estimates of land use intensity by natural region are given in appendix table C.6.

10. It may seem counterintuitive that land values are higher in CAs than in LSC areas, but this is precisely because CA land is overused while LSC land is abundant. This observation is fully consistent with the model in Figure II.1, which shows how the overuse of CA land is due to its extreme scarcity and high marginal value from the farmer's point of view, relative to LSC land, which is more abundant, has a lower marginal value, and is therefore used less intensively by commercial farmers.

11. These are examples of the well known "two-thirds" rule in engineering, which follows from the idea that the costs of equipment tend to rise in proportion to surface area while output rises with volume, thus yielding increasing returns. But this applies only to mechanical inputs; most inputs in agriculture, such as land, labor, fertilizer and so forth show strongly diminishing returns.

For a general study of returns to size and scale in agriculture, see Berry and Cline (1979).

12. Details of Zimbabwe's resettlement process are provided in Kinsey (1983), Weiner et al. (1985), Cliffe (1986), and Palmer (1990); an excellent survey of general land reform issues is Binswanger and Elgin (1989).

13. The average cost of resettlement has been about Z$6,000 per household (in constant 1989 dollars), in about equal shares for infrastructure, administration, and land purchase. But budget limits have not been the primary restraint on the pace of resettlement. During the 1980s donor funds for resettlement routinely remained unspent, as planning and other bottlenecks were more constraining (MLARR, Monitoring and Evaluation file data).

14. LSC farm sizes and proportions cropped vary greatly by region; in the high potential areas some farms are small and may be mostly cropped, whereas in the driest areas ranches cover tens of thousands of hectares and have no cropped area at all.

15. Average population density in the CAs is 0.33 persons per hectare, but is roughly 0.7 in Natural Regions I and II, 0.4 in Region III, 0.3 in Region IV, and 0.2 in Region V (for details see Masters 1990b, page 1.25). Cropped areas, herd sizes, and productivity are detailed in Part IV and in MLARR (1990).

16. For the 1989 harvest year, the MLARR survey found average farm incomes in Natural Regions IV and V to have been $585 (of which $290 was the implicit value of herd appreciation), while farm incomes in Region II averaged $1327 (of which $121 was herd appreciation). Non-farm incomes were similar in both regions (averaging $374), leaving total household incomes over twice as high in Region II than in Region IV/V (MLARR 1990).

17. The prohibition on land sales also gives farmers less collateral with which to obtain loans, a well-known problem in situations of communal property. In Zimbabwe the AFC uses stop-orders on marketing board accounts in an attempt to ensure repayment, but defaults are still common. Recently the AFC has been expanding its group lending schemes, using joint liability to generate peer pressure (Bratton 1986; AFC 1990).

18. There are many detailed descriptions of CA farming systems. Two of the most useful published works are Steinfeld (1988) and Cousins (1989), detailing livestock-crop interactions. Large-scale surveys have been undertaken by numerous institutions, whose reports are largely unpublished; some examples are Agritex (Chipika 1988 and Truscott 1985), DR&SS (e.g. Shumba 1985), SADCC/ICRISAT (Hedden-Dunkhorst 1990), the UZ Department of Agricultural Economics and Extension (Stanning 1989b), the UZ Department of Economics (Amin and Chipika 1990), the UZ/MSU Food Security Research Project (Rohrbach 1988 and annual conference proceedings), and the Zimbabwe Institute of Development Studies (Sunga et al. 1990). An older study of enduring value is Massell and Johnson (1968).

19. Mharapa (1985) cites E. R. Sawer, the first editor of the *Zimbabwe Agricultural Journal*, as writing in 1909 that rice "has for a century formed the staple food for the Mashona: the swampy areas in Eastern Rhodesia being pitted with old rice fields now being abandoned in favor of the more recently introduced maize crop."

20. The history of irrigation and irrigation policy is reviewed in Rukuni (1986).

21. These results are the author's calculations from cost and return data given in FAO/Harare (1990), Annex p. 5.11 and 5.12. Each project's net present value was not explicitly presented in the original.

22. The principal sources on the history of Zimbabwe's agricultural research establishment are Weinmann (1973, 1975), Tattersfield (1982), and Billing (1985). Excellent reviews of crop breeding results are given in Metelerkamp (1987) and Friis-Hansen and Mpande (1990).

23. Veterinary service expenditure is mostly on tsetse-fly control, but it involves the control of tick-borne infectious diseases through cattle dipping as well. Subsidies were particularly heavy between 1969 and 1973, when large compensatory payments of Z$10 to Z$20 million annually were made to tobacco producers (Billing 1985).

24. Subsidies were briefly cut back during the 1975–1977 period but rose again in 1977 and 1978 when food crop subsidies climbed to Z$47 million (Table C.4).

25. Examples include "Maize Still Undelivered" (*Herald* [Harare], 5 December 1989) and "Rains Damage Undelivered Cotton" (*Herald* [Harare], 29 October 1990).

26. For example, "Haulage Fleets Worst Hit By Spares Shortage" (*Herald* [Harare], 26 April 1990).

27. An exception is "Bad Roads Hamper Produce Delivery in Wedza" (*Herald* [Harare], 15 June 1990).

28. Sabotage operations were carried out by the Mozambique National Resistance (MNR, or Renamo in its Portuguese acronym), a group founded in the late 1970s by the Rhodesian intelligence service, primarily to provide information on Zimbabwean nationalists in Mozambique. In 1980 funding and logistical support was taken over by the South African military, and in the early 1980s Renamo activities expanded to include both the destruction of East-West transport routes and a general insurgency. The Mozambican government was unable to contain the guerrillas, and in 1990 they began negotiations with Renamo for an end to what had become one of Africa's bloodiest conflicts. (For details of the economic impact of the Mozambique war, see Martin 1988.)

29. The electricity used to synthesize ammonia now uses about one-fifth of total national electricity consumption. But as long as total electricity demand remains below the capacity of Zimbabwe's established hydroelectric and domestically mined coal plants, continued ammonia synthesis is likely to remain

profitable. Only when the country begins to need new electricity generation capacity would it become desirable to retire what is now among the last electrolysis fertilizer plants in the world. At that point, it is likely that domestic production of urea by gasification of locally mined coal would be most efficient, although some direct imports of urea might be cost-effective (UNDP 1987; JICA 1989).

30. Contemporary studies on smallholder soil fertility were pioneered by Grant (1981), followed by numerous other articles in the *Zimbabwe Agricultural Journal* through the mid-1980s.

31. A cross-section result such as this is merely indicative; risk should be studied in time series for particular locations, controlling for other determinants of fertilizer use such as relative prices, credit, livestock availability and soil type. Unfortunately, no such time series data are as yet available.

32. The smaller increases after 1981 are mostly due to resettlement area purchases. Data by subsector begin in 1987, at which point the RAs accounted for 33,000 mt (27%) of smallholder sales. Thus it seems likely that all of the 34,000 mt increase in total smallholder sales between 1981 and 1985-1987 was in fact used in RAs and that CA demand has been almost completely unchanged since 1981 (see appendix Table C.8).

33. Herbicides do substitute for labor in weeding, but are used almost exclusively in the LSC sector.

Part III

Agricultural Product Markets

Zimbabwe's agricultural product markets, like the entire sector, are marked by strong dualism. The contrast is generally between formal markets controlled by parastatal marketing boards and informal markets confined within rural areas. Within formal markets government intervention is highly visible, as large transfers from the government treasury are needed to keep the marketing boards solvent. But even larger income transfers are caused by the restrictions on private trade that protect the marketing boards from competition. In this chapter both policy effects are explored, proceeding again from the general to the specific. The analysis begins with an overview of demand and supply forces, then covers prices and marketing systems for each product.

PRODUCT DEMAND AND SUPPLY

As in all low-income countries, farm products account for a large share of consumer spending: A 1985 survey found that food took an average of 52 percent of all expenditure in rural areas and 32 percent in urban areas (CSO 1988, p.10).[1] Food prices are therefore a major influence on consumers' real income, especially in rural areas.

Food is also a major item in international trade, along with several nonfood farm products. The country's first major export was maize: by 1909 over 1,000 mt per year was sold. But maize exports were quickly followed and surpassed by tobacco, which reached 1,000 mt in 1914. Tobacco exports grew steadily, being usually the largest agricultural export until UDI in 1965. But then international sanctions were imposed, which were particularly effective against tobacco, annual export earnings from which were cut from Z\$7-9 million (US\$10-12 million) in the early 1960s to less than Z\$2 million (US\$3 million) in the late 1960s. The government responded with a temporary program of heavy subsidies but also intensified the development of alternative crops for the relatively dry, sandy soils on which tobacco had been grown. Maize and cotton were the most successful tobacco substitutes, during the 1960s and early 1970s in LSC areas and during the 1980s in smallholder areas.

During the late 1970s, the escalating war forced many farmers to abandon some or all of their fields, in both smallholder and LSC areas. As shown in Figures III.1 through III.5, agricultural production was well below trend levels, setting the stage for very rapid growth in the 1980s. Formal marketings reached unprecedented heights in 1981 for both LSC and smallholder farmers (including RA, SSC, and CA producers), as almost perfect weather coincided with a return to rural peace, easily available inputs, relatively high pre-announced prices, and other factors. Subsequently, LSC maize and cotton marketings declined and were overtaken by smallholder marketings.

The LSC production decline was due in part to white emigration and in part to the relatively greater profitability of other crops under LSC conditions. The smallholder increases were due partly to the replacement of some LSC farms with RAs and partly to improved technology and increased availability of inputs and credit. An additional and perhaps essential factor was the rapid expansion of marketing board intake facilities into the CAs. Combined with relatively favorable depot prices in 1980-1982 and again in 1985, this sharply raised effective farmgate prices. Table III.1 summarizes several of the main factors affecting the growth of smallholder marketing in this period, including a producer price index for the major government-controlled crops.

As shown in Figure III.1, maize marketings in the 1980s were particularly striking in their wild fluctuations, as the effect of rainfall variation on production was magnified by its effect of consumption and retentions for home and on-farm use. On average smallholders are estimated to retain about half of their maize for home consumption and local sales, while LSC farmers retain about a quarter for livestock feeds. But this proportion rises in bad years, when farmers meet on-farm and local demand before selling into the national market.

Sorghum and pearl millet offer an important alternative to maize, especially in very dry areas.[2] Open-pollinated varieties, with little improvement from scientific breeding, are grown by smallholders for use in beverages and porridges, at home and in local sales.[3] Smallholders typically sell little (under 10 percent of production) into the formal market. The GMB intake of sorghum is dominated by LSC production of soft red sorghum hybrids, used almost exclusively in industrially-produced opaque beer. As shown in Figure III.2, formal marketings of sorghum rose sharply in 1985 and 1986. Much the same factors contributed to this burst as to the simultaneous growth in maize marketings. But there was even less demand for this sorghum than for the maize, and much of it had to be sold for feed at a substantial discount.

Table III.1
Selected Influences on Smallholder Crop Sales, 1978–1988

	1978	1979	1980	1981	1982	1983	1984	1985	1986	1987	1988
Annual Rainfall											
National average (mm)	980	556	644	861	440	403	464	746	695	474	798
Percent of mean	145	82	95	127	65	59	69	111	103	70	118
Smallholder Input Use											
Fertilizer ('000 mt)	25	25	27	90	96	98	106	128	124	124	111
New AFC loans (Z$m.)			2	8	15	19	42	51	59	78	63
GMB Intake Network											
Permanent depots		34	34	51	50	45	48	52	60	61	66
Seasonal collection points								121	56	17	45
Producer Price Index (1980=100)											
Current prices	79	89	100	111	136	136	155	183	199	205	219
Deflated by CPI	93	93	100	98	109	88	84	91	87	79	79

Note: Dates are harvest years (end of crop years, start of marketing years).

Sources: Grain Marketing Board, Department of Meteorological Services, and Central Statistical Office file data. Producer price index is the author's calculation, as detailed in Appendix Table C.10.

Figure III.1
Formal Maize Marketings, 1950–1988

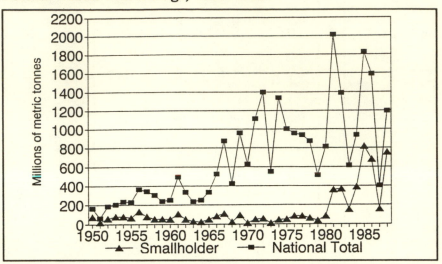

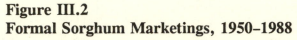

Source: GMB *Annual Reports* and file data.

Figure III.2
Formal Sorghum Marketings, 1950–1988

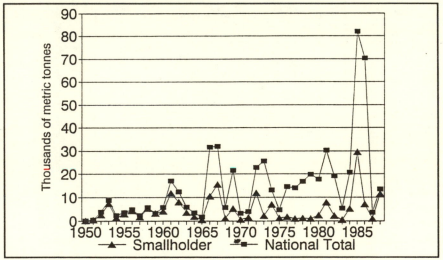

Source: GMB *Annual Reports* and file data.

Groundnuts (peanuts) are a traditionally important crop, which has now been almost completely displaced in formal markets by cottonseed (see Figure III.4) and soybeans (Figure III.5).[4] Groundnuts are still profitable on informal local markets for direct food use and in export markets for confectionery-grade nuts, but from the mid-1980s the Grain Marketing Board has had administrative difficulties in meeting either type of demand. There have been constraints in seed production as well as product grading, processing, and marketing (AMA 1989). As a result, domestic food use is now dominated by informal markets, and export volumes have shrunk rapidly.

For cotton, there is virtually no informal market, so the data in Figure III.4 represent production as well as formal sales. In the 1960s, improved varieties combined with chemical pest control methods, accompanied by effective seed production and product marketing, brought rapid growth in cotton supplies. In 1980, after the war, this growth was resumed. The driving force has been export demand for lint, but the domestic oil expressing and textile industries have also grown rapidly. Those industries became increasingly important politically, and in the mid-1980s they were protected from high export prices, partly at the expense of producers and partly through subsidies to the Cotton Marketing Board (see Figures III.7 and III.12). Cotton production continued to grow through 1988, but then fell sharply at the 1989 and 1990 harvests, because of farm-level profitability and marketing constraints.

Two other nontraditional crops, wheat and soybeans, were introduced in the UDI period. Rainfed wheat production in the hot summer season remains unsuccessful due to rust diseases, but the area under irrigation for growth in the cool, dry winter months has expanded rapidly. Soybeans became popular in part as a short-season crop to use this area in the summer. The smallholder sector, with little field irrigation, grows little wheat or soybeans.

PRICES AND MARKETING SYSTEMS

Market prices for most products covered in this study have been controlled by the official marketing boards, which handle virtually all shipments of controlled products along main roads. (Groundnuts are the notable exception, because of the large parallel market.) This situation is unusual in Africa, where marketing boards with legal monopolies often in fact handle only a fraction of actual sales and do not fully control prices. The relative strength of Zimbabwe's boards is closely linked to their history of offering favorable prices and marketing services to farmers, often at the expense of local consumers. Since there is little opportunity to smuggle crops into the country, this gives the boards control over the entire market. In contrast, marketing boards elsewhere often give their clients a strong incentive to seek out parallel channels, by offering unfavorable prices or weak marketing services.[5]

Figure III.3
Formal Groundnut Marketings, 1964–1988

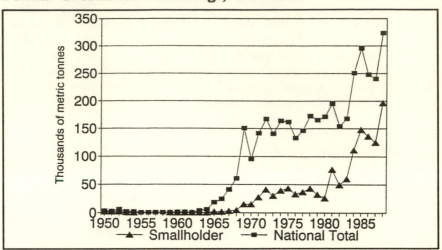

Note: Data for 1950–1964 are not available.
Source: GMB *Annual Reports* and file data.

Figure III.4
Formal Cotton Marketings, 1950–1988

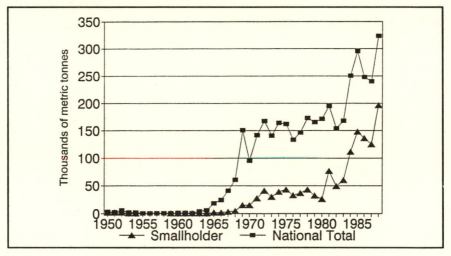

Source: GMB *Annual Reports* and file data.

Figure III.5
Formal Wheat and Soybean Marketings, 1970–1988

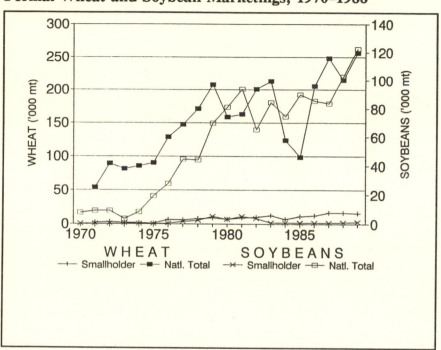

Source: GMB *Annual Reports* and file data.

    The producer orientation of Zimbabwe's boards is closely linked to the historical influence of white settler farmers on the Rhodesian government. From 1890 onwards, settler farmers were politically important as a large and well organized group of voters, from whose ranks were drawn many prominent politicians. Their political importance was heightened by their claim to be the rural frontier, against the far more numerous, disenfranchised African population. The competing economic interests of the mining companies, who would have preferred lower product prices, were politically handicapped because they were almost entirely foreign-owned.

    The Rhodesian situation was very different from most other parts of Africa, where the colonial powers had a more urban and more foreign foundation.[6] Rhodesia's exceptional rural bias was gradually weakened as the white urban population grew and locally owned nonfarm industry became economically more important, a trend that culminated in the anti-export, import-substitution bias of UDI.

For African smallholders, the pro-farm heritage of the marketing boards was a mixed blessing. It ensured relatively favorable pricing and technically efficient operations, but also an infrastructure and marketing system heavily biased toward the large-farm sector. This is perhaps most clearly shown by the history of the Grain Marketing Board (GMB), which began operations in 1931 as the Maize Control Board (MCB), Africa's first statutory marketing board (Jones 1987). Before then, settler maize production had expanded rapidly in an open market, driven by strong export demand primarily for starch manufacture in England. In the 1920s, one-quarter to one-half of marketed maize was exported. But the global depression of 1930 put an abrupt stop to the maize boom, as world maize prices plummeted.

The MCB was charged with the task of protecting farmers from the collapsing export market, initially on a temporary basis. This was accomplished by giving the MCB monopoly powers over domestic and export markets, enabling it to keep domestic prices above and more stable than export realizations. Local sales were restricted through quotas, allocated preferentially to whites on smaller farms. A larger proportion of sales from African and the largest white farms went into the export pool, at a lower and more variable price.

The quota system was abandoned in 1941, but other means remained to segment supply and favor white farmers. For example, after 1948, a 10 percent Native Development Fund levy was imposed on all African maize sold to the MCB.[7] But the most important separation between white and African farmers was probably geographical. Most land given to settlers was near the railroad lines along the fertile highlands, while most African reserves were in remote dry areas far from roads and towns. This gave the settlers better access to urban markets, which was enhanced by locating the MCB depots in the heart of European farming areas.

The geographical advantages of European farmers were substantially amplified by the system of uniform, panterritorial prices at all depots generally used by marketing boards. Such a system is common in administered markets in part because it appears fair (transport costs are shared equally among all participants) and in part because it is easy to administer. But to equalize prices at different depots, the marketing board must undertake all of a larger-than-otherwise transport burden between surplus and deficit areas. This extra transport raises prices in surplus areas and lowers them in deficit areas. Since almost all settler grain production was in the surplus "maize belt" of the north, the pan-territorial system served mainly to raise their prices and enhance their already-strong geographical advantage, at the expense of most city dwellers (in Harare and the other towns of the north) as well as most African farmers (in the dry, southern reserves).

In accomplishing its income-transfer effect, panterritorial pricing serves to eliminate incentives for private transport. Similarly, the boards' system of pan-seasonal pricing eliminates incentives for private storage. These two effects combine with the relatively high national price levels, efficient operations, and financial solvency of the boards to make good their promise of control over Zimbabwean marketing and effectively eliminate private competition.

In 1951, the MCB was renamed the Grain Marketing Board (GMB) and its mandate extended to several other products. As of 1990, the GMB had a statutory monopoly over local and foreign trade in maize, groundnuts, wheat, soybeans, sunflower, coffee, and white sorghum (the "controlled crops") and also offered a floor price for red sorghum, pearl and finger millet, rice, and beans (the "regulated crops"). (Between 1984 and 1989, all sorghum and millets were controlled.) The GMB purchases and sells at a network of permanent depots and seasonal collection points, contracting for transport between them from the railroad and private road transporters. Its only major processing activity is the grading and shelling of groundnuts for export; the GMB also usually sells empty grain bags and buys them when full.

The only other marketing board that is important for this study is the Cotton Marketing Board (CMB), which operates in close cooperation with the GMB as the sole buyer of raw cotton and processor of lint and seed. The CMB exercises much tighter control over cotton than the GMB does over grains, by certifying and distributing all planting seed to ensure a homogeneous product, setting crop-destruction deadlines to limit pest populations, and carrying out its own processing. There is also a Tobacco Marketing Board, whose function is to oversee the activities of the privately owned tobacco auction houses, processors, and exporters.

Other boards not figuring highly in this study include the Dairy Marketing Board (DMB), which is the sole buyer, seller, and transporter of raw milk in most areas and is also the largest processor of milk products, and the Cold Storage Commission (CSC), which is a residual buyer of cattle and goats as well as the largest processor and sole exporter of beef. Pork is handled by a single private producer cooperative, while the formal poultry market is dominated by two private firms.

The only controlled crop with a significant illegal parallel market is groundnuts, for which the GMB is essentially only a residual buyer and exporter. Beef and goat meat have a legal informal market, operating alongside the CSC. Most of the other important uncontrolled products, chiefly sugar, tea, flowers, and vegetables (all mostly exported), and barley (grown under contract to local breweries), are dominated by large-scale producers.

Prices for marketing board products are generally announced once a year, before the principal harvest. The announcement follows three to four months of negotiation between the board, the farmers organizations, MLARR (for producer prices) and the Ministry of Industry and Commerce (for consumer prices). These two ministries then make independent recommendations to the Ministerial Economic Coordinating Committee (MECC) of Cabinet, which occasionally makes further modifications.

The negotiation process changes somewhat from year to year, adapting to changed circumstances.[8] Typically negotiations begin with a submission to MLARR from the farmers' organizations, requesting specific prices to reach target levels of return based on average-cost budgets.[9] A separate submission to MLARR is made by the marketing boards, requesting a generally lower price based on their stock levels and anticipated prospects for trade, domestic sales, and financial performance. The MLARR reviews both proposals and then makes its own recommendation to the Ministerial Economic Coordinating Committee (MECC) and the cabinet.[10]

Price negotiations are begun just after planting. At this time the CSO's Crop Forecasting Committee estimates anticipated harvest quantities, which may then also be considered in price-setting. A larger area planted and better weather tend to lower price levels, which helps the government hold down the board's buying costs and the next year's plantings. But prices are almost never reduced in nominal terms, and each announcement provides a floor price for the following year. Later, after the harvest, the minister may make a "preplanting" policy speech promising a higher price for next year to encourage production or a price freeze to reduce it.

Zimbabwe's negotiation process generally appears to take into account all the major forces that would influence an open-market price. Supply, demand, storage, and trade pressures all come to bear on price formation, but their effects are delayed by the bureaucratic processes involved. Consumers are generally underrepresented in the negotiation process but favored by the slow adjustment of negotiated prices to inflation elsewhere, as well as the real exchange rate appreciation identified in Part I.

Figure III.6 shows that the recent trend for most prices has been just slightly below inflation, at least since the peaks reached in the early 1980s. The principal relative-price changes over the full UDI and post-independence period have been a temporary premium paid for cotton and groundnuts between 1973 and the early 1980s and a temporary premium paid for maize between 1980 and 1985.

Individual crops are covered in more detail in Figures III.7 through III.12, which show nominal producer, consumer, and border prices. (Average results for selected periods are shown in Appendix Table C.5.) Producer and consumer prices are for Grade A products at any board depot; border prices are net of trade costs typically at Harare. These price graphs confirm that negotiated domestic prices generally have followed border values, but with considerably more stability in the sense that there are rarely nominal declines in domestic official prices. There are, however, some periods of significant nominal protection or disprotection of important crops.

Figures III.7 through III.12 also show marketing board operating costs assigned to each crop, including handling, storage costs, inter-depot transport, and overhead. These costs have risen quickly in the 1980s; where costs exceed

Figure III.6
Real Average Prices Paid by Marketing Boards, 1966–1989

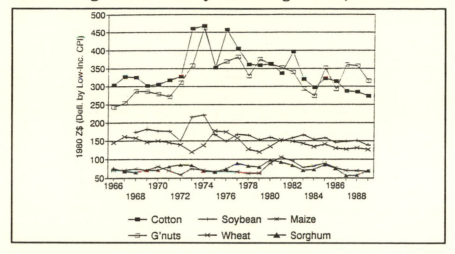

Source: Author's calculations from GMB and CMB data, detailed in Appendix Table C.10.

domestic and export marketing margins the boards have incurred substantial losses (see Figure III.13 and Appendix Table C.4). This is particularly true for the grains, partly on account of capital and transport costs incurred in expanding the intake network after 1980 and partly on account of interest costs on the large surplus stocks accumulated after the 1981, 1985, and 1986 harvests.

Figure III.7 shows that producer and consumer prices for maize were kept below border prices during the war, but have generally been above border prices in the 1980s. The two exceptions are one year of high-priced imports (1984), and one year of high-valued exports (1988). Zimbabwe's trade prices for maize are highly variable, and the marketing board has succeeded in stabilizing the domestic market while following the export trends.

Cotton prices—expressed in Figure III.8 as cents per kilogram, rather than in dollars per ton—followed border values extremely closely until 1983, when the domestic textile industry was protected from increases in lint export values caused in part by devaluation. As a result, the CMB did not pass on the full increase to producers either, and raw seed cotton prices fell below their implicit export values as well.

With groundnuts (Figure III.9), the disprotection of the 1970s was continued in the 1980s, in part because of strong pressure from the oil expressing industry to hold consumer prices low and in part because of its limited constituency among LSC farmers.[11] Sorghum (Figure III.10) has been exported

Figure III.7
Prices and Board Costs for Maize, 1966–1988

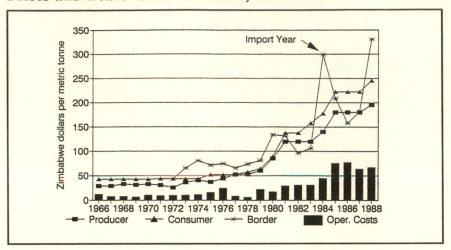

Source: Figures III.7-III.12 are calculated from GMB and CMB data, in Takavarasha and Rukovo (1991).

Figure III.8
Prices and Board Costs for Cotton, 1966–1988

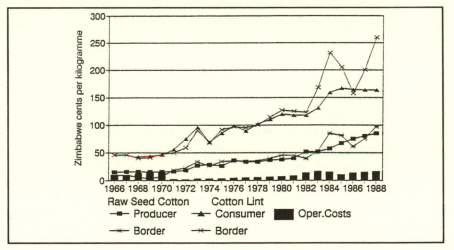

Figure III.9
Prices and Board Costs for Groundnuts, 1966–1988

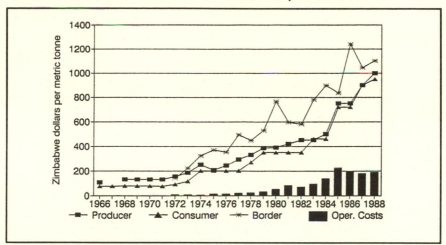

Figure III.10
Prices and Board Costs for Sorghum, 1966–1988

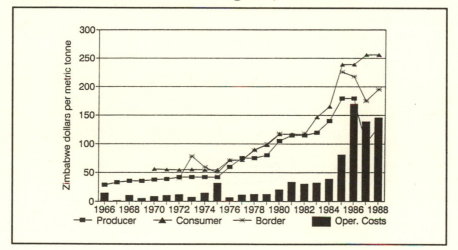

in small quantities at values similar to domestic consumer prices until the late 1980s, when the domestic marketing margin was expanded in an attempt to cover storage costs on unsalable stocks.

For wheat (Figure III.11), an importable, trade parity has generally been maintained at the consumer-price level, and producers have paid the domestic marketing margin. In the late 1980s, however, low import prices were not passed on to consumers, thus protecting producers. Disprotection for soybeans (Figure III.12) was substantial in the 1970s and became even more so in the 1980s, when exports were cut off altogether because of domestic oilseed shortages at the relatively low controlled prices.

Government-imposed domestic prices interact with border prices and board operating costs to determine the government's losses (or, occasionally, profits) on trading each product. The main product subsidies are shown in Figure III.13, in real terms (nominal figures are given in Appendix Table C.4). These subsidies were actually disbursed in a variety of ways, including some government payments to processors through the Ministry of Trade and Commerce, some government payments directly to marketing boards, and some government-guaranteed borrowing by marketing boards.

Within the grains subsector, Figure III.14 shows that the initial 1981–1982 maize and, to a lesser extent, wheat subsidies were initiated primarily as Ministry of Trade and Commerce (MTC) payments to industrial processors to maintain the relatively low processing margins allowed by retail price controls on flour. These were phased out in the mid-1980s, however, and replaced by relatively low grain prices from the Grain Marketing Board which effectively postponed the need for direct budget allocations until such time as it would become necessary for MLARR to cover the board's debts.

Among other products, after UDI there was almost a decade of large payments to tobacco producers, accounting for 5-12 percent of total government expenditure in the 1968-1973 period (Table A.4). These were followed by large subsidies to beef producers, and heavy maize subsidies that began in 1979. But total subsidies stayed under 5 percent of government expenditure until the costs of purchasing and storing the exceptional 1981 harvest, which along with consumer subsidies (Figure III.14) tripled real spending to 8.5 percent in the 1981–1982 fiscal year.

In the 1980s, the older maize and beef subsidies were compounded by significant new dairy and wheat subsidies, as government attempted to hold down the cost of these relatively expensive urban-consumed foods. In the late 1980s, maize subsidies were reduced but the other subsidies proved more persistent. The one crop yielding significant positive profits was cotton in 1985, which was just enough to offset, for example, the losses on dairy.

In 1990, as part of the government's larger structural adjustment program, the Minister of Finance, Economic Planning and Development announced the "government's intention to wipe out subsidies, except in exceptional carefully

Figure III.11
Prices and Board Costs for Wheat, 1966–1988

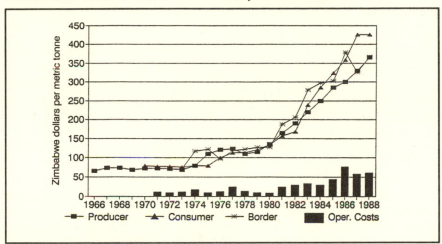

Figure III.12
Prices and Board Costs for Soybeans, 1966–1988

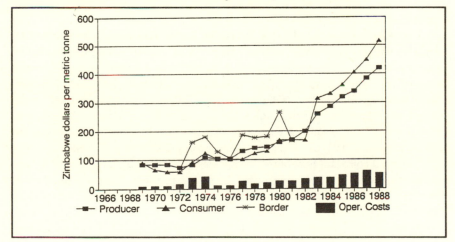

Figure III.13
Subsidies and Parastatal Losses on Agricultural Products,
Deflated by Low-income CPI

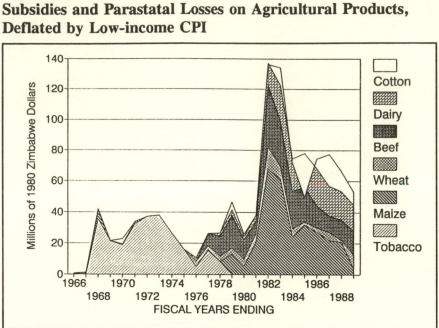

Source: Table C.4, calculated from MLARR file data.

targeted cases, by the end of 1994/95" (GOZ 1990). Accomplishing this will be virtually impossible without moving away from the longstanding system of annual nationwide fixed prices toward a more flexible system of regional and seasonal price flexibility. This could be done through rationalizing prices within the controlled market, but is more likely to be accomplished through some degree of decontrol. Liberalization offers one way to escape the political pressures that tend to squeeze a marketing board's margins and also to avoid the almost impossible task of predicting break-even prices ahead of time.

The full costs and benefits of the Rhodesian system of market controls cannot be measured by marketing board losses or profits. After all, the boards generally had little profit or loss during most of the pre-independence period. The marketing boards generated benefits as the mechanism by which the post-independence government was able to procure large quantities of smallholder maize and cotton in the 1980s. The resulting surpluses made the country famous as an agricultural success story, an African country that actually increased its farm export earnings in the 1980s, while the rest of Africa turned into a net importer.[12]

Figure III.14
Subsidies on Maize and Wheat, 1976–1989

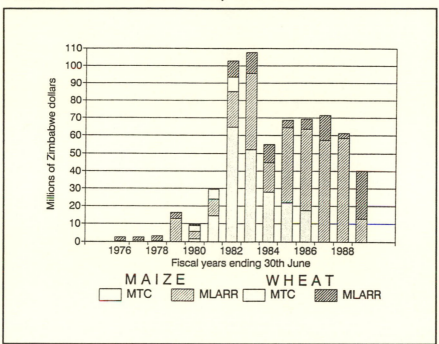

Source: Calculated from MLARR file data.

The costs of the Rhodesian system can be found only in disaggregation. Indeed, soon after the country's post-independence aggregate success was noted, it was found to contrast sharply with household-level data (Rukuni and Eicher 1986). A "food security paradox" was observed, of aggregate national abundance with household-level scarcity (Jayne et al. 1990).[13] Throughout the 1980s, despite growth in smallholder farm production, the country continued to experience extreme and widespread rural poverty. Chronic malnutrition severely stunts growth in a third of rural children (CSO 1989),[14] while acute malnutrition was—until 1990—by far the greatest cause of child deaths (Mason 1990).[15]

To help bridge the gap between full GMB granaries and rural malnutrition, internal "drought relief" food aid is used, even in relatively good rainfall years. Most of this grain is given freely to selected households by local officials, but some has been distributed through food-for-work programs.

Table III.2
Drought Relief Food Aid in Zimbabwe, 1982–1983 to 1988–1989

Fiscal Year	1982–1983	1983–1984	1984–1985	1985–1986	1986–1987	1987–1988	1988–1989
Drought relief maize (mt)	46,300	223,900	78,100	9,384	32,614	127,107	9,759
(% of GMB sales)	3.0	14.7	9.1	1.1	2.7	8.6	1.0

Source: FAO/Harare (1990).

Drought relief shipments have been large but inadequate to fill grain deficits in many communal areas. The remainder is bought commercially, paid for with remittances or sales of other crops and livestock. As private shipment of grain was banned (and transport sufficiently scarce that there was little illegal trading), inflows consisted mostly of industrially milled maize flour costing over twice the official producer price of grain.[16] Large net inflows of maize meal would not occur if private shipments of grain were easier or if the GMB were supplying the rural demand for grain through sales from rural depots. The board is legally allowed to sell everywhere, but there are few depots in grain-deficit areas.[17] In general, the GMB's rural staff has been oriented towards buying, while the facilities and personnel to make sales are concentrated in the urban depots.

The extension of the GMB into CAs after independence must have provided an attractive price for surplus growers; otherwise they would not have delivered so much grain into the depots. But deficit households would not have been helped and could even have been hurt if GMB intake reduced availability and raised prices on informal local markets.[18] Although the GMB presence is clearly preferable to no market at all, more complete rural markets—with substantial selling as well as buying—would have assisted both sides of the market more equitably and efficiently.

The GMB clearly succeeded as a procurement service for grain into the cities or for export trade. This was, indeed, its original intention. But providing all the small-volume marketing services needed in rural areas was not the board's mandate and would be difficult for any centralized organization. Large benefits could be achieved by expanding intra-rural trade, bringing buying and selling prices closer together.

The Effects of Panterritorial GMB Pricing

The impact of the GMB's system of panterritorial pricing can best be seen by comparing it with the alternative of no intervention. Figure III.15 presents a simple analytical model with which to predict what would happen without panterritorial pricing. It shows Zimbabwe divided into two regions: the "North," which has a maize surplus, with lower production costs (represented by the supply curve) relative to consumption requirements (represented by the demand curve), and the "South," which has a maize deficit, with higher production costs relative to consumption requirements. The model shows that if no transport were possible, each region would have to be self-sufficient, leading to a very large gap between the Northern and Southern maize prices. The use of transport gives people in the North and the South access to each other, thus narrowing the price gap.

Figure III.15
The Effects of Panterritorial Pricing

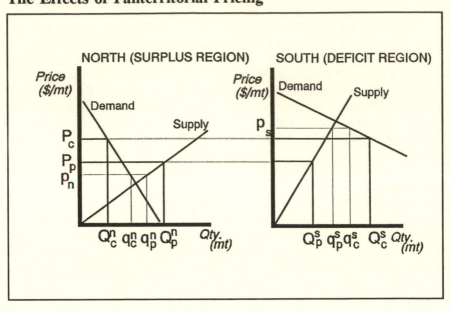

Under panterritorial pricing, the government sets uniform prices for consumers (P_c) and producers (P_p). The margin between the two prices covers most of the GMB's average marketing and storage costs, plus losses or profits from international trade. Since the GMB handles both within-region and between-region sales, actual average costs are typically less than the full cost of between-region transport. But in practice the government sets GMB margins that are lower than actual average costs, leaving a shortfall to be financed by the central government. These subsidies are often viewed as the major food policy issue—but the hidden transfers between market participants may be even more important, as can be seen from Figure III.15.

If the GMB did not exist and private traders competed among one another, they would move grain from North to South until the gap between prices in the North (p_n) and the South (p_s) just equalled the cost of transport. Within each area there would be virtually no gap between producer and consumer prices, because no transport is required. The two regional prices (p_s and p_n) would then rise and fall in tandem until total national production ($q^n_p + q^s_p$) equals total consumption ($q^n_c + q^s_c$), plus or minus any exports and stock changes which are omitted from this simple model.

We can now use this model to assess the effects of intervention. Relative to the competitive case, panterritorial pricing reduces consumption (to Q^n_c) and increases production (to Q^n_p) in the North, while reducing production (to Q^s_p) and increasing consumption (to Q^s_c) in the South. This raises the North's surplus (to $Q^n_p - Q^n_c$) and the South's deficit ($Q^s_c - Q^s_p$), increasing the amount shipped between regions.

To sustain the panterritorial system, the government must not only subsidize any difference between the GMB's revenue and its expenses, but also prohibit private traders from competing with the GMB *within* each region. Long-distance trading *between* regions is not an issue: As long as the GMB's margin ($P_c - P_p$) is smaller than the full cost of transport ($p^s - p^n$), private traders have no reason to enter this market. Private traders would like to compete with the GMB in short-distance trading such as around major cities, which they can easily do for less than the GMB's margin. But the GMB's survival depends on being able to use profits from such low-cost activities to subsidize its higher-cost marketing routes—and those hidden cross-subsidies may be much larger than any visible subsidies received from the government.

In terms of social welfare, the effects of panterritorial pricing can be approximated by changes in producer and consumer surplus: the shaded areas in Figure III.15. In the North, panterritorial pricing raises prices from p_n to P_c (for consumers) and P_p (for producers). Consumers lose the area with upward-sloped shading, and producers gain the area with downward-sloped shading. In the South, the opposite occurs: Panterritorial pricing lowers prices from p_s to P_c and P_p. The resulting producers' loss is shown with upward-sloped shading and the consumers' gain with downward-sloped shading. In both regions, the cross-hatched area is transfered from consumers to producers, and each region's net loss or gain is the difference between the remaining loss (with upward-sloped shading) and the gain (with downward-sloped shading).

In each region, and in the nation as a whole, welfare losses occur because of missed opportunities for low-cost local trading: Losses are proportional to the GMB margin ($P_c - P_p$) times the quantity traded locally (i.e., consumed in the North or produced in the South). Some offsetting welfare gains occur because of lower-cost long-distance transport: these gains are proportional to the difference between private traders' long-distance margin ($p_s - p_n$) and the GMB's margin ($P_c - P_p$) times the quantity traded between regions (i.e., $q^n_p - q^n_c$ or $q^s_c - q^s_p$).

To summarize the results of Figure III.15, panterritorial pricing (a) increases the North's dominance of the market and the amount of transport, (b) requires the government to restrict *local* rather than long-distance trade, and (c) causes large transfers to producers in the North, at the expense of consumers in the North and producers in the South.

Consumers in the South benefit to the extent that they actually have access to grain at the "panterritorial" price. But many Southern consumers cannot buy grain at P_c: They are either too far from a depot or their depot has depleted its stocks, so they are forced to buy industrial roller meal at much higher prices (see Stanning 1989a, p. 94). Deficit households cannot buy from nearby farmers, because the ban on grain transport along major roads prevents the growth of wholesale markets; farmers with any significant surplus have had to sell it to the marketing board at price P_s. Some may be sold to neighbors and shopkeepers, but only to satisfy the immediate local area. This option raises the overall average price received by farmers in deficit areas, but not as high as P_c or P_s.[19]

Regional price variation is particularly important in the market for maize, because areas may be either in net surplus or net deficit. Thus the opportunity cost of grain may have transport costs added (for deficit areas) or subtracted (for surplus areas). In contrast, most non-grain crops are always sent to urban processors, so their opportunity costs are always urban prices minus transport. The more subtle spatial variation for "subsistence" crops (which may be processed within rural areas) than for "cash" crops (which must be sent to town) may be among the most important economic differences between them.

To estimate the opportunity costs of maize in each region, a national model of maize supply and demand by district was developed by the author and a colleague (Masters and Nuppenau 1993). The national model is similar to the two-region model of Figure III.15 but includes 34 districts, 41 transport routes, and possibilities for trade and storage.[20] The model results give the regional pattern of prices (as well as production, consumption, and transport patterns) required to reach equilibrium in all districts, given their supply and demand schedules and the transport costs between them. This result simulates the outcome of a liberalized maize market, yielding both opportunity costs of grain by location and guidelines for improved price setting by the marketing board.

The exact regional pattern of equilibrium opportunity costs depends on export values (which raise prices at the border), storage demand (which raises prices at storage locations), and drought (which raises prices in the southern half of the country). But in general, opportunity costs in the far northern surplus areas are 25-35 percent below prices in the far southern deficit areas.[21] Allowing such price differences to be felt by producers and consumers would allow national maize requirements to be met with a 15 percent savings in domestic transport costs and a net welfare gain on the order of US$14 million, or 4 percent of current producer plus consumer surplus from maize. This gain would recur every year, with a present value ten times larger (assuming an infinite horizon and a real interest rate of 10 percent).

It would be possible to capture some of the potential welfare gains from regional pricing within the current marketing rules. For example, the GMB could calculate a set of desired price premiums (for deficit-area depots) and discounts (for surplus areas) relative to some reference depot (say, at Harare). For simplicity, there might be only four or five categories of depots, and the few regional premium or discount rates could be pre-announced, as is currently done with price differences between product grades. Then every year only the reference-depot price would have to be negotiated and announced, as is now done with Grade A prices.

Administered regional prices could only capture a portion of the potential welfare gains, since it would be difficult to model supply and demand at each location accurately. Regional pricing might also be politically difficult to introduce in a controlled market, because of its administrative simplicity and the rhetorical "fairness" of a uniform price. But the analysis presented here indicates that panterritorial pricing in the maize market has strongly worsened income distribution, by favoring the relatively well-off northern farmers (in the "maize belt") and southern city-dwellers (in Bulawayo and smaller towns, industrial sites, and mines), at the expense of everyone else. The greatest losers include both poor urban people (in townships around Harare) and poor rural people (in the southern CAs).[22]

Despite the clearly negative income-distribution effects of panterritorial pricing, it seems likely that its administrative and political advantages prevent the introduction of regional pricing within the current controlled marketing system. Regional pricing would probably arise only in the context of market deregulation. Various reform proposals were made throughout the 1980s—notably Child, Muir, and Blackie (1985), Blackie (1986), and Muir-Leresche and Takavarasha (1989)—but none was implemented until the early 1990s (for details, see Masters 1994). Thus, prices used in Part IV initially take the panterritorial system as given and then examine the effects of a wide range of possible variations.

Seasonal Prices and Storage

Controlled-market prices for all crops are panseasonal, but informal market prices vary over time, rising after harvest to cover storage costs until the product is consumed. This seasonal rise includes the value of physical losses (both quantity and quality), handling costs, and the capital costs of the stock and its storage facility. Since storage has an element of uncertainty, a risk premium may also be included.

With panseasonal pricing, the marketing board encourages farmers to deliver early and end-users to buy late, so that almost all formal-market storage is undertaken by the marketing boards themselves. This is analogous to panterritorial pricing, which leads the board to undertake all interregional transport. Farmers and users use their own transport and storage only for convenience and to cope with the frequent delays in pickup or delivery to and from the boards.

But unlike panterritorial pricing, which creates net welfare costs by changing the location of consumption and production and increasing the transport burden, panseasonal pricing in the Zimbabwean context probably has little effect on quantities stored or aggregate welfare. Harvest times are fixed by the weather, and consumption for staple crops is continuous. Thus panseasonal pricing merely shifts the burden of storage from the private sector to government, without changing the total amount of grain in storage each month. The major effect of price policy on storage quantities would occur through annual price levels, not panseasonal pricing as such.

In Zimbabwe, the marketing board seems to have low storage costs. Although most stocks are held in bags (or, for cotton, bales) under tarpaulins, physical losses can be kept well under 5 percent by moisture control and fumigation. Financial storage costs to the marketing boards are also low, as they are able to borrow internationally at very low rates. Thus the total opportunity cost of government storage, including all types of cost, is probably under 15 percent per year in real terms. Costs and physical losses would rise above that when stocks get so large that stock rotation slows down, but this would be a consequence of annual price levels and not panseasonality.[23]

Private storage costs in the formal sector are probably similar to marketing board costs, but storage costs in the CAs are certainly much higher. CA farmers face both higher physical losses and higher costs of capital. The available data on storage losses are limited, but some surveys indicate that although losses are small in the dry winter after harvest, they rise quickly in the rain and heat of the next cropping season.[24] Grain stocks held over a full year might lose 10-30 percent of their mass (Giga 1987, Giga and Rukuni 1989, Giga and Katerere 1986) and suffer loss of value from quality deterioration. Capital costs for CA farmers are even more difficult to estimate, but they are certainly higher than for the marketing boards if only because of higher risks.

By bringing stocks into central storage, panseasonal pricing probably reduces the average cost of holding them. Doing so requires the marketing board to assume responsibility for stockholding, but it also makes the board's work easier by increasing the time available to plan the year's domestic transport and international trade operations. If planning is a more severe bottleneck than capital and storage facilities, from the board's point of view the convenience yield of holding the stock outweighs the storage costs, thus inverting the usual pattern of seasonal price variation.

Introducing seasonal prices would induce farmers and end-users to undertake more private storage and undoubtedly reduce the board's storage costs and capital requirements. But this might raise the board's transport and trade costs, because it would shorten the board's planning horizon. It would also probably raise average storage costs. Thus unlike panterritorial pricing, the panseasonal pricing policy probably has little effect on national efficiency.

CONCLUSIONS

In the 1980s, Zimbabwe's agricultural product markets performed well in terms of aggregate growth. This national success was achieved essentially by extending the procurement efforts of the country's statutory marketing boards deep into smallholder areas, drawing unprecedented quantities of maize, cotton, and other crops from CA farmers. Marketing costs were high, but the expansion of GMB intake was a good thing for the many farmers who could easily produce a surplus of grain.

Rural households wanting to buy grain, however, were not helped by the GMB's maize procurement, and some may have been hurt. To assist both buyers and sellers, a more complete rural grain market would be needed, facilitating both grain sales and grain purchases throughout the countryside. Lowering rural grain purchase prices not only would promote equity by lowering the relative cost of food, it would also promote efficiency by allowing farmers to produce whatever crops they choose, with confidence that they could buy the foodgrains they needed at a reasonable and stable price.

It would be very difficult to provide low-cost, intra-rural trade within a controlled market. Volumes would probably be too low and too uncertain for a centralized board to operate effectively and at low cost. Some degree of deregulation will be needed, to allow more timely shipments of grain around the country, filling whatever effective demand were felt.

Deregulation of grain flows would benefit the poorest rural people in the southern CAs and the poorest urban people in the northern cities. The principal losers would be northern producers, in whose interests the current system was first established in 1931. The transition would not be simple, but maize market policy eventually could be far more equitable and efficient than it is today. This would, in turn, allow further growth of marketed cotton, groundnuts, and other crops from the communal areas, because farmers growing these higher-valued crops could be confident that they could buy maize from the market if they run short. Farmers would be free to pursue their comparative advantage, which would be a powerful source of increased incomes for farmers and for the nation.

NOTES

1. The diet is dominated by maize, which in direct food use accounts for about 45 percent of total calories and 72 percent of cereal calories. The basic meal consists of a stiff porridge of maize-meal (or, more traditionally, millet or sorghum flour), with a "relish" of green vegetable (rape, cabbage, pumpkin leaves, or okra, cooked preferably with onion and tomato) or meat (beef, chicken, or goat, generally in stew). Milk (typically soured), eggs, and fish are also used as relishes.

Wheat bread and rice are widely preferred substitutes for maize, but because of import restrictions they are not always available. Import substitution has been possible in the case of wheat (see Figure III.5) but not for rice—although some rice is grown by smallholders in small plots of wet clay ("vlei") soils and by the parastatal Agricultural Development Authority (ADA).

2. Finger millet is also widely grown for brewing purposes but is rarely eaten as a food. For a detailed study of sorghum and millets in Zimbabwe, see Masters 1990b.

3. Porridges and beer are typically made from either maize or pearl millet flour, with malt flour from germinated finger millet or sorghum added to increase energy density and allow alcoholic fermentation. A hot, runny porridge is used as a breakfast and weaning food, often served with added peanut butter or milk. Non-alcoholic malt drinks are widely consumed by children and as a midday snack in the fields. Alcoholic beer (typically consumed after either three or seven days of fermentation) and distilled liquor are produced both for home use and for sale to neighbors.

4. Groundnuts were traditionally used as a cooking base for relish, in the form of hand-ground peanut butter. This purpose is now usually fulfilled by industrial vegetable oil, although peanut butter is often also added to almost any type of stew. Groundnuts are also a common snack, consumed boiled or roasted along with bambara nuts, cowpeas, and maize kernels.

5. An additional reason for the dominance of Zimbabwe's boards is the absence of much traditional marketing activity; in general Central and Southern Africa seems to have had less of a mercantile history than West, East, or North Africa.

6. This study's emphasis on the colonial roots of Zimbabwe's marketing institutions is very different from the contemporary influences highlighted by many researchers, such as Bates (1981), in studies of other African countries. Both colonial and contemporary forces are important, but in Zimbabwe colonial influences are both more recent and more present than in the African countries that attained independence a generation earlier and had a smaller colonial population.

7. Moyana (1984, p. 15) writes that "although a Development Fund levy was deducted from African produce, there was virtually no visible development initiated by the government in the African area." The fund's direct descendent, the District Development Fund (DDF), is today responsible for local roads and bridges, but it is financed from the central government budget, rather than a commodity tax.

8. For a discussion of the recent trends in price levels and price negotiations, see Wright and Takavarasha (1989) and Takavarasha and Rukovo (1991); for the politics of price-setting, see Herbst (1990).

9. There are now two farmers' organizations: the Zimbabwe Farmers Union (ZFU), formed of the former Commercial Farmers Union (CFU) representing LSC farmers and the Zimbabwe National Farmers Union (ZNFU) representing SSC farmers, and the National Farmers Association of Zimbabwe (NFAZ), representing CA farmers. There is no association for resettlement area farmers. Since 1986 the three unions' Joint Presidents Agricultural Committee (JPAC) have submitted a common proposal. The proposal is drafted mostly by the staff of the CFU, but its acceptability to the government depends crucially on the support of the smallholder unions.

10. The MLARR recommendations are based in part on an average-cost budget for each crop; the quantity weights are rarely revised, however, so the budgets serve more as indexes of input prices for each crop than as guides to resource allocation.

11. The extremely narrow, often negative marketing margin appears to be an artifact of the methods used to account for quality differences and shelling losses.

12. In the decade between 1976 and 1985, Africa as a whole moved from net agricultural exports of US$3.2 billion to net agricultural imports of over US$4.5 billion. In contrast Zimbabwe raised its net farm exports from US$350 million to over US$450 million (FAO, *Trade Yearbook*, various years).

13. Iliffe (1990) chronicles the history of rural poverty in Zimbabwe, while contemporary surveys of rural consumption and incomes include Stanning (1989b) and Jackson and Collier (1988). These works show clearly the fallacy of aggregation in drawing household-level conclusions from national or regional data.

14. In 1988 stunting, defined as being two standard deviations below the WHO standard median height-for-age, was found in 33.6 percent of rural and 14.3 percent of urban children aged 3-60 months (CSO 1989). Weight-for-age malnutrition was found in roughly half as many children (NSCFN 1990).

15. In 1988 and 1989, among children one to five years of age, malnutrition was the main cause of about 350 deaths per year in clinics and hospitals, while respiratory and diarrheal infections caused 150 and 100 deaths respectively. Malaria and measles, in contrast, caused less than fifty deaths each. (An unknown number of child deaths occurred outside clinics.) Preliminary reports suggest that AIDS probably surpassed all other causes of child mortality in 1990 and will almost certainly continue to do so throughout the 1990s.

16. Informal markets within CAs (marketing area B) are legal, but grain may not be transported across commercial-area boundaries. Since virtually all main roads are in commercial areas (area A), the rule effectively blocks all non-GMB grain shipments into deficit CAs.

17. The depot network is supplemented by seasonal collection points, but all grain admitted to collection points must be shipped to a depot for final grading before it can be sold.

18. There is unlikely to be a price effect on informal markets as long as GMB intake does not affect marginal flows and marginal values. But in practice, Jayne et al. (1990) suggest that some areas have increased their purchases of industrial maize meal, perhaps at increased marginal cost, because of outflows through the GMB. The observation of such backflows is largely a function of the level of aggregation and in particular on the costs of local marketing relative to the costs of trade with town.

A simultaneous flow of grain toward town and backflow of maize-meal to rural areas is not likely to occur at the village level, say within walking distance, among people who could easily trade with one another. Backflows would be expected only at a more aggregate level, encompassing both a group of surplus farmers who might find few buyers other than the GMB, and a group of deficit households who find little grain available other than industrially milled maize meal shipped from town. There is ample evidence that this sort of grain back-flow regularly occurs at the highly aggregate level of Natural Regions (Masters 1990b), but probably also at the more disaggregated level of Districts and Communal Areas (Jayne et al. 1990). A more direct route between surplus and deficit households within these areas would require a lower cost rural marketing and storage network than now exists.

19. In the 1989 MLARR survey results used for the PAM budgets in Part IV, the average maize price received by farmers, weighted by quantities sold, was Z$255/mt in low-potential (generally maize-deficit) areas. This was 20 percent above the average price received in high-potential areas, Z$213/mt.

20. For simplicity, the national model uses a single panterritorial price instead of the two prices (P_c and P_p) of Figure III.15. Thus the national model ignores the effects of that fixed margin in local markets, in order to focus on inter-regional price differences.

21. The equilibrium regional price differences for maize predicted by the model are similar to but not exactly the same as actual differences in average maize prices received by CA farmers in different areas. (The actual average price difference between low- and high-potential areas was just under 20 percent in the 1989 MLARR survey.) In deficit areas, for example, both the actual average price received and the hypothetical equilibrium price are intermediate between the prices paid by deficit households and lower prices paid by the GMB.

The difference between the average and the equilibrium price corresponds roughly to the difference discussed in Chapter 2 between the Harberger weighted-average rule for calculating marginal shadow values in project appraisal and the market equilibrium concept that is used to analyze the effects of policy.

22. The popular appeal of panterritorial pricing seems to derive not from its economic effects, but from something else. Perhaps its simplicity reassures people that they are not being cheated. Whatever its appeal, panterritorial pricing is the main advertising slogan for a major chain of Zimbabwean discount clothing shops, which claims to offer "One Price Nationwide!"

23. Models of optimal interannual maize storage for Zimbabwe are given in Buccola and Sukume (1988) and Pinckney (1990).

24. CA grain stocks are typically kept in a special pole-and-mud hut, raised up on logs or boulders to limit moisture levels and animal damage and subdivided into several compartments, each of which is sealed with cow dung to limit insect damage. Traditionally, pesticides from the ash or green leaves of various plants were used; today the principal grain pesticide is Malathion. Its use is common but not universal, however, as acquired resistance may have reduced its effectiveness (Wrigley 1981); some survey results suggest treatment reduces losses by only about 10 percent over a year (Giga and Katerere, 1986).

Part IV

Policy Analysis Matrix Results

Parts I, II, and III of this book are largely independent analyses of the effects of economy-wide, agricultural and product-market policies on farmers. In this chapter, the combined effects of all these policies at the farm level are assessed, using the Policy Analysis Matrix (PAM) approach.

WHAT IS A PAM?

The PAM is an innovative method for analyzing the effects of policy, in contexts where the data needed for traditional economic models are not available. It was first developed in a study of Portuguese agriculture (Pearson et al. 1987); soon thereafter a detailed exposition appeared (Monke and Pearson 1989), along with applications to Ecuador (Byerlee 1989) and Indonesia (Nelson and Panggabean 1991), among others.

The PAM itself is a matrix of budgets showing average revenues, costs, and profits for the production and marketing of a particular commodity. The first budget uses market prices or private opportunity costs to measure the private (financial) profitability of the system, and the second uses national opportunity costs to measure its national (economic or social) profitability. The third budget shows the differences (divergences) between the private and national budgets: These are either transfers within the national economy or net losses to national income, caused by government actions (such as taxes and quotas) or inactions (such as failures to regulate monopolies).

PAM entries add up both horizontally (private minus national values equal transfers) and vertically (revenues minus costs equal profits), so that the full matrix can be calculated from any eight of the fifteen entries in Table IV.1.[1] The choice of which items to measure exogenously and which to calculate endogenously depends on the data and models available to the researcher.

Table IV.1
The Structure of the Policy Analysis Matrix

	Private Budget (at market prices)	National Budget (at national opp. costs)	Divergences: Transfers and Net Losses
Output revenue	A	F	K
Labor costs	B	G	L
Capital costs	C	H	M
Tradable input costs	D	I	N
Profits	E	J	O

Source: Adapted from Monke and Pearson (1989).

Several PAMs are typically constructed for each commodity, representing different farming systems or locations. These systems can then be ranked by total average costs, forming a stepwise approximation of the national supply curve. Figure IV.1 shows this study's actual results for maize, from low-potential communal areas (System A), high-potential communal areas (System B), and large-scale commercial areas (System C).[2] Each segment of this average-cost curve represents an aggregate production and marketing system, within which there is both high- and low-cost production. A marginal-cost supply curve would be a smoother, steeper curve, because of decreasing marginal physical products and increasing marginal prices for the inputs being used.[3]

Revenues are shown in Figure IV.1 as the product's market price, cutting across the stepwise supply curve. Systems with average costs below the price line have positive average profits (entry E in Table IV.1), meaning that the resources used in that system are earning returns above their value elsewhere. On the other hand, resources in the noncompetitive system C could earn slightly higher returns elsewhere. Noncompetitive systems can be expected to decline over time as the owners of those resources seek higher incomes in other activities.

Private budgets forming stepwise average-cost curves (as in Figure IV.1) are conventional elements of applied production economics, typically used to construct optimization models of a particular market, sector, or whole economy (as in Hazell and Norton 1986). The main innovation and analytical strength of the PAM approach lies in recalculating the budgets at national opportunity costs, which allows comparative advantage and policy effects to be analyzed without a complex optimization model.

Figure IV.1
Average Cost of Maize Production at Market Prices

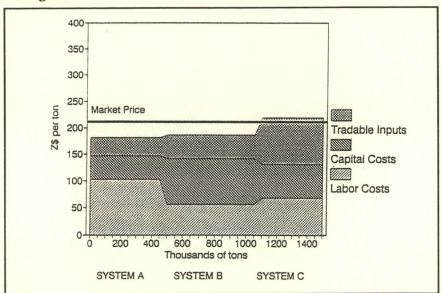

Source: Calculated from PAM results in this chapter.

The estimation of national opportunity costs is done in two steps. First, for all individual budget items such as fertilizer or transport, item-specific transfers or opportunity costs are estimated, using either tax and subsidy data for transfers or potential trade and domestic values for opportunity costs. Then, these itemized costs are grouped into the three macroeconomic categories, and economy-wide transfers in the markets for capital, labor, and foreign exchange are applied.

The second set of budgets, showing the national opportunity costs of all resources used in each activity, forms an opportunity-cost supply curve as in Figure IV.2. For the new budgets revenue is also calculated in terms of national opportunity cost, which in this example has risen much more than average costs, giving all systems positive national profits. Even System C is highly profitable at national values, relative to other activities in the economy.

The PAM itself is a framework of accounting identities, making no behavioral assumptions. The PAM is not an economic model; its function is to provide a theoretically consistent set of accounts in which to combine the results of other models. Specifically, each matrix of budgets combines an input-output model of farm and marketing activities for a commodity system with a set of

Figure IV.2
Average Cost of Maize at National Values

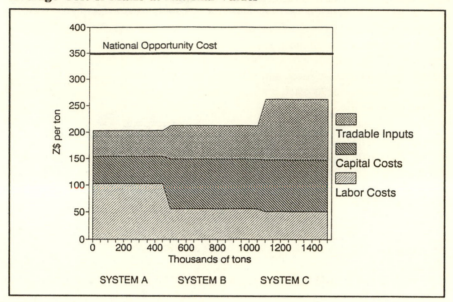

Source: Calculated from PAM results in this chapter.

economic models, showing market prices and opportunity costs for the inputs and outputs in that system. A few general characteristics of these models are reviewed below.

Physical Budgets

The first type of model used in the PAM is a set of average input-output coefficients, forming a physical budget describing a commodity system. The actual economy has a continuum of physical input-output relationships (approximated, for example, in a continuous production function), that for PAM-based research is segmented into discrete systems using average quantities of inputs and outputs. There are two main dimensions to this aggregation.

One dimension of aggregation is the size of the commodity system, in terms of quantity produced or area under production. Every field, farm, or region is in some way unique, but for analytical convenience only a limited number of PAMs can be built. The appropriate number is a compromise between detail and simplicity. This study uses three farming systems—low-potential CAs, high-potential CAs, and LSC areas—to show the main directions of variation in Zimbabwean agriculture.

A second dimension of aggregation is the length of the marketing chain to and from the farm. To measure private farm income and incentives it would be easiest to measure inputs and outputs at the farm gate. But to identify national opportunity costs the commodity system must include enough off-farm activities for inputs and outputs to reach national markets. Tradable products must be processed and transported to reach trade opportunities, and intermediate inputs must be broken down into their tradable, capital, and labor components. Where off-farm and intermediate cost items are small, measuring them exactly will be of little consequence for the entire system. But for important off-farm activities, such as transport, fertilizer, and processing of some crops, measuring total costs and decomposing them into capital, labor, and tradables are important aspects of the physical budgets in a PAM. These nonfarm data are not needed in many other types of farm budgets (Brown 1979).

Market Prices and National Opportunity Costs

The second type of model used in the PAM provides the prices and opportunity costs at which inputs and outputs may be valued. Following Harberger (1971), values are derived from the interaction of marginal opportunity costs in production and consumption.[4] Divergences between market prices and national opportunity costs can all be considered to be policy-induced transfers, whether they were actively created by government actions (such as a tax or regulation) or were passively allowed to persist by government inactions (such as a failure to correct market failures). If suitable models and data were available to distinguish between the direct effects of policy and the effects of uncorrected market failures, the total divergence could be broken down into these two types of transfers. Further analysis could also account for the effects of policies offsetting market failures.

The PAM itself offers no method by which to distinguish between types of divergences, and PAM results do not depend on this distinction as long as national opportunity costs are measured directly. When the divergences themselves are estimated, only the most visible policy-induced divergences are likely to be included in the PAM. And in general, market failures are impossible to measure. Since measurable things are usually marketable, a common reason for markets to fail is difficulties in measuring quantities or prices.

In all cases, the estimation of counterfactual national opportunity costs and divergences is subject to debate. As a practical matter, the measurement of opportunity costs often reduces to the availability of data and trustworthy models. The methods used in the PAM are derived from applied welfare economics (e.g., Warr 1977, 1982) and the practical experience of cost-benefit analysis practicioners (e.g., Little and Mirrlees 1969; Dasgupta, Marglin, and Sen 1972). In general the following rule of thumb is used: If marginal quantities of a good may profitably be traded internationally, its optimal price is its currently observed value in trade; otherwise, a domestic opportunity cost must be found.

The structure of the PAM is designed to take advantage of these optimal-pricing rules, by separating tradable from nontradable costs. This makes it possible to estimate national opportunity costs for the entire commodity system without constructing a complete optimization model of the whole economy. The result is only an approximation but may be as accurate as a complete model given the very limited data available.

The PAM provides both flexibility and analytical insight, but like any method it is subject to important limitations. One simplification is that the PAM uses average input-output coefficients, which may not be the same as the marginal values that would apply if quantities changed. Input-output coefficients would in fact be constant for inputs that had constant marginal productivity or were always used in fixed proportions. But to the extent that inputs can be substituted for one another, PAM results overstate the marginal costs and benefits of policies.

A second source of error derives from the absence of interaction effects among the various prices. The PAM does include economy-wide and sectoral effects—for example, through the interest rate, the real exchange rate, and wages—but the impact of policy on each price is measured individually, and the interaction between prices is not explicitly modeled. If suitable models to capture such cross-price or general equilibrium effects were available, their results could be integrated into the PAM. But again, it is precisely because the data and models needed to measure these effects are not available that the PAM approach is needed.

Both input substitution and general-equilibrium adjustments take time to occur and would tend to dampen the effects of policy in any one market. By omitting them the PAM shows itself to be most accurate as a short run measure, highlighting effects that can be expected to decline over time as market participants adjust to the policies. But this is precisely the point of PAM results: to show the direction and approximate magnitude of the incentive and income effects of policy before adjustment occurs, without modeling the adjustment process itself.

A third limitation is the omission of risk or uncertainty. The prices and yields of riskier crops could be reduced using some risk discount, but the information needed to calculate the costs of risk is virtually unobtainable. This study shows that it is difficult enough to make an accurate measurement of average costs and benefits; the impact of risk must then be judged subjectively or with other analytical methods.

Beyond these simplifications the PAM is subject to the wider limitations of social science in general, particularly that controlled experiments are not possible. National profits and transfers in the PAM are estimates based on historical information, using economic models to estimate national opportunity costs for each budget item. Those outcomes did not, in fact, occur; national opportunity costs are estimates of what market prices would have been under counterfactual conditions. The PAM then makes a simple comparison between those national opportunity costs and the market prices that were actually observed.

Finally, it must be noted that PAM results, like the results of other methods, depend on the objectives of the research. As this is a study of the effects of policy in general, national opportunity costs are defined as optimal prices—the values that would have resulted from a Pareto-optimal allocation of resources throughout the economy. This approach provides the most complete possible picture of the effects of policy, by assuming that all government interventions are subject to change. But such a general picture is of general value only. For a more specific analytical purpose, such as evaluating a particular policy change, project, or activity, it would no longer be appropriate to use economy-wide optimal prices. Second-best marginal values, calculated using the Harberger (1969) weighted-average pricing rule or some other method—should be used instead, under the specific set of conditions that would reflect the actual environment for the options under consideration.

In the context of a particular policy choice, inputs that have completely inelastic supplies would have a marginal value of zero, while goods that are subject to quantitative restrictions in trade would be valued at local rather than border prices. Which budget items are to be considered fixed (and hence have a zero value) and which trade restrictions are to be taken as given (thus making the item nontradable) depends on the problem to be addressed. But to analyze a particular policy decision, the results of this general study should be adapted by replacing optimal values with the appropriate second-best marginal prices. Major changes in the conclusions are unlikely, however, since the sensitivity analyses indicate that most results of the study are quite robust in the face of changes in important parameters.

THE PAM IN ZIMBABWE

In this study, budgets are presented for nine major field crops (maize, sorghum, pearl and finger millet, cotton, groundnuts, sunflower, wheat, and soybeans), in the three major farming systems (LSC, low-potential CA, and high-potential CA). Not all crops are produced in all farming systems; a total of sixteen budgets are compiled, covering Zimbabwe's principal crop enterprises.

The dividing line between areas of high and low agroeconomic potential is around 700 mm/year of average rainfall (Torrance 1981). In addition to higher rainfall, the high-potential regions generally have richer soils (with more organic matter) and more reliable and longer season lengths (Hussein 1987). Prices and marketing conditions also vary with agroecological conditions, particularly because the high-potential regions generally produce a surplus of grain, whereas the low-potential areas often import grain from the rest of the country.

In terms of Zimbabwe's standard Natural Region classification, high-potential farming systems correspond roughly with Natural Regions I, II, and some parts of III, and the low-potential region with most of III, IV, and V (see map in the appendix and Vincent and Thomas 1961). But drawing exact boundaries would be arbitrary. As with any agroecological classification, there is typically no sharp demarcation on the ground between high- and low-potential regions. The rainfall, evaporation, soils, and other determinants of agricultural potential all vary continuously over space and time and are only imperfectly correlated with one another.

Two relatively fixed and easily measured influences are latitude and altitude. Agricultural potential is generally highest in the north, because much of Zimbabwe's rainfall is brought from north to south by the Inter-Tropical Convergence Zone (ITCZ). The ITCZ moves southward from the equator to bring rains and start the growing season and then cycles back towards the equator for the winter. Thus the more southern areas tend to receive less rainfall, less reliably, and over a shorter season. A second general influence is altitude, with higher agricultural potential along the spines of high plains between Bulawayo and Harare and between Harare and Mutare. At lower altitudes, there tend to be higher temperatures, less rainfall, and more evaporation.

Although there are no simple boundaries between low- and high-potential regions, the distinction between them captures the two poles of communal area farming. The three types of budgets presented here (CA low-potential, CA high-potential, and LSC) refer to Zimbabwe's three key farming systems. These systems use different production techniques in different locations, but compete for common resources and produce substitutable crops. Figure IV.3 summarizes these substitution possibilities in terms of production and consumption.

Cotton, maize, and groundnuts are at the center of this study, in the sense that they are grown in both LSC and smallholder systems over a wide range of environments. Sunflower and the small grains (sorghum and millets) are almost entirely grown by smallholders, most commonly in low-potential regions. Wheat and soybeans are almost entirely grown by LSC farmers. They are somewhat complementary in that they can both be grown within a single year, but other rotations are also used.

In terms of consumption, LSC production is almost entirely sold onto formal markets. Smallholder production is entirely market-oriented in the case of cotton and mostly so for sunflowers. Maize is produced for both home consumption and sale, but sorghum and millet are produced primarily for home consumption and informal sales. The nine crops in Figure IV.3 covered by this study are not, of course, the only important agricultural products in Zimbabwe. Others have been discussed in Parts II and III, but these are more specialized products that have limited substitution possibilities with the major field crops, typically because of high fixed capital requirements or restricted markets.

DATA SOURCES

In creating representative budgets, every effort has been made to draw on standard Zimbabwean sources. Budgets for the LSC sector are compiled primarily with material from the Commercial Farmers Union, supplemented by data from private agricultural management consultants. As the CFU prepares crop budgets primarily for the annual price negotiations with government, it might be expected that costs would be somewhat overestimated and yields underestimated. Nonetheless, the budgets are widely accepted as representative for the sector, and their general accuracy is confirmed by evidence from input suppliers and from farm management consulting firms. There has been no formal survey of farm management in the LSC sector since the late 1970s.[5]

Figure IV.3
Principal Substitutions Among Major Field Crops

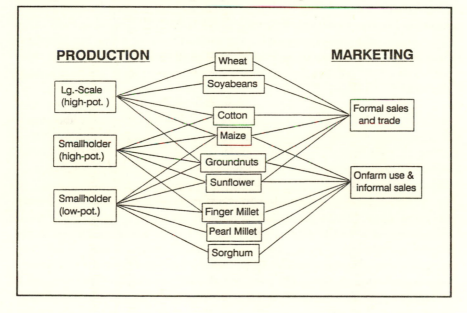

For the CA sector, budgets are drawn primarily from data collected in the first MLARR Communal Areas Farm Survey, on which the author provided technical assistance between October 1988 and December 1990. Prior to this survey, there had been no large-scale attempt to measure input use, yields, and crop sales across a range of environments in Zimbabwe. The successful completion of the MLARR survey and the analyses of the resulting data presented in MLARR (1990), in Chigume and Jayne (1990), and in this study represent significant additions to the empirical base for agricultural economics in Zimbabwe. Because of the importance of the data presented here, this section will focus primarily on the CA budgets.

The survey covered eight sites chosen randomly from around the country (see map in the appendix). Three sites are in high-potential areas,[6] one is in an intermediate area,[7] and four are in low-potential areas.[8] The low-potential sites do not include any of Zimbabwe's driest areas in Matabeleland, because military activity made survey work impossible in that region when the sample sites were selected in 1986–1987.

A sample of 60 households at each site was selected using the CSO sample frame from the 1982 national census, divided between two enumeration areas about 10 km in diameter and about 20 km apart. One full-time enumerator was stationed at each site, visiting each household every four to eight weeks from October 1988 (a month or two before planting began) to September 1989 (after almost all marketings were complete).

The initial sample included only farmers who were present and had made harvests in the previous year. An average of 8 households per site subsequently dropped out of the sample, typically because of illness or migration. Thus the final sample of 414 includes only farmers who had some area harvested in both 1988 and 1989 and does not represent the full spectrum of communal area residents.

The eight enumerators were supervised by two local economists and a foreign advisor. The enumerators met together with their supervisors at the ministry head office before the season for a week of training, then again three times during the year to submit completed questionnaires and discuss their work. The enumerators were also visited by their supervisors in the field two or three times each at various intervals.

Three separate questionnaires were used, covering pre-, mid-, and end-season cropping issues. (Livestock questions were asked continuously.) Most questions were answered numerically; although the questionnaire was written in English, interviews were conducted in Shona using local terms. Interviews generally involved the entire household, with the enumerator reporting the respondents' best collective estimates. The enumerator made personal estimates of land area (by pacing) and container volumes (by hand-spans or visual estimates) when respondents expressed doubt. All input use (including labor time) was reported by plot, but since farmers commonly join crops from several plots together for transport, threshing, and storage, harvested quantities were reported for all plots together.

During the season, completed questionnaires were reviewed by the supervisors and entered into a computer database by staff typists. The resulting data tables were then checked against the original questionnaires, corrected, and used to calculate various tables of results. Although considerable care was taken in questionnaire design, enumerator training, supervision, and data analysis, some measurement error is inevitable.

Errors in area planted arose particularly in cases of intercropping, for which the area occupied by each crop had to be estimated for the results to be given on a pure stand basis. There were also important errors in harvested quantities, particularly when farmers postponed the threshing of grain until the off-season so that grain yields had to be estimated from unthreshed and unbagged produce, but also when the enumerator had to estimate how much of the harvest had already been consumed before the interview.

DESCRIPTION OF SURVEY SITES

Selected background data for the communal area PAM budgets are given in Table IV.2. The 1989 harvest year had average rainfall in the high-potential regions, while rainfall in the low-potential sites was about one standard deviation below normal. This is somewhat unusual, as rainfall levels are usually correlated throughout the country (Masters 1990b, p. 1.7).

In general, the low-potential sites have much lower population density, giving more land per farm and greater planted area per household. But the low-potential areas have sparser infrastructure, and a broad range of indicators all point clearly to much more severe poverty than in the high-potential areas. There are larger households, more migration, and particularly more female-headed households in low-potential areas than in high-potential areas.[9]

In the low-potential sites, there is virtually no use of formal credit and far less ownership of implements beyond the basic ox-plow than in the high-potential areas. A slightly larger share have an irrigated household garden, and a larger proportion declared their intention at the start of the season to have one or more intercropped plots.[10]

Low-potential area farmers generally put more emphasis on livestock than high-potential area farmers, but they actually had smaller livestock herds in 1989—largely because their cattle and goat herds declined during the 1980s, while herds in the high-potential areas increased. The low-potential decline occurred entirely in the two driest survey sites, Nyajena and Zvishavane areas,

Table IV.2
Selected MLARR Survey Site Data, 1989 Harvests

		Low-potential	High-potential	All areas
Normal Rainfall	mm	645	798	734
1988–1989 rainfall	% of normal	65	99	86
Population Density (1982)	/km2	39.3	55.6	45.6
Infrastructure				
Distance to dust road	km	2.1	1.5	2.1
Distance to tar road	km	20.4	13.2	20.0
Distance to water source	km	1.1	0.5	0.9
Household Characteristics				
HH members	no./HH	10.5	9.6	9.8
Nonresident HH members	% of total	23.3	18.7	20.2
Female HH heads	% of HH	40.3	29.1	35.6
Credit Use				
Used AFC credit 1987–1988	% of HH	3.6	42.8	18.6
Using AFC credit 1988–1989	% of HH	1.3	34.5	13.9
Asset Ownership and Land Use				
Ox-plow	no./HH	1.1	1.2	1.1
Ox-cultivators	no./HH	0.2	0.7	0.3
Ox-carts	no./HH	0.3	0.5	0.4
Own garden	% of HH	47.9	43.5	43.9
Use intercropping	% of HH	23.7	5.7	15.2
Livestock Ownership				
Livestock units (250kg)	/HH	6.9	7.9	7.18
Of which: Cattle	%	69.8	91.6	78.9
Goats	%	21.6	6.3	14.7
Donkeys	%	6.8	0.2	4.5
Historical Trends				
Cattle: 1980–1981	no./HH	7.1	6.3	6.7
Cattle: 1987–1988	no./HH	6.3	8.4	7.0
Goats: 1980–1981	no./HH	8.2	0.8	5.0
Goats: 1987–1988	no./HH	9.8	2.8	6.7
Hiring draft: 1980–1981	% of HH	20.0	20.8	22.5
Hiring draft: 1987–1988	% of HH	18.3	14.7	18.2
Owning ox-cart: 1980–1981	% of HH	23.8	36.3	28.9
Owning ox-cart: 1987–1988	% of HH	28.9	46.3	36.0

		Low-potential	High-potential	All areas
Whole Farm Financial Results				
Crop production value	Z$/HH	572	1950	1001
+Livestock appreciation	Z$/HH	290	121	212
+Livestock trading	Z$/HH	105	61	76
- Total variable costs	Z$/HH	319	758	496
- Overhead expenditure	Z$/HH	63	46	58
=Net farm income	Z$/HH	585	1328	735
+Non-farm income	Z$/HH	381	498	374
=Total HH income	Z$/HH	966	1826	1109
Total own labor hours	hours/HH	1478	1352	1437
Net crops income per hour	Z$/hour	0.13	1.25	0.31

Source: MLARR survey data. "All Areas" includes Chirumanzu, an intermediate site.

where farmers had difficulty restocking after the severe three-year drought in 1982-1984 reduced herd sizes.

In the low-potential sites, the evidence of declining cattle herd sizes, only slightly offset by an increase in goat herd sizes, is consistent with a small net decline in agricultural wealth. But other indicators suggest an improvement over the decade, as the proportion of low-potential farmers hiring draft animals declined and the proportion owning their own ox-carts rose. Some of these changes are due to life-cycle changes within the sample households, and some are recall errors. But on balance it appears that net agricultural wealth has changed little and has perhaps fallen in the low-potential areas, while it has clearly risen substantially in the high-potential areas.

Income and expenditure results for the 1989 harvest year show the low-potential region farmers earning income from crops of less than a third as much—and total household income about half as much—as the high-potential area sample. The low-potential farmers were able to earn more than high-potential farmers from improving their livestock, but most of these earnings were reinvested in herd expansion.

PHYSICAL BUDGETS: INPUT USE AND YIELDS

Table IV.3 provides a summary of the major input-output relationships in the communal-area farming system.

The farming system is dominated by maize in the high-potential regions and by maize plus the small grains (pearl millet, sorghum, and finger millet) in the low-potential regions. All coarse grains together cover a larger share of plantings in the areas of low potential (74 percent) than of high potential (67 percent), with the remaining area given to oilseeds. But in the low-potential areas grains are planted primarily for subsistence needs, with the oilseeds earning most (57 percent) of the crop sales revenue, whereas in the high potential areas this relationship is reversed and maize earns most (77 percent) of the crop sales revenue.

Groundnuts and bambara nuts are typically planted in small plots by many farmers, whereas cotton and sunflowers are planted by fewer farmers each with larger areas. Several high-potential area farmers in the sample were experimenting—so far unsuccessfully—with soybeans, and a few farmers in one site (Chiweshe) had developed a highly lucrative burley tobacco crop.

Labor allocations on a per-hectare basis show that cotton and groundnuts are very labor intensive, particularly at harvest, while sunflowers are given little effort. But among the grains per-hectare averages are misleading: in per-ton terms, harvesting labor requirements for high-yielding maize are much lower than for the low-yielding small grains, largely because the small grains require more threshing effort.

Table IV.3
Physical Budgets for CA Production by Region, 1988–1989

	Maize			Pearl Millet			Sorghum		
	Low	High	All	Low	High	All	Low	High	All
Households Planting	219	146	411	117	3	125	59	1	61
Area per HH									
Planting (ha/HH)	1.6	2.0	1.7	1.3	0.2	1.2	0.7	0.4	0.7
Failed (%)	12	10	10	25	100	25	4		5
Total Labor (hrs/ha)	386	370	411	343	46	351	306	328	308
Labor Allocation (hrs/ha)									
Manuring	19	2	12	..	3	..	3		3
Preplowing	13	12	19	7	21	8	7		9
Planting	60	48	56	64		63	63	70	62
Chem. application		1	..		21				
Weeding	126	91	113	118		120	79	50	80
Harvesting	170	217	210	153		159	155	208	154
Labor Type (hrs/ha)									
Adult family	327	336	354	269	46	274	280	310	281
Adult hired	11	13	14	10		12	13		13
Child family	96	43	86	119		121	27	35	28
Child hired	2	..	2	7		7			
Inputs (kg/ha)									
Seeds	19	29	23	13	10	13	10	18	10
Fertilizer	17	240	115		3	..			
AN	7	109	52						
8-14-7	10	129	62		3	..			
Other		2	1						
Gypsum									
Yield (mt/ha planted)	0.6	3.2	1.8	0.2		0.2	0.2	0.7	0.2
Field-Home Transport (km)									
Per mt	0.7	0.6	0.6	1.0		0.9	0.4	1.5	0.4
Per HH	1.0	0.9	1.0	1.2		1.1	0.4	1.5	0.4
Sales (% of harvest)	19	80	67	27		26	3		3
Home-Market Transport (km)									
Per mt	10	26	25	22		48			
Per HH	11	25	24	27		19	1	57	15
Memo Items									
% of HHs planting	99	100	99	53	2	30	27	1	15
% of total area	42	64	51	18	..	11	5	..	3
% of total labor	46	56	46	18	..	9	4	..	2
Avg. price (Z$/mt)	255	213	220	278		278	260		260
% of produc. value	43	76	65	7		2	2		1
% of sales value	33	77	72	8		1	..		..

	Finger Millet			Groundnuts (unshelled)			Cotton		
	Low	High	All	Low	High	All	Low	High	All
Households Planting	114	30	187	181	82	293	1	53	54
Area per HH									
Planting (ha/HH)	0.6	0.4	0.6	0.6	0.4	0.5	2.0	1.5	1.5
Failed (%)	8	..	10	8	5	10		16	16
Total Labor (hrs/ha)	485	388	545	673	578	658	1032	627	637
Labor Allocation (hrs/ha)									
Manuring	1		1	2		2		1	1
Preplowing	9		20	9	1	14	18	28	28
Planting	38	34	33	85	66	83	14	57	56
Chem. application					..	..		61	59
Weeding	100	57	136	144	128	146	455	212	218
Harvesting	337	297	355	433	383	414	545	268	275
Labor Type (hrs/ha)									
Adult family	374	359	408	560	542	561	692	567	571
Adult hired	76	18	92	35	16	29	324	42	49
Child family	69	22	89	152	39	134	32	34	34
Child hired	1	..	1	3		2			
Inputs (kg/ha)									
Seeds	13	19	14	34	37	34	18	37	36
Fertilizer		9	1	3		2	300	124	128
AN		1	..	1		1		22	21
8-14-7		8	1	2		2		7	7
Other							300	95	100
Gypsum									
Yield (mt/ha planted)	0.4	0.6	0.4	0.5	0.4	0.5	0.8	0.5	0.5
Field-Home Transport (km)									
Per mt	0.5	0.4	0.6	0.6	0.3	0.6	0.2	0.6	0.6
Per HH	0.7	0.7	0.9	1.0	0.6	0.9	0.2	1.2	1.2
Sales (% of harvest)	7		7	32	11	27	100	100	100
Home-Market Transport (km)									
Per mt	8		15	21	1	29	58	32	33
Per HH	5		10	34	2	25	58	32	33
Memo Items									
% of HHs planting	51	21	45	82	56	71	..	36	13
% of total area	9	3	8	14	7	12	..	17	6
% of total labor	12	2	9	26	10	17	1	25	8
Avg. price (Z$/mt)	370	370	370	688	886	768		906	906
% of produc. value	7	1	4	30	5	13		14	9
% of sales value	2		..	40	1	6		18	15

	Sunflowers			Bambara Nuts			Soya	Tobacco	Whole Farm		
	Low	High	All	Low	High	All	All	All	Low	High	All
Households Planting	50	32	84	130	8	145	17	7	222	146	414
Area per HH											
Planting (ha/HH)	0.7	0.8	0.8	0.4	0.2	0.3	0.4	0.5	3.7	3.2	3.3
Failed (%)	26	9	19	17	12	17	57	13	14	12	13
Total Labor (hrs/ha)	312	254	287	573	831	506	200	1296	353	428	451
Labor Allocation (hrs/ha)											
Manuring	..		..						9	1	7
Preplowing	8	2	5	6		6		20	9	13	17
Planting	61	25	45	104	58	92	48	135	50	50	59
Chem. application								27		11	4
Weeding	68	22	49	235	155	200	90	93	101	109	124
Harvesting	175	205	187	228	618	208	62	1021	185	244	241
Labor Type (hrs/ha)											
Adult family	264	235	252	482	732	428	195	1111	295	390	382
Adult hired	8	8	8	3	14	3	..	143	18	19	23
Child family	78	20	53	174	172	151	9	85	80	39	91
Child hired	..	2	1	1		1			2	..	2
Inputs (kg/ha)											
Seeds	11	14	13	36	23	32	29	3			
Fertilizer		26	11				23	474	8	182	68
AN		11	5				4		3	75	28
8-14-7		15	6				19	53	4	86	33
Other								421	1	21	8
Gypsum									..		..
Yield (mt/ha planted)	0.3	0.5	0.4	0.4	0.4	0.4	0.2	1.0			
Field-Home Transport (km)											
Per mt	0.4	0.4	0.4	1.1	0.4	1.1	0.5	0.3	0.5	0.6	0.6
Per HH	0.6	0.8	0.7	1.3	0.7	1.3	0.5	0.5	0.7	0.9	1.0
Sales (% of harvest)	88	98	81	10		9	88	98			
Home-Market Transport (km)											
Per mt	32	28	30	14		5	32	142	9	26	26
Per HH	28	26	28	15		15	..		11	24	24
Memo Items											
% of HHs planting	23	22	20	59	5	35	4	2	100	100	100
% of total area	4	6	5	6	..	3	1	..	100	100	100
% of total labor	4	3	3	9	1	4	..	1	100	100	100
Avg. price (Z$/mt)	455	455	455	524		524	423	1380			
% of produc. value	4	2	2	8		2	..	1	100	100	100
% of sales value	13	3	3	3		..	..	2	100	100	100

Notes: Low-potential sites are Buhera, Nyajena, and Zvishavane. High- potential sites are Chirau, Chiweshe, and Kandeya. All Sites total includes these plus Chirumanzu. Input use is per hectare planted. Child labor is weighted by one-half in totals.

Sources: Calculated from the MLARR, Farm Management Research Section Communal Lands farm survey, 1989 harvest year.

Hired labor is, as noted in Part II, only a small part of total labor except in the lucrative, labor-intensive cases of cotton and finger millet. Children, here defined as under fifteen years of age, are much more important than hired workers, particularly in cultivating groundnuts and bambara nuts.

Seed rates are generally proportional to agroecological potential. For maize, seed rates are higher than the generally recommended 25 kg/ha in the high-potential areas and lower than that in the low-potential areas. Other crops follow a similar pattern, as farmers seek to match plant populations with the moisture and nutrient content of their soils.

Manuring efforts are focused on maize, and chemical fertilizer is used almost exclusively on maize and to a lesser extent cotton. Crop chemicals, as shown in the PAM budgets below, are used almost exclusively on cotton, although a few farmers used a grain pesticide (typically Malathion) on maize.

Yield levels are higher than in the high-potential area than in the low-potential area for almost all crops. The gap is greatest for maize, which shows a five-fold difference thanks to the interaction of rainfall and fertilizer with modern hybrid varieties. But these survey results show that in the low-potential areas, even in this relatively dry year, the modern maize hybrids still yield more than the virtually unimproved sorghum and millet varieties. The survey also found that maize requires much less labor than alternative grains, particularly at harvest. In addition, maize is easier to process and may also be a preferred food; these factors have ensured the dominance of maize over the small grains in all but the driest, most remote parts of the country (Masters 1990b).

POLICY ANALYSIS MATRIX RESULTS

To make direct comparisons of resource productivity in the low- and high-potential CAs and in LSC farming areas, it is necessary to attach values to each product and each input. In the PAM framework, productivities are compared at market prices to measure private profitability and at national opportunity costs to measure national profitability. Only the results of these comparisons are given here; the underlying data and calculations are detailed in the appendix budget notes.

Table IV.4 shows the private profitabilities of alternative crops in descending order. In both the low- and high-potential CAs these market-price profits are strongly positive for maize and negative for all other crops. In the LSC systems, market-price profits are strongly positive for wheat, slightly positive for cotton, and negative for all other crops.

The absolute level of profits in these budgets is determined by setting average whole-farm profits to zero. The difference between total revenues and total costs is considered a return to land, since in the long run land is a fixed factor whose value equals the level of farm profits.[11] The resulting implicit value of

Table IV.4
Profits at Market Prices, 1989 (Z$/ha)

| Communal Areas | | | | | | |
Low-potential		High-potential		Large-scale Commercial	
Mz	+115	Mz	+81	Wh	+136
Gn	-18	Gn	-109	Co	+26
Sf	-54	Sf	-109	Mz	-39
Fm	-101	Fm	-149	Gn	-42
Sg	-118	Co	-156	Sb	-48
Pm	-160				

Note: The abbreviations used here and in later tables are: Co-Cotton, Mz-Maize, Sb-Soybeans, Gn-Groundnuts, Pm-Pearl Millet, Sg-Sorghum, Fm-Finger Millet, Sf-Sunflower, Wh-Wheat.
Source: Author's calculations, from data in the appendix PAM budgets.

land is Z$10/ha in low-potential CAs, Z$150/ha in high-potential CAs, and Z$90/ha in LSC areas. The difference between the high-potential CAs and the LSC areas is largely due to different tenure rules, given that both are in similar natural regions (see Part II for details).

In these budgets, as average farm profits are fully absorbed by the cost of land, the profitability of any individual activity reflects only differences from the average for that type of land. These differences could be due to transient weather or price surprises, to slow adjustment to recent trends in yield and technology, to differences in risk and other variables missing from the crop budgets, or simply to measurement error.

Table IV.4 shows that, in both low- and high-potential CAs, maize is by far the most profitable crop, despite the below-average rains in the low-potential regions of 1989. The low profitability of cotton in the high-potential CAs is due to the unusually low average yields, only 500 kg/ha, recorded in the survey; with higher yields costs but also profits would be higher. And in the LSCs, wheat is shown to be by far the most profitable crop, despite a relatively high capital cost attributed to irrigated land.[12]

Net profits at national opportunity costs are ranked in Table IV.5. All profits are substantially higher, primarily because the foreign exchange premium raises the values of all outputs and the few tradable inputs, relative to the costs of labor and land. In the CA budgets national opportunity costs of domestic resources are the same as market prices. However, in the LSC sector, the opportunity cost of labor is below market wages because of employment

Table IV.5
Profits at National Opportunity Costs, 1989 (Z$/ha)

| | Communal Areas | | | Large-scale Commercial | |
	Low-potential		High-potential		
Gn	+298	Mz	+425	Gn	+1487
Mz	+229	Co	+194	Co	+1386
Sf	+2	Gn	+52	Wh	+947
Fm	-39	Sf	-18	Sb	+813
Sg	-101	Fm	-56	Mz	+486
Pm	-149				

restrictions, while the opportunity cost of land is above market prices because of subdivision restrictions. In both cases, national opportunity costs have been set by the ruling market prices in the much larger CA sector, to Z$0.32/hr for labor and Z$150/ha for land.

Using opportunity costs instead of market prices changes relative incentives for several important crop substitutions. In the low-potential CAs groundnuts become more profitable than maize, and in the high-potential CAs cotton becomes just slightly less profitable than maize. In the LSC budgets both groundnuts and cotton rise to become more profitable than wheat.

The PAM method is useful not only in calculating private and national profitabilities but also in comparing the determinants of those results in terms of consistent categories that can be compared across different enterprises. The full PAMs in Table IV.6 show, for example, that the generally higher private returns to land in communal area production are due to much lower use of capital and tradable inputs, which more than outweighs lower crop yields. Total labor use per hectare in the CAs is also lower than in the LSC budgets, because of the high use by LSC farmers of labor that is embodied in other inputs. When calculated per ton or per dollar of output, however, labor use is higher in the CAs than on LSC farms.

The full PAMs of Table IV.6 also show the sources of the difference between private and national profits. For all budget categories except LSC labor, market prices are below opportunity costs. This reflects the pervasiveness of scarcity in the economy, with prices repressed by direct controls. But as the degree of price repression is generally greater for products than for inputs, farmers earn lower private than national profits.

Table IV.6
Policy Analysis Matrix Results, 1989 Harvest Year

	Low-Potential CAs				High-Potential CAs				Large-Scale Commercial			
	Market Prices	Opp. Costs	Trans-fers	(%)	Market Prices	Opp. Costs	Trans-fers	(%)	Market Prices	Opp. Costs	Trans-fers	(%)
Maize												
Output	408	554	-146	-26	682	1109	-427	-39	1193	1958	-765	-39
Labor	165	165			180	180			382	284	98	35
Capital	72	82	-10	-12	277	302	-25	-8	360	548	-188	-34
Tradables	56	78	-22	-28	144	201	-58	-29	490	640	-150	-23
Profit	115	229	-114	-50	81	425	-345	-81	-39	486	-525	-108
Cotton												
Output					453	859	-406	-47	1607	3177	-1570	-49
Labor					248	248			569	400	169	42
Capital					241	260	-19	-7	426	640	-214	-33
Tradables					119	157	-37	-24	586	750	-164	-22
Profit					-156	194	-350	-180	26	1386	-1360	-98
Groundnuts												
Output	344	691	-347	-50	354	553	-198	-36	1467	3178	-1710	-54
Labor	260	260			208	208			648	444	204	42
Capital	53	61	-8	-13	195	203	-9	-4	413	635	-223	-33
Tradables	49	72	-22	-31	61	89	-29	-32	448	611	-163	-22
Profit	-18	298	-317	-106	-109	52	-161	-311	-42	1487	-1528	-98

	Low-Potential CAs				High-Potential CAs				Large-Scale Commercial			
	Market Prices	Opp. Costs	Trans-fers	(%)	Market Prices	Opp. Costs	Trans-fers	(%)	Market Prices	Opp. Costs	Trans-fers	(%)
Sunflower												
Output	137	205	-68	-33	228	341	-114	-33				
Labor	128	128			104	104						
Capital	45	49	-4	-9	196	203	-7	-4				
Tradables	18	25	-8	-30	37	52	-16	-30				
Profit	-54	2	-56	-3168	-109	-18	-91	-501				
Pearl Millet												
Output	56	83	-28	-33								
Labor	144	144										
Capital	45	50	-5	-10								
Tradables	26	39	-12	-32								
Profit	-160	-149	-10	7								
Sorghum												
Output	52	78	-26	-33								
Labor	117	117										
Capital	32	46	-4	-8								
Tradables	11	16	-5	-30								
Profit	-118	-101	-18	17								

	Low-Potential CAs				High-Potential CAs				Large-Scale Commercial			
	Market Prices	Opp. Costs	Transfers	(%)	Market Prices	Opp. Costs	Transfers	(%)	Market Prices	Opp. Costs	Transfers	(%)
Finger Millet												
Output	148	222	-74	-33	222	333	-111	-33				
Labor	184	184			147	147						
Capital	47	51	-5	-9	195	201	-6	-3				
Tradables	19	26	-8	-30	29	42	-12	-30				
Profit	-101	-39	-62	157	-149	-56	-92	-163				
Wheat												
Output									2190	3630	-1440	-40
Labor									413	355	57	16
Capital									965	1400	-434	-31
Tradables									677	928	-251	-27
Profit									136	947	-812	-86
Soybeans												
Output									1000	2094	-1094	-52
Labor									291	233	57	25
Capital									367	528	-161	-30
Tradables									391	520	-129	-25
Profit									-48	813	-861	-106

Source: Author's calculations from data in the appendix.

These PAM results are calculated on a per-hectare basis. But for farmers facing physical shortages of particular inputs other than land, returns to those non-land factors may be more revealing than returns to the enterprise as a whole. In Table IV.7 PAM profits (returns per hectare) are compared with returns to family labor and returns to total variable costs. These measures might be the primary concerns of farmers constrained by shortages of labor, seasonal finance, or both.

The return to family labor is calculated as profits, after paying all costs except family workers, per hour of family work. As such it applies only to the CA budgets. Cases where the returns to family labor are below the CA-average wage, Z$0.32/hr, generally reflect activities with negative net profits. In a few extreme cases returns to family labor are themselves negative, implying that inputs other than labor are also receiving below-average returns. The ranking of crops by returns to labor is similar to the ranking by net profits, except that for low-potential areas national returns to labor are higher in maize than in ground-nuts. Hence, for farmers in low-potential communal areas who are particularly constrained by labor shortages, maize might be preferred.

Returns to variable costs show net profits per hectare as a percentage of all costs except depreciation on fixed assets and on-farm labor. Since input use is relatively limited in the CA budgets, returns to variable costs are high: The private rate of return in maize, for example, is 89 percent in the low-potential regions and 26 percent in the high-potential regions. In contrast, the returns to variable costs in the LSC budgets are small. Although these averages do not necessarily correspond to marginal returns, they do suggest that working capital is much scarcer for communal farmers (who face high implicit seasonal interest rates and use little capital) than for LSC farmers (who face lower implicit interest rates and use larger amounts of capital).

The PAM results are calculated on a per-hectare basis in Table IV.5 and a per-hour or percentage basis in Table IV.6. But such figures are of interest only relative to one another within each farming system, across activities that share the same denominator for profits. Absolute, unit-free measures of profitability, allowing comparisons across different sectors, can be provided by combining PAM entries into ratio indicators. Table IV.8 provides the principal such indicators: the first five columns are different measures of transfers to or from farmers; the last column measures national profitability.

In Table IV.8, the nominal protection coefficient (NPC) is defined as the ratio of output value at market prices to its estimated national opportunity cost. Here this opportunity cost is measured at nominal exchange rates in order to show product-market effects alone, in isolation from exchange-rate effects. NPCs in Table IV.8 are generally near or slightly below one, suggesting that farmers generally receive slightly less than export, import, or equilibrium self-sufficiency values. The NPC is above one for maize in the low-potential CAs, because informal-market prices in these net deficit areas are above export

Table IV.7
Net Returns to Factors of Production, 1989 Harvest

		Low-Potential Regions			High-Potential Regions		
		Returns at Market Prices (a)	Returns at Opp. Costs (b)	Transfers (% of b)	Returns at Market Prices (a)	Returns at Opp. Costs (b)	Transfers (% of b)
Maize							
Land and management	(Z$/ha)	115.14	229.05	-50	80.94	425.46	-81
Family labor	(Z$/hr)	0.59	0.89	-34	0.53	1.50	-64
Variable costs	(%)	89	142	-37	26	108	-76
Cotton							
Land and management	(Z$/ha)				-155.91	194.29	-180
Family labor	(Z$/hr)				0.06	0.65	-92
Variable costs	(%)				-67	67	-199
Groundnuts							
Land and management	(Z$/ha)	-18.33	298.27	-106	-109.19	51.79	-311
Family labor	(Z$/hr)	0.26	0.76	-66	0.12	0.41	-71
Variable costs	(%)	-19	236	-108	-100	35	-383

	Low-Potential Regions			High-Potential Regions		
	Returns at Market Prices (a)	Returns at Opp. Costs (b)	Transfers (% of b)	Returns at Market Prices (a)	Returns at Opp. Costs (b)	Transfers (% of b)
Sunflower						
Land and management (Z$/ha)	-54.47	1.78	-3168	-108.93	-18.13	-501
Family labor (Z$/hr)	0.10	0.29	-64	-0.13	0.24	-156
Variable costs (%)	-100	3	-3846	-122	-16	-655
Pearl Millet						
Land and management (Z$/ha)	-159.66	-149.26	7			
Family labor (Z$/hr)	-0.22	-0.19	17			
Variable costs (%)	-228	-188	37			
Sorghum						
Land and management (Z$/ha)	-118.39	-100.86	17			
Family labor (Z$/hr)	-0.09	-0.03	191			
Variable costs (%)	-264	-189	40			
Finger Millet						
Land and management (Z$/ha)	-100.83	-39.29	157	-148.71	-56.44	-163
Family labor (Z$/hr)	0.08	0.23	-67	-0.08	0.17	-150
Variable costs (%)	-176	-56	212	-186	-57	-225

Large-Scale Commercial

		Returns at Market Prices (a)	Returns at Opp. Costs (b)	Transfers (% of b)
Maize				
Land and management	(Z$/ha)	-38.75	486.41	-108
Variable costs	(%)	-5	49	-110
Cotton				
Land and management	(Z$/ha)	25.99	1386.42	-98
Variable costs	(%)	3	114	-98
Groundnuts				
Land and management	(Z$/ha)	-51.59	1486.42	-103
Variable costs	(%)	-5	142	-104
Wheat				
Land and management	(Z$/ha)	135.66	947.17	-86
Variable costs	(%)	10	56	-82
Soybeans				
Land and management	(Z$/ha)	-47.80	813.33	-106
Variable costs	(%)	-6	90	-107

Table IV.8
Indicators of Policy and Comparative Advantage, 1989

		NPC	EPC	PC	PSE	SRP	DRC
Maize	CA Low-potential	1.10	0.74	0.50	-0.28	-0.21	0.52
	CA High-potential	0.92	0.59	0.19	-0.51	-0.31	0.53
	LSC	0.91	0.53	-0.08	-0.44	-0.27	0.63
Cotton	CA High-potential	0.79	0.53	-0.80	-0.77	-0.41	0.72
	LSC	0.76	0.42	0.02	-0.85	-0.43	0.43
Groundnuts	CA Low-potential	0.75	0.48	-0.06	-0.92	-0.46	0.52
	CA High-potential	0.96	0.63	-2.11	-0.45	-0.29	0.89
	LSC	0.69	0.40	-0.03	-0.04	-0.48	0.42
Sunflower	CA Low-potential	1.00	0.67	-30.68	-0.41	-0.27	0.99
	CA High-potential	1.00	0.67	6.01	-0.40	-0.27	1.06
Pearl Millet	CA Low-potential	1.00	0.67	1.07	-0.19	-0.12	4.34
Sorghum	CA Low-potential	1.00	0.67	1.17	-0.34	-0.22	2.63
Finger Millet	CA Low-potential	1.00	0.67	2.57	-0.42	-0.28	1.20
	CA High-potential	1.00	0.67	2.63	-0.42	-0.28	1.19
Wheat	LSC	0.91	0.56	0.14	-0.37	-0.22	0.65
Soybeans	LSC	0.72	0.39	-0.06	-0.86	-0.41	0.48

Source: Author's calculations from data in the appendix.

values.[13] NPCs are particularly low for cotton, groundnuts, and soybeans, although not in the case of groundnuts in high-potential CAs, where a substantial higher-priced informal market for groundnuts exists.

A more complex indicator of transfer effects is the effective protection coefficient (EPC), which compares value added (in the sense of output minus tradable inputs) in private and national terms. Here national opportunity costs are measured at the estimated equilibrium exchange rate, because exchange rate policy is the principal instrument used to regulate tradable input prices. Largely because of the high premium on tradables, EPCs in Table IV.7 are substantially below NPCs and are all less than one, showing net transfers from farmers to others in the economy.

The profitability coefficient (PC), which is analogous to the EPC but is measured at the level of net profits, yields very unstable results because the denominator is typically small and may be negative. The producer subsidy equivalent (PSE) and subsidy ratio to producers (SRP) are more reliable measures of total net transfers, showing private profits minus national profits as a proportion of private revenue in the PSE and national revenue in the SRP. These results show substantial net transfers from farmers, generally above 30 percent of the market-price revenues (as shown by the PSE) and 20 percent of their national opportunity-cost revenues (SRP).

The standard unit-free way to present national profitability is the Domestic Resource Cost (DRC). This is the ratio of domestic factor costs to value added, both measured at national opportunity costs. DRCs attempt to measure the "cost of production" of foreign exchange in each activity and are a typical way in which direct measurement of comparative advantage is attempted. The lower the DRC, the less is the domestic cost of earning or saving a unit of foreign exchange, and the more comparative advantage is enjoyed by that activity.

For convenience, the DRCs from Table IV.8 are repeated and ranked in Table IV.9. Since all costs and benefits have, as far as possible, been included in domestic costs (the numerator) and in value added (the denominator), these DRCs can legitimately be compared across farming sectors—and indeed with other sectors of the economy. Because most major cropping activities enjoy DRCs below two-thirds, Zimbabwe's farming sector as a whole has a strong comparative advantage (Table IV.9).[14]

The only crops shown in Table IV.9 not to be productive earners of foreign exchange are sunflowers, millets, and sorghum. This conclusion may in part be due to incomplete accounting of full costs and benefits in the budgets. For example, the budgets use a single value for land in each area. This assumes that all crops are planted on fields of similar quality. But the crops shown here to be unprofitable may in fact have been planted on below average quality land, perhaps because farmers expect them to be less sensitive to land quality than other crops.

Table IV.9
Domestic Resource Costs of Alternative Activities

Groundnuts	(LSC)	0.42	Cotton	(CA-High)	0.72
Cotton	(LSC)	0.43	Groundnuts	(CA-High)	0.89
Soybeans	(LSC)	0.48	Sunflower	(CA-Low)	0.99
Groundnuts	(CA-Low)	0.52	Sunflower	(CA-High)	1.06
Maize	(CA-Low)	0.52	Finger Millet	(CA-High)	1.19
Maize	(CA-High)	0.53	Finger Millet	(CA-Low)	1.20
Maize	(LSC)	0.63	Sorghum	(CA-Low)	2.63
Wheat	(LSC)	0.65	Pearl Millet	(CA-Low)	4.34

Source: Calculated from PAM budget data in the appendix.

Sunflowers, millets, and sorghum are clearly low-input, low-yield crops for most farmers. These crops appear to be relatively unattractive for different reasons. Sunflower is still a new crop; several improved varieties have been released, but farmers may not yet have learned to exploit their full yield potential. With sorghum and millets, on the other hand, farmers plant virtually unimproved traditional varieties. It is possible that 25-100 percent improvements in yields could be realized in the next five or so years, from a switch to modern hybrids. This would be unlikely to turn small grains from the low-potential regions into a net export to other regions, but the improved small grains would be efficient substitutes for current shipments of maize from high- to low-potential areas (Masters 1990b). Today, farmers continue to plant these low-yielding crops in part for very limited, high value uses in home brewed beverages and in part to be used as insurance food crops if their own maize harvests fail and they are then unable to purchase maize.

An important result of the data in Table IV.9 is that the top tier of enterprises, with DRCs around one-half, includes activities from all three farming sectors. The most efficient foreign exchange earners, with very similar DRCs, are the LSC crops of groundnuts and cotton, closely followed by soybeans. Not far behind are groundnuts from low-potential CAs and maize from both low- and high-potential CAs. The relatively high level of DRCs for most crops in high-potential communal areas is due primarily to these areas' very high opportunity cost of land. Unless there is a rapid decrease in rural population density, however, it is unlikely that land values will fall. The sensitivity analyses presented later in this chapter address the effects of different relative land prices that might result from alternative land policies. But despite the high value of high-potential CA land, all farming sectors have more than one highly efficient activity, indicating substantial opportunity for economic growth.

PAM results on a whole-farm average basis are presented in Table IV.10, using aggregate cropping patterns to weight the individual crops planted in each sector. Transfers lower the farm costs of purchased inputs and capital, while leaving labor costs unchanged or higher. This reduces employment and worsens the distribution of income, while it increases demand for imported inputs and capital. The substitution effect is strongest in the LSC sector, but is also felt in smallholder agriculture.

In LSC farms, the effect of transfers is to raise average labor costs by a third, while capital and tradable input costs are reduced by almost a quarter. Relative to capital, the price of labor to the employer is raised by 71 percent (1.32/0.77 - 1); and relative to tradable inputs wages are raised by 74 percent (1.32/0.76 - 1). In CA farms, the shift in relative input prices is much smaller, since labor costs include no transfers and CA farmers receive only half the proportional reduction in capital costs realized by LSC farmers. As a result, the use of inputs and capital instead of labor is much less favored in the CA than in the LSC sector.

PAM RESULTS UNDER ALTERNATIVE CONDITIONS AND POLICIES

So far, crop profitability and comparative advantage have been analyzed under 1988–1989 conditions and policies. Now, a range of potential future conditions and policy options may be considered, to assess the sensitivity of PAM results to selected changes. Generally, in these simulations a single price or quantity is altered, and the PAM shows the impact of that variable on profitability and comparative advantage. The PAM itself does not incorporate behavioral models to estimate the new levels of other prices or quantities that would arise in response to each change. Those adjustments would have to be modeled separately, either explicitly or implicitly.

Three types of change are considered. First, in the realm of macroeconomic conditions and policies, the effects of changing exchange rates and wages is assessed. Then, within the agricultural sector, the impact of changing land tenure rules and crop yields is discussed. Finally, for individual products, the impact of alternative price regimes is addressed. A multitude of specific policy-change scenarios could be investigated, but the few selected for discussion here capture the main dimensions of potential change.

MACROECONOMIC CONDITIONS AND POLICIES

The three principal macro prices are exchange rates, wages, and interest rates. As shown in the previous chapter, interest is a relatively small share of total costs for most farmers and is relatively similar across crops. Thus, interest

Table IV.10
Whole-Farm Policy Analysis Matrix Results

	Low-Potential CAs				High-Potential CAs				Large-Scale Commercial			
	Market Prices	Opp. Costs	Trans-fers	(%)	Market Prices	Opp. Costs	Trans-fers	(%)	Market Prices	Opp. Costs	Trans-fers	(%)
Output	273	409	-137	-33	576	953	-378	-40	1395	2526	-1130	-44
Labor	173	173			188	188			415	313	102	32
Capital	59	66	-8	-12	157	178	-21	-12	481	611	-130	-23
Tradables	41	59	-17	-30	123	171	-48	-28	516	680	-164	-24
Profit	0	111	-112	-100	107	416	-309	-74	-17	922	-939	-104

Note: Crop weights are drawn from Table IV.2 for the CA budgets, and Table II.4 for the LSC budgets, with all percentages re-scaled to include the listed crops only:

Low-Potential CA: Mz 45.7%, Pm 19.6%, Gn 15.2%, Fm 9.8%, Sg 5.4%, Sf 4.3%.

High-Potential CA: Mz 66.0%, Co 17.5%, Gn 7.2%, Sf 6.2%, Fm 3.1%.

LSC: Mz 40.2%, Co 22.0%, Sb 20.7%, Wh 14.6%, Gn 2.4%.

Source: Calculated from PAM budget data in the appendix.

rate changes are unlikely to have a major impact on the relative short-run profit-ability of alternative crops. Interest rates will have an important impact only over the longer run, affecting the direction of investment and technical change. This may bring a bias for or against particularly capital-intensive crops. But the greatest potential effects of macroeconomic changes on farm comparative advantage over the next five or more years are likely to come from potential changes in exchange rates and wages, as detailed below.

Devaluation

A change in the nominal exchange rate, such as a devaluation, alters the local-currency prices of foreign goods and thereby changes the local-market prices for all goods with foreign substitutes. The magnitude and timing of price transmission from the exchange rate and border prices to the domestic market can vary greatly. A few items, said to be "fully traded" (Joshi 1972, p. 12) are entirely substitutable with an import or export and so will have almost immediate and complete price transmission: A 20 percent devaluation would yield a 20 percent local-price increase. At the other extreme, "nontradable" items are not at all substitutable with traded goods. For nontradables the devaluation causes a local-price change only through shifts in domestic supply and demand; most commonly, devaluations would raise a nontradable's price by shifting its supply schedule upward, through increased relative prices of tradable inputs and substitutes.

The price effects of a devaluation are also affected by government controls on quantities traded (which would limit substitution to or from imports and exports) as well as direct controls on local prices. In Zimbabwe, for most major agricultural items both types of restrictions apply. In the short run, such controls block all direct price transmission; any change would be a policy choice. But typically over time the government is forced to pass along price changes, to accommodate the accumulation of excess supply or demand. Therefore, it is assumed here that trade and price controls fully accommodate the devaluation and pass along the exchange rate change to the domestic market.

In the local market, price transmission is assumed to follow a simple short-run pattern. For tradable items, prices rise by the full extent of devaluation, through substitution with items actually traded. For intermediate items that are not fully traded, price transmission is assumed to be proportional to tradable input content, as demand is assumed perfectly inelastic. Finally, wages and interest rates are assumed to be unaffected by the devaluation, as it is assumed that the money supply does not expand so that tradable-good price rises do not become generalized inflation.

This stylized picture of price transmission allows the effects of a devaluation to be conveniently modeled within the PAM: the output and tradable-input categories fully absorb the exchange rate change. Over time, however, adjustment after devaluation would erode this initial relative-price change, raising relative domestic factor prices and yielding smaller effects than those suggested here.

For simplicity, only three levels of devaluation are illustrated in Table IV.11 below. The 50 percent rate compensates for the degree of exchange rate misalignment found in Part II. For comparison, a 60 percent rate is also shown, corresponding to a full restoration of the pre-UDI internal real exchange rate, as a 100 percent devaluation would match the parallel market foreign exchange premium. In general, the level of devaluation is shown to have little effect on relative profitability among crops, given the assumption that all product prices rise in the same proportion. But even under this strong assumption the change in relative input costs is sufficient to bring new profitability rankings for two of the three farming systems. In the high-potential CAs, cotton rises from last to third, as devaluations raise cotton profitability past sunflowers and finger millet. In the LSC areas, devaluation raises the profitability of groundnuts relative to maize, switching the relative position of these crops.

The strongest effect of devaluation is to raise the profitability of all farm activities. On a whole-farm average basis, per-hectare profits rise by over two dollars in the low-potential CAs, four dollars in the high-potential CAs, and eight dollars in the LSC areas, for each percentage point of devaluation. When multiplied times the area under each farming system, each percentage point of devaluation yields about Z$4.3 million for low-potential CA farmers, Z$3.9 million for high-potential CA farmers, and Z$2.5 million for LSC farmers. These nominal income changes would be offset by higher prices for tradable goods consumed on the farm. Their exact magnitude also depends on the assumption that the devaluation is applied equally to all tradable goods. But even with highly variable degrees of price transmission, devaluation raises the prices of tradable outputs and inputs relative to nontradable domestic factors and thereby enhances the profitability of farming.

The Exchange Rate Premium

A second critical macroeconomic issue is the extent of current exchange rate overvaluation. There is considerable debate over the methods and results needed to measure this important element of comparative advantage measurements. In Table IV.12 four different degrees of overvaluation are shown, corresponding to the target equilibrium rates that follow from the various analytical approaches described in Part II and used for the nominal devaluations simulated in Table IV.11. The zero percent exchange rate premium corresponds to the multilateral RER approach, the 50 percent and 60 percent premiums to the

Table IV.11
Impact of Devaluation on Private Profitability

	Low-Potential CAs				High-Potential CAs					Large-Scale Commercial			
Percentage Devaluation	0	50	60	100	0	50	60	100		0	50	60	100
Private Profits (Z$/ha)													
Maize	115	291	326	467	81	350	404	619		490	313	383	664
Groundnuts	-18	129	158	276	-109	38	67	185		448	468	570	977
Sunflower	-54	5	17	64	-109	-13	6	82					
Pearl millet	-160	-145	-142	-130					Wheat	677	892	1044	1649
Sorghum	-118	-98	-94	-78					Soya	391	257	318	562
Finger millet	-101	-36	-23	29	-149	-52	-33	44					
Cotton		116	139	231	-156	11	44	177		516	536	638	1047
Whole farm average	0	116	139	231	7	233	278	459		-1	439	526	878

Source: Calculated from PAM budget data in the appendix.

Table IV.12
Impact of the Exchange Rate Premium

	Low-Potential CAs				High-Potential CAs				Large-Scale Commercial			
Exchange Rate Premium (%)	0	50	60	100	0	50	60	100	0	50	60	100
National Profits (Z$/ha)												
Maize	71	229	261	387	125	425	486	726	95	486	565	878
Groundnuts	92	298	339	504	-103	52	83	206	692	1487	1646	2281
Sunflower	-58	2	14	61	-114	-18	1	78				
Pearl millet	-164	-149	-146	-134								
Wheat									94	947	1118	1800
Soya									327	813	911	1299
Sorghum	-121	-101	-97	-80	-153	-56	-37	40				
Finger millet	-104	-39	-26	26	-39	194	241	427				
Cotton					57	316	367	575	634	1386	1537	2139
Whole farm avg.	-5	112	135	228					276	843	956	1410
Domestic Resource Costs (DRC)												
Maize	0.78	0.52	0.49	0.39	0.79	0.53	0.50	0.40	0.89	0.63	0.60	0.50
Groundnuts	0.78	0.52	0.49	0.39	1.33	0.89	0.83	0.67	0.60	0.42	0.40	0.33
Sunflower	1.48	0.99	0.93	0.74	1.59	1.06	1.00	0.80				
Pearl millet	6.49	4.34	4.07	3.26								
Wheat									0.95	0.65	0.61	0.50
Soya									0.69	0.48	0.46	0.38
Sorghum	3.93	2.63	2.47	1.97	1.79	1.19	1.12	0.90				
Finger millet	1.80	1.20	1.13	0.90	1.08	0.72	0.68	0.54				
Cotton					0.89	0.60	0.56	0.45	0.61	0.43	0.41	0.34
Whole farm avg.	1.02	0.68	0.64	0.51					0.78	0.54	0.51	0.43

Source: Calculated from PAM budget data in the appendix.

internal RER approach, and the 100 percent premium to the parallel-market premium.

In this analysis, the exchange rate premium is assumed to apply equally to all crops, as in the devaluation example. As a result, different levels of overvaluation have little effect on relative profitability and comparative advantage among the crops. Only in LSC areas are rankings affected; the per-hectare profitability of wheat rises from fifth to third, passing maize and soybeans. But wheat achieves high per-hectare profits at the cost of very high capital-intensity; with the DRC measure, wheat remains in fifth place among the listed crops and has only a very small relative increase in comparative advantage as the exchange rate premium rises.

The most significant effect of altering the level of exchange rate overvaluation is to change the measured level of comparative advantage for all farm activities. If it were believed, for example, that there is currently no significant overvaluation—as would be suggested by the conventional multilateral RER approach—the column under the zero percent exchange rate premium in Table IV.12 would be correct, showing most smallholder cropping to be economically inefficient. On the other hand, accepting the 100 percent black market premium as correct would show almost all farm activities to be highly efficient. The appropriate result, provided by a 50 percent rate (as indicated by the internal RER approach), falls between these two extremes.

The Opportunity Cost of Labor

The opportunity cost of family labor in the communal areas has hitherto been estimated on the basis of returns per hour from the 1989 farm management survey. That implicit wage has also been used for the opportunity cost of unskilled LSC labor, on the grounds that CA labor is the primary alternative to formal employment for unskilled workers. But these data could have been mismeasured and are perhaps not fully applicable to LSC workers. Table IV.13 explores the sensitivity of the PAM results to alternative labor-cost scenarios.

Four levels of labor cost are shown, applying to family labor in both private and national CA budgets and to unskilled labor in the national LSC budgets.[15] The first case shows an opportunity cost of labor of zero, representing the extreme "surplus labor" model in which workers are assumed to have no productive alternative to the activities studied here. The other cases show implicit wages that are 50 percent, 100 percent, and 150 percent, respectively, of the baseline level. These figures are chosen only to illustrate the full potential extent of variation in labor values.

Relative profitability among crops is affected only slightly by wage rate changes. In the low-potential CAs, rankings are generally unchanged as wages rise, except that the relative position of sunflower rises to exceed groundnuts in

Table IV.13
Impact of Labor Costs

Family Labor Cost ($/hr)	Low-Potential CAs				High-Potential CAs				Large-Scale Commercial			
	0.00	0.16	0.32	0.48	0.00	0.16	0.32	0.48	0.00	0.16	0.32	0.48
Private Profits (Z$/ha)												
Maize	222	168	115	62	191	136	81	26	-39	-39	-39	-39
Groundnuts	166	74	-18	-111	67	-21	-109	-197	-42	-42	-42	-42
Sunflower	31	-12	-54	-97	-32	-71	-109	-147				
Pearl millet	-72	-116	-160	-204								
Sorghum	-27	-73	-118	-164	-31	-90	-149	-208				
Finger millet	31	-35	-101	-167	32	-62	-156	-250				
Wheat									136	136	136	136
Soya									-48	-48	-48	-48
Cotton					133	70	7	-56	26	26	26	26
Whole farm avg.	115	58	-0	-58					-1	-1	-1	-1
National Profits (Z$/ha)												
Maize	335	282	229	176	535	480	425	371	593	540	486	433
Groundnuts	483	391	298	206	228	140	52	-36	1707	1597	1487	1376
Sunflower	88	45	2	-41	58	20	-18	-56				
Pearl millet	-62	-105	-149	-193								
Sorghum	-9	-55	-101	-147								
Finger millet	93	27	-39	-105	61	2	-56	-115				
Wheat									1009	978	947	916
Soya									876	844	813	782
Cotton					382	288	194	100	1569	1478	1386	1295
Whole farm avg.	227	169	112	54	442	379	316	252	953	898	843	788

Family Labor Cost ($/hr)	Low-Potential CAs				High-Potential CAs				Large-Scale Commercial			
	0.00	0.16	0.32	0.48	0.00	0.16	0.32	0.48	0.00	0.16	0.32	0.48
Domestic Rsc. Costs (DRC)												
Maize	0.30	0.41	0.52	0.63	0.41	0.47	0.53	0.59	0.55	0.59	0.63	0.67
Groundnuts	0.22	0.37	0.52	0.67	0.51	0.70	0.89	1.08	0.33	0.38	0.42	0.46
Sunflower	0.51	0.75	0.99	1.23	0.80	0.93	1.06	1.20				
Pearl millet	2.38	3.36	4.34	5.32								
Sorghum	1.15	1.89	2.63	3.37					Wheat	0.63	0.64	0.65	0.66
									Soya	0.44	0.46	0.48	0.50
Finger millet	0.53	0.86	1.20	1.54	0.79	0.99	1.19	1.40				
Cotton					0.46	0.59	0.72	0.86	0.35	0.39	0.43	0.47
Whole farm avg.	0.35	0.52	0.68	0.85	0.43	0.52	0.60	0.68	0.48	0.51	0.54	0.57

Source: Calculated from PAM budget data in the appendix.

terms of private profits and to exceed finger millet in national profits, while maize rises to first place, exceeding groundnuts in terms of the DRC measure. In the high-potential CAs, the relative position of sunflower rises from last to second place in terms of private profitability and from last to fourth in terms of DRCs, but national profitability per hectare is unchanged. In the LSC budgets, private profitability is not altered at all, national profitability rankings remain constant, and in the DRC rankings wheat rises from last to fourth place, exceeding maize.

Changing labor costs has a greater effect on relative profitability across farming systems than across crops, largely because the CA systems have much greater direct labor use than the LSC systems. Thus, at a zero opportunity cost of family labor, the CA systems show appreciably greater economic efficiency than the LSC system, with an average whole-farm DRC of 0.35 in low-potential CAs and 0.43 in high-potential CAs, in comparison with 0.48 for LSC farms. At Z$0.16/hr, or half of the baseline labor cost, the average whole-farm DRCs for all farming systems are about equal.

Finally, Table IV.13 shows that removing the link between CA and LSC opportunity costs of labor does not significantly alter most results. If LSC farmworkers are assumed, for example, not to have any productive alternatives (a labor opportunity cost of zero) while CA wages remain at Z$0.32/hr, there is no change at all in the relative rankings of profits or DRCs. The relative profitability and comparative advantage results of this study are generally insensitive to measurement errors in labor costs.

SECTORAL CONDITIONS AND POLICIES

In this section two alternative scenarios for sectoral change will be explored using the PAM framework. First, changes in land tenure policies and patterns of land use will be considered, as they affect the relative value of land for each farming system. Second, changes in crop varieties, technology, and climate will be considered, by simulating alternative crop yields under the given input regimes.

Land Values

Previously in this study the private cost of land has been set equal to the level at which private whole-farm profits would be approximately zero—Z$10/ha in the low-potential CAs, Z$150/ha in the high-potential CAs, and Z$90/ha in the LSC areas. These land costs reflect different average land productivities under differing land use conditions and tenure rules. In particular, within the areas of high agro-ecological potential, CA land values are much higher than

LSC land values. The greater intensity of land use in the CAs appears to be partly due to severe restrictions on LSC farm subdivision. To show the effects of relaxing these tenure restrictions, national opportunity costs for LSC lands were set equal to the cost of land in high-potential CAs.

Per-hectare land costs are subtracted directly from per-hectare activity profits, so by definition changes in land costs cannot affect profitability rankings. But land costs can matter for comparative advantage, as illustrated in Table IV.14. For each farming system, DRCs are calculated under land costs of zero and at three alternative levels: Z$10, Z$20, and Z$30 in the low-potential CAs; Z$50, Z$100, and Z$150 in the high-potential CAs; and Z$50, Z$90, and Z$150 in the LSC areas. These levels, like the alternative wage and exchange rate levels shown earlier, have been chosen arbitrarily to reflect the likely range of possible errors in land valuation.

Within each farming system, land values have little impact on relative comparative advantage across crops. In the low-potential CAs, DRC rankings are unchanged, and in the high-potential CAs, sunflowers improve to pass groundnuts as land costs rise from zero to Z$50/ha. In the LSC areas, wheat falls from third to fourth, past soybeans and maize, as land costs rise—but this result is largely due to the assumption that the winter-irrigated land under the wheat crop remains five times as valuable as the rainfed land under summer crops.

Changing the cost of land does not affect the relative comparative advantage of the low-potential CAs compared with the other two systems. But at low land costs of Z$0 to Z$50, the high-potential CA farming system enjoys almost the same comparative advantage as the LSC system; it is only at relatively high levels of land values that the LSC systems become economically more efficient. This result reflects the idea that as land becomes more scarce, it becomes more profitable to substitute off-farm inputs such as fertilizer for land.

Crop Yields

The baseline yield levels are 1989 averages for the CA budgets and CFU estimates for the LSC farming systems. Wide variation in yields can be expected, both across farmers and across years. Yield variation could arise for a multitude of reasons, including variation in climate, land quality, pest and weed competition, the timing and accuracy of farm operations, the use of purchased inputs, and genetic potential for crops planted with retained seeds.

Under alternative yield conditions farmers might choose different input combinations, changing the crop budgets. But without a model of farm production choices it is not possible to generate those new input levels endogenously. Within the average-cost model of farm production used here, it is possible to simulate only the effects of yield surprises, which by definition are not linked

Table IV.14
Impact of Land Values on Comparative Advantage

Land Values (Z$/ha)	Low-Potential CAs				High-Potential CAs				Large-Scale Commercial			
	0	10	20	30	0	50	100	150	0	50	90	150
Domestic Rsc. Costs (DRC)												
Maize	0.50	0.52	0.54	0.56	0.37	0.42	0.48	0.53	0.52	0.56	0.59	0.63
Groundnuts	0.50	0.52	0.53	0.55	0.56	0.67	0.78	0.89	0.36	0.38	0.40	0.42
Sunflower	0.93	0.99	1.05	1.10	0.54	0.72	0.89	1.06				
Pearl millet	4.12	4.34	4.57	4.79					Wheat 0.37	0.46	0.54	0.65
Sorghum	2.47	2.63	2.79	2.95					Soya 0.39	0.42	0.45	0.48
Finger millet	1.15	1.20	1.25	1.30	0.68	0.85	1.02	1.19				
Cotton					0.51	0.58	0.65	0.72	0.37	0.39	0.40	0.43
Whole farm average	0.65	0.68	0.71	0.74	0.40	0.47	0.53	0.60	0.41	0.46	0.49	0.54

Source: Calculated from PAM budget data in the appendix.

to input use. These surprises could be induced by any transient factor, such as weather or pests. In Table IV.15, the only cost item affected by yield shocks is product transport, calculated on a per-ton basis. Harvesting costs might be expected also to rise with higher yields, but the magnitude of this link is unclear.

Yield surprises have relatively little impact on private profitability rankings in the CAs, where the most privately profitable crop remains maize even if maize yields fall or other yields rise by well over 25 percent. Comparisons across farming systems are also not very sensitive to yield variation. Yield changes would affect private profitability rankings within LSC areas, however, as well as national profitability and domestic resource cost rankings within both LSC and CA areas. In particular, a 25 percent yield improvement in cotton is sufficient to give it similar comparative advantage as maize. Persistent changes in yield response, such as those that would be produced by changes in crop varieties, would have similar effects to the extent that input use remained relatively constant.

PRODUCT-MARKET CONDITIONS AND POLICIES

Changes in demand, trade opportunities, and the marketing system could produce substantial, relatively rapid changes in relative prices and crop profitability. Like yield surprises, new price expectations are likely to induce some changes in input use. But as input response cannot be estimated in the PAM itself, all budget items except revenue were held constant. The price-change results shown in Table IV.16 are therefore similar to the yield-change effects of Table IV.15, except that price changes have no impact on transport costs.

Price changes could occur from shifts in aggregate domestic supply and demand, if changing trade volumes caused changes in trade prices or a switch between exports, no trade, and imports. Such changes are possible, but generally unpredictable. Price changes could also occur from shifts in regional or larger global markets. Some indication of trends in world prices can be derived from price projection models such as those published by the World Bank (1988), but unpredictable surprises from changing weather conditions and other factors are likely to dominate the more predictable influences such as aggregate income and demand.

Within Zimbabwe, relative-price changes could arise from changes in market policy, particularly from the introduction of differing regional maize prices, as noted in Part III. Some regional price differences already occur, because of informal local markets that supplement panterritorial formal markets. Broader regional pricing would generally enlarge these differences, further raising prices in and around deficit regions and lowering prices in and around surplus regions. This change would occur almost inevitably if the maize-market regulations were

Table IV.15
Impact of Yield Changes

Product Yield (% of norm)	Low-Potential CAs				High-Potential CAs				Large-Scale Commercial				
	-25	0	25	50	-25	0	25	50		-25	0	25	50
Private Profits (Z$/ha)													
Maize	29	115	201	287	-57	81	219	357		-305	-39	228	494
Groundnuts	-99	-18	62	142	-193	-109	-25	59		-391	-42	308	658
Sunflower	-85	-54	-24	7	-160	-109	-57	-6					
Pearl millet	-172	-160	-148	-136					Wheat	-391	136	662	1188
Sorghum	-129	-118	-107	-96					Soya	-287	-48	192	431
Finger millet	-134	-101	-68	-35	-198	-149	-99	-50					
Cotton					-264	-156	-48	60		-316	26	368	710
Whole farm avg.	-59	-0	59	118	-114	7	128	248		-318	-1	316	633
National Profits (Z$/ha)													
Maize	110	229	348	467	188	425	663	901		29	486	943	1400
Groundnuts	132	298	464	630	-81	52	185	317		712	1487	2261	3036
Sunflower	-46	2	49	96	-97	-18	61	140					
Pearl millet	-168	-149	-131	-112					Wheat	64	947	1830	2714
Sorghum	-118	-101	-84	-67					Soya	302	813	1325	1836
Finger millet	-90	-39	11	62	-132	-56	19	95					
Cotton					-14	194	402	611		635	1386	2138	2889
Whole farm avg.	20	112	203	294	105	316	526	736		241	843	1445	2048

Product Yield (% of norm)	Low-Potential CAs				High-Potential CAs				Large-Scale Commercial			
	-25	0	25	50	-25	0	25	50	-25	0	25	50
Domestic Rsc. Costs (DRC)												
Maize	0.68	0.52	0.43	0.37	0.71	0.53	0.43	0.37	0.97	0.63	0.47	0.38
Groundnuts	0.71	0.52	0.41	0.34	1.25	0.89	0.69	0.57	0.60	0.42	0.33	0.27
Sunflower	1.35	0.99	0.79	0.65	1.47	1.06	0.84	0.69				
Pearl millet	7.72	4.34	3.03	2.34								
Sorghum	3.71	2.63	2.04	1.68								
Finger millet	1.63	1.20	0.95	0.80	1.63	1.19	0.95	0.79				
Wheat									0.96	0.65	0.49	0.40
Soya									0.71	0.48	0.37	0.30
Cotton					1.03	0.72	0.56	0.46	0.61	0.43	0.34	0.28
Whole farm avg.	0.92	0.68	0.55	0.46	0.81	0.60	0.48	0.40	0.80	0.54	0.41	0.34

Source: Calculated from PAM budget data in the appendix.

Table IV.16
Impact of Product Price Changes

Product Yield (% of norm)	Low-Potential CAs				High-Potential CAs				Large-Scale Commercial			
	-25	0	25	50	-25	0	25	50	-25	0	25	50
Private Profits (Z$/ha)												
Maize	13	115	217	319	-89	81	251	422	-331	-39	253	545
Groundnuts	-104	-181	68	154	-198	-109	-21	68	-400	-42	317	676
Sunflower	-89	-54	-20	14	-166	-109	-52	5				
Pearl millet	-174	-160	-146	-132					Wheat -403	136	674	1213
Sorghum	-131	-118	-105	-92					Soya -294	-48	199	445
Finger millet	-138	-101	-64	-27	-204	-149	-93	-38				
Cotton					-269	-156	-43	70	-369	26	421	815
Whole farm avg.	-68	-0	68	136	-137	7	151	295	-343	-1	341	684
National Profits (Z$/ha)												
Maize	90	229	368	506	148	425	703	980	4	486	969	1451
Groundnuts	126	298	471	644	-86	52	190	328	701	1487	2272	3058
Sunflower	-49	2	53	104	-103	-18	67	152				
Pearl millet	-170	-149	-128	-108					Wheat 49	947	1845	2743
Sorghum	-120	-101	-81	-62					Soya 294	813	1333	1853
Finger millet	-95	-39	16	72	-140	-56	27	110				
Cotton					-20	194	409	624	600	1386	2173	2959
Whole farm avg.					77	316	554	792	218	843	1467	2092

Product Yield (% of norm)	Low-Potential CAs				High-Potential CAs				Large-Scale Commercial			
	-25	0	25	50	-25	0	25	50	-25	0	25	50
Domestic Rsc. Costs (DRC)												
Maize	0.73	0.52	0.40	0.33	0.76	0.53	0.41	0.33	1.00	0.63	0.46	0.37
Groundnuts	0.72	0.52	0.41	0.33	1.27	0.89	0.68	0.56	0.60	0.42	0.32	0.26
Sunflower	1.39	0.99	0.77	0.63	1.51	1.06	0.82	0.67	Wheat 0.97	0.65	0.49	0.39
Pearl millet	8.14	4.34	2.96	2.25					Soya 0.72	0.48	0.36	0.29
Sorghum	3.84	2.63	2.00	1.61								
Finger millet	1.68	1.20	0.94	0.77	1.67	1.19	0.93	0.76				
Cotton					1.04	0.72	0.55	0.45	0.63	0.43	0.33	0.26
Whole farm avg.	0.96	0.68	0.53	0.43	0.86	0.60	0.46	0.37	0.82	0.54	0.41	0.33

Source: Calculated from PAM budget data in the appendix.

relaxed, but it could also be introduced deliberately as GMB policy. In either case, prices would generally rise in the low-potential CAs and fall in the high-potential CAs and LSC areas. The magnitude of the relative price change depends on a range of other conditions and policies but typically remains within a range of 25 percent around 1989 panterritorial levels (Masters and Nuppenau 1993).

Like changing relative yields, changing relative prices have little effect on private profitability rankings in the CAs. Maize remains the most privately profitable crop in both low-potential and high-potential CAs despite relative price changes well beyond 25 percent. This does not imply that there would be no production response to changed relative prices. These budgets are aggregate averages, and adjustments would occur at the margin. But the insensitivity of aggregate-average crop rankings to relative prices does suggest that adjustments would be limited and that wholesale changes in CA cropping patterns are unlikely. The dominance of maize is too extreme for its profitability to be much affected by relatively small product-price changes. Larger relative-profitability changes would arise in LSC areas, but since maize is already not a very highly profitable crop for LSC farmers the impact of these changes on area planted is likely to be muted.

CONCLUSIONS

The PAM results explored here show that government policies impose a heavy burden of taxation on the production of Zimbabwe's main field crops. But these transfers do not fall equally on all farm activities; within the farm sector transfers encourage substitutions among crops and inputs that tend to worsen the level and distribution of national income. Among alternative crops in each region, transfers generally favor food grains (maize and wheat) over industrial crops (oilseeds and cotton). While it is necessary to ensure adequate food supplies, the current pattern of incentives encourages local self-sufficiency at considerable cost in terms of the level and distribution of farm income. Within the CAs, transfers limit the development of regional specialization, in groundnuts from the low-potential regions and maize and cotton in higher-potential areas, which would allow all areas to earn increased real incomes. In the LSC area, transfers make capital-intensive importable wheat the most privately profitable crop, when labor-intensive exportable groundnuts and cotton provide higher national profits. The net contribution of the entire farm sector to the trade balance, industrial growth, national income, and equity would be greater if incentives reflected a crop mix better suited to each subsector.

The net transfers out of agriculture are even more important than the substitution effects among crops and inputs. The average net rate of transfer, at over Z\$120/ha in low-potential CAs, Z\$300/ha in high-potential areas, and

Z$860/ha in LSC farms, represents a very large absolute reduction in farmers' incomes, welfare, and investable savings. The crops included in this average are produced on about 1.9 million hectares annually in the low-potential CAs, 0.85 million hectares in the high-potential CAs, and 0.28 million hectares in the LSC sector. The total transfers suggested by these PAMs, of roughly Z$230 million from low-potential CA farmers, Z$255 million from high-potential CA farmers, and Z$240 million from LSC farmers, represent a total of $725 million—over half of measured agricultural GDP and over 7 percent of total national GDP.

For all farmers, but especially in the CAs, much of this increase in nominal income would be offset by higher prices for goods consumed, thus reducing the net welfare gain. Furthermore, it would be neither feasible nor desirable for these transfers to be reduced absolutely to zero. But some reduction from their currently very large magnitude would contribute to faster growth in agricultural production, rural incomes, and welfare.

The sensitivity analyses explored in this chapter confirm that Zimbabwe has a strong pattern of comparative advantage in oilseeds and maize in low-potential CAs, maize and cotton in high-potential CAs, and oilseeds and cotton in the LSC areas. Under particular farms and for small quantities, other crops could be more profitable. But for the bulk of farm area, this general pattern appears to be robust under a broad range of assumptions and conditions. In their most profitable crops, the various types of farms have similar DRCs of around one-half, indicating similar degrees of comparative advantage (or rates of contribution to national income). The per-hectare returns to land and management are higher in the high-potential than in the low-potential areas, indicating that better-quality land is more valuable than lower-quality land, but farming everywhere can make a significant contribution to national income.

NOTES

1. In other PAM applications, the matrix is usually presented with its rows and columns transposed; these are reversed here for ease of presentation in the empirical crop budgets.

2. Here capital costs include returns to land; land values account for most of capital costs in the high-potential CAs, but take a somewhat smaller share in the other two systems.

3. An insightful paper contrasting average-cost budgets and marginal supply response is Pasour (1980).

4. Prices and opportunity costs should be marginal values, estimated differently from input-output data, which are aggregate averages. But in practice, several prices may be observed simultaneously, and it may not be known which is the marginal one. In such cases an average price is used.

5. The CSO does maintain a continuous postal survey to determine area planted and yields for crop forecasting, but results have not been published for several years.

6. The three high-potential sites are in Chiweshe CA near Bare business center, Chirau CA near Murombedzi district center, and Kandeya CA (Mt. Darwin area) near Dotito district center (a cotton-specialty area). These first two are in Natural Region IIa, while the Kandeya site straddles Regions II and III.

7. Chirumanzu CA near Holy Cross Mission.

8. The low-potential sites are in central Buhera district near Mudanda business center, northern Mutoko district near the Mudzi district boundary, Nyajena CA near Renco mine, and Zvishavane District near Buchwa mine. The first three are in Region IV, while the Zvishavane site is in Region V.

9. Female-headed households include cases where the head was reported to be either a woman or a nonresident man. It was clear, however, that many male resident household heads hold that title in name only, with much of the decision-making as well as of the work being undertaken by nominally subservient wives and daughters.

10. The actual incidence of intercropping is much higher. The difference is probably partly due to farmers' reluctance to declare their true practices given the discouragement of intercropping by the extension service and partly due to the improvised nature of some intercropping.

11. It would have been possible to construct budgets ignoring the value of land or giving it a fixed value and attributing the remaining profits to labor and management instead. In that case, returns to labor would vary across areas, while land costs were constant. Comparisons across areas would not be affected, since labor and land costs are not separated in the measures of profitability.

The distinction between land and labor costs matters only for comparisons between relatively labor-intensive crops (like groundnuts) and land-intensive crops (like maize). Labor rates for the LSC budgets are known from payroll data but have had to be imputed for the CA budgets. As there is no other reliable data source on returns to labor in the CAs, the same budget data must be used to estimate labor costs that are used for the land rates.

To provide as accurate a breakdown as possible, labor has been valued at the survey-wide average returns to family labor before subtracting land costs (Z$0.32/hour), which in the context of the crop budgets shown here is just enough to leave a small return to land. The procedure is arbitrary, but it seems realistic because the resulting wage is close to the separately estimated average cash-equivalent rate for hired CA labor (Z$0.35/hour) and about equal to half the formal-sector wage. Details of these procedures are given in the appendix budget notes.

12. The charge for developed wheat land is five times that of summer-crop land, based on farm valuation estimates detailed in the appendix budget notes.

13. These results refer to the current situation of panterritorial pricing, in which marketing costs are spread equally so that national opportunity costs are equal at all depots. If opportunity costs were allowed to vary by region following some spatial-equilibrium model, opportunity costs as well as market prices would be higher in most low-potential regions.

14. This statement refers to agriculture's comparative advantage as compared with the totality of other activities in the Zimbabwean economy. Assessing agriculture's comparative advantage against particular other sectors cannot be done without also calculating DRCs for them. But if the national opportunity costs used for these DRC calculations are correct, the weighted-average DRC for nonagriculture would have to be greater than one.

15. The indirect use of off-farm labor is not subject to wage variation, because it has been measured directly through input costs.

Conclusions

Agriculture fared better in Zimbabwe than in most other African countries during the 1980s, but the analysis presented in this study indicates that further improvements in both equity and growth are possible, through the exploitation of Zimbabwe's full agricultural comparative advantage. Three central issues dominate the country's opportunities for faster and more equitable growth: real exchange rate depreciation in the macroeconomy, land tenure reform in the agricultural sector, and regional grain flows in the product markets. Each is briefly reviewed here. At the end of the chapter, some conclusions are drawn regarding the analytical methods used in the study.

ECONOMY-WIDE POLICIES: THE REAL EXCHANGE RATE

The principal macroeconomic issue found in this study is the real exchange rate: the prices of tradable goods (such as most farm products) relative to non-tradables (most production costs). Zimbabwe's rapid economic growth in the early post-independence period caused wages, construction costs, and the prices of other nontradables to rise much faster than the prices of tradables, which were kept low by the import licensing system retained from UDI. This decline in the prices of tradables relative to nontradables—experienced by farmers as a worsening of their domestic terms of trade—was found to be the greatest single influence on overall agricultural profitability and competitiveness for both large-scale and smallholder farmers.

Reversing the decline in farmers' domestic terms of trade could be accomplished with a combination of nominal devaluation (to raise the prices of tradables) and reduction in inflationary pressures (to lower the relative prices of other goods). This real depreciation would then have to be passed on to farmers through the marketing boards and other pricing agents. Real depreciation entails a reduction in consumption of tradables by the urban population, at least in the

short run. This is harsh medicine, but in this case the disease is still worse than
the cure. Without real depreciation agricultural production and exports would
continue to stagnate, with a continued shortage of foreign exchange. The government would then either have to maintain tight import licensing, thus perpetuating
sluggish growth, or have to borrow abroad, thus accumulating foreign debts that
would eventually have to be repaid. In either case, the need for real depreciation
would have merely been postponed, not avoided.

The government's 1989 trade liberalization program attempted to expand
imports without depreciation, but this resulted in a burst of imports with no
corresponding growth in exports. In 1991, the government sought to finance this
growing trade deficit with help from the World Bank and the IMF, through a
full-scale economic structural adjustment program (ESAP) involving rapid devaluation. But domestic inflationary pressures were not immediately reduced, so the
effect of devaluation on tradable-goods prices was quickly offset by rising
nontradable-goods prices, and little if any real depreciation has occured.

For real depreciation to be sustainable, Zimbabweans must be convinced
that the government is committed to both devaluation and inflation reduction.
Reducing inflationary pressures is the more difficult of the two measures, but
it can probably be accomplished with a reduction in the government deficit to
decrease aggregate demand, accompanied by the opening of bottlenecks in production to increase aggregate supply.

Other aspects of the macroeconomy, notably wages and interest rates, are
important particularly for large-scale farmers and others in the formal sector.
But smallholders are generally self-employed and borrow little from the formal
sector, so they are only indirectly affected by labor and credit-market policy.
For smallholders, by far the most important macroeconomic force is the real
exchange rate, which largely determines their terms of trade with the rest of the
economy.

THE AGRICULTURAL SECTOR: LAND TENURE AND FARM SIZES

The key sectoral issue found in this study is the need for more equal farm
sizes. The extreme inequality between smallholder and commercial farming
areas is found to be highly inefficient as well as inequitable, but it is perpetuated
by the maintenance of colonial rules restricting the subdivision of LSC farms.
Subdivision restrictions were originally implemented under the Land Apportionment Act in the 1930s, to protect settler farmers from African competition. They
continue to do so, by preventing smallholders from moving into LSC areas. This
problem dominates the farming sector, distorting the pattern of input and factor
use and constraining total factor productivity.

The post-independence government has not ignored the problem of land
distribution. In fact, Zimbabwe has undertaken one of the largest and fastest

peacetime resettlement land reforms in history. This prodigious effort absorbed much of the government's attention during the 1980s, but by the end of the decade the resettlement process had slowed sharply, partly because the easiest resettlement opportunities had been exhausted and the development of new schemes was increasingly difficult. A further reason for the slowdown in resettlement was that the schemes were visibly failing to relieve land pressure in the communal areas, because their population densities and cropping intensities were little better than the LSC farms they were replacing. This limits the improvement in efficiency and equity provided by resettlement, particularly in comparison with the CAs, where despite lower average land quality the density of population and the intensity of land use remain two to three times greater than in the resettlement or commercial farming areas.

To increase commercial-area land use more efficiently and more quickly, a more opportunistic pattern of subdivision would be necessary. Currently, many LSC operations have a small area of very intensively cropped land, while slightly less productive lands are left for low-input grazing. If landowners were allowed to sell or lease parcels of their underused land, smallholder buyers or renters would plant more crops and put more effort into livestock herding. Some LSC farmers might give up their core operations and divide their entire farm into parcels, but many would maintain profitable core operations while selling or leasing only parts of their farms.

A system of voluntary, decentralized resettlement would require a relaxation of current restrictions on farm subdivision, to allow the registration of very small parcels. Institutional innovations would also be needed, such as a land bank to finance the purchase of smallholdings, and possibly a progressive land tax to motivate the sale or lease of underused lands. Education, health, and other public services for smallholders in commercial areas would have to be provided. Conditions would inevitably change over time and institutional arrangements would have to evolve, under the overall goal of increasing land use intensity by providing farmers with more open access to land.

Several aspects of the agricultural sector other than land are also important, such as crop improvement research, rural transport, and input marketing. But inequality in land distribution draws these inputs towards the LSC subsector, where there is an artificial abundance of land on a few large farms. A more equitable distribution of land would help to induce a more efficient and sustainable pattern of input use and agricultural investment across all types of farmers.

PRODUCT MARKETS: INTERREGIONAL GRAIN FLOWS AND THE NATIONAL MARKETING SYSTEM

The main opportunity for more equitable and efficient product markets is found in inter-regional grain flows, particularly for white maize. After independence, the marketing board network inherited from the colonial regime was dramatically expanded into the communal areas, and total intake from small-holders rose rapidly. This helped net sellers, but the gains were not widely spread, and a large number of rural people continued to suffer from extreme poverty and malnutrition. Inequality in resource distribution has been aggravated by an asymmetrical marketing system: Official marketing boards are better at procuring rural grain surpluses for shipment to town than at marketing grain between rural areas. Furthermore, since private transporters have been prohibited from shipping grain and there is relatively little illegal trading, rural food demand can often be satisfied only with industrial maize-meal at much higher cost. This asymmetry in marketing favors farmers in surplus areas but discriminates against the majority of farmers who live in or near deficit areas.

The asymmetrical grain marketing system is a constraint particularly on the incomes of the most resource-poor rural people in the driest areas. They have the potential incomes with which to buy grain, from sales of livestock and oil-seeds as well as nonfarm income and migrant's remittances. But with panterritorial pricing there has been little grain available for them to buy, so they must devote as much of their land as possible to grains in an often futile attempt to reach household self-sufficiency. In this way the constraint on grain movements reduces the real incomes of the poor. The high cost of purchased grains also increases their vulnerability to drought, because their own grain yields are very unstable relative to their other sources of income and national maize prices.

Panterritorial pricing also discriminates against grain surplus farmers in or near deficit regions, who receive much less from the marketing board than what nearby consumers are forced to pay for their purchases. To bridge the marketing constraint between surplus and deficit households in rural areas, a more flexible system is needed. In particular, there needs to be more intrarural shipment of grain. This objective could be achieved either through reformed marketing board operations or through liberalizing the rural grain market. Either method could be used to expand the grain flows that are needed to reflect local conditions better than the current marketing system.

Over all crops, nominal national-average prices were generally found to be less distorted than in many countries with government-set prices. This could be because the government conducts lengthy price negotiations involving representatives of all major market participants. These negotiations often come close to replicating the interaction of supply and demand in a competitive market. As a result, local prices generally follow border values, although with less year-to-year variation because nominal prices almost never decline. Negotiated prices tend to lag behind inflation in other goods, but this is shared by all exportables and is due more to exchange rate overvaluation than the agricultural pricing system.

For individual crops, however, some significant misalignments were found. In the cases of soybeans, groundnuts, and cotton, producer prices were systematically kept lower than border-equivalent prices. This was a deliberate government policy to support agro-industries. Raising relative oilseed and cotton prices to their full export parity levels would undoubtedly squeeze profits in those industries. But it would stimulate the primary production of these crops, which are very efficient, labor- and land-intensive foreign exchange earners. For groundnuts, low formal market prices have led to the rise of a substantial parallel market, absorbing most smallholder sales. In this context, simply raising formal-market prices would not have the full desired effect unless informal-market prices also rose. Policies to unify the two markets, perhaps through deregulation of the formal market, could help to achieve this objective.

Another oilseed, sunflowers, is relatively new to Zimbabwe and is grown primarily by smallholders as a low-input, low-risk crop. It is found in this study to give extremely low yields and low profits, which suggests either that available varieties are unresponsive to higher input levels or that farmers are not yet fully skilled in handling this new crop. If farmer learning, plus further agronomic and breeding research, does not result in dramatic improvements for sunflower profitability, it must be concluded that this is only a niche crop with limited potential for growth. Soybeans, with which a few smallholders are already experimenting, might yet prove to be a more profitable oilseed for smallholder production.

Among the grains, national-average prices are generally well balanced, but this study provides some interesting results in terms of comparative advantage. For white maize, the study indicates that Zimbabwe's greatest comparative advantage is in smallholder production, from both high- and low-potential areas. This is true of competitiveness as well, and production in these areas is rising while LSC maize area is declining. The change to more smallholder production is reducing the cost of maize, but it is increasing the variability of marketed production, since CA maize producers receive less and more variable rainfall and have less supplementary irrigation than do LSC maize growers.

The coarse grains other than white maize, principally sorghum and millets in CAs and yellow maize grown in LSC areas, are used primarily for on-farm and rural consumption—as food and beverages (sorghum and millets) or as animal feeds (especially yellow maize). Limited urban demand has troubled the government's repeated attempts to control their marketing. It is likely, therefore, that these crops would do best in uncontrolled markets mostly within rural areas. But particularly for sorghum and millets, government crop improvement efforts could still make considerable contributions to rural welfare, since more productive grains for drought-prone areas would be very valuable.

For wheat, this study finds relatively lower comparative advantage than summer crops, but this result depends crucially on the valuation of irrigation development. Once irrigation is in place and the value of wheat land is ignored, wheat production is highly profitable. But for new irrigation development, only the lowest-cost sites and methods are likely to be profitable. The expansion of summer crops for export to pay for wheat imports is likely to be more profitable.

The empirical results of this study clearly cannot be reduced to a matter of relative crop prices. Each crop's relative input and factor use, location and marketing system are equally important in determining comparative advantage. The study shows that policy must take into account all these factors to yield the greatest possible degree of equitable growth and that policy analysis must do so as well if comparative advantage is to be measured accurately.

METHODOLOGY: MEASURING COMPARATIVE ADVANTAGE AND POLICY EFFECTS

The PAM is an unusual method for contemporary economics. Instead of a single, complex, highly specified optimization model, the PAM uses a simple accounting framework to combine the results of many small models: average input-output coefficients, market prices, and national opportunity costs. A few conclusions about this approach can be drawn from the results of this study.

Perhaps the first consequence of the PAM's unusual structure is that much of the analytical work is done outside the matrix itself. The most important policy issues found in this study, for example, are initially analyzed not in the PAM but in separate studies of the macroeconomy (Part I), agricultural sector (Part II), and product markets (Part III). The PAM is used only later (Part IV), to provide empirical measures of the impact of all policies together on farm incomes and incentives, the returns to land in different farming systems, and the relative profitability of different crops in each system.

The nature of the PAM does not determine which issues in the macroeconomy and the agricultural sector prove to be most important. But the PAM does require that the full spectrum of determinants of farm income and incentives be explicitly considered. A PAM cannot be completed without measuring the quantities, market values, and national opportunity costs for capital, foreign exchange, land, labor, and all inputs and outputs in the various farming systems and marketing channels being considered. In this way, the PAM combines analysis of price policy with analysis of more structural issues (following, for example, Delgado and Mellor 1984). All factors may not be correctly measured, but the PAM ensures that they are explicitly taken into account—and also permits any new information about them to be used later in updating the old results.

The methods used in this study that have the greatest empirical impact on its results are the techniques used to measure the real exchange rate (in Part I); the analytical model used to show links between land tenure rules, land use intensity, and input intensity (in Part II); and the spatial equilibrium model used to analyze the impact of panterritorial pricing (in Part III). When this study was first conceived in 1986, none of these issues was recognized as especially important. But insights from the PAM provided the motivation to draw up improved models of these specific issues.

The example of this study confirms the value of the PAM as an open-minded research agenda, providing a flexible but theoretically consistent framework to show the effects of a wide range of influences on farm incomes and incentives. The PAM has provided valuable insights into policy options for equity and growth in Zimbabwean agriculture and makes a promising contribution to the methodology of policy analysis and applied welfare economics.

Appendix A

Notes and Sources for the Policy Analysis Matrix Budgets

OVERVIEW

The policy analysis matrix (PAM) budgets condense most of the calculations behind the PAM into a single page, with a minimum of side-calculations (see budgets in Appendix B). For convenience, the rows and columns of the PAM are transposed from their conventional layout so that the rows list the budget items, in terms of their PAM category (capital, labor, and tradable inputs).

The capital and labor categories include both the resources used directly in each activity and the resources used indirectly in inputs and marketing services. The tradable-input category includes only the tradable component of inputs and marketing services, which is calculated from an itemized listing at the end of the activity budget.

The initial two columns list the budget items and their units. The third column shows market prices, the next shows a conversion factor for item-specific transfers, and the next shows the proportion of the item that is tradable and hence directly affected by exchange-rate transfers. These three columns are used to calculate the item's national opportunity cost, shown in the next column. Then the relevant quantity is shown, which in the three right-hand columns is multiplied by market prices and opportunity costs to generate the PAM.

OUTPUT

Two rows are given for the activity's output: the first shows a market price and the second shows a national opportunity cost. (This same two-row system is used for ammonium nitrate fertilizer, the other major item whose opportunity cost is figured by a side-calculation.) Because the opportunity cost is calculated separately, the item-specific conversion factor is 1, showing no divergence. As all products are considered entirely tradable, the full foreign exchange premium applies.

Market prices for output in the LSC budgets are based on official GMB prices and on survey averages in the CA budgets. For LSC producers, the market price is the GMB's Grade A price for the 1989 harvest, multiplied by the blend factor used by the CFU to reflect the average quality delivered by LSC farmers and the discounts used by the GMB for qualities below Grade A. For CA budgets, the market price is usually the average price observed for the 1989 harvest in the MLARR survey, over both official and parallel marketings from each area.

National opportunity costs are the same for LSC and CA producers, using the same quality conversion factors. This is generally the actual border price in terms of U.S. dollars, minus domestic operating costs of the marketing board, all converted into Zimbabwe dollars at the end-1989 nominal exchange rate. To see medium-term expected prices, the 1980–1988 average is generally used. Over this period the year-to-year coefficient of variation differs widely among these products: Maize is the most unstable, and wheat is the least unstable. Table A.1 summarizes these calculations.

LABOR

In the LSC budgets, there are separate listings for "basic" labor (general employees, usually employed full-time), "tractor driver and mechanic" (specialized workers, also usually employed full-time), and the "indirect" labor used in the intermediate inputs and transport listed at the bottom of the budgets. There are also separate categories for temporary harvest workers figured on a per-ton basis, in maize and in cotton. For maize, general workers are used, whereas for cotton contract labor is used at an average contract price based on 90 percent of crop at 7.5 cents per kg, 10 percent at 8.5 cents per kg, and 10 percent of total wages to contractor. For basic labor, the market price is the average daily wage for a mixed team of workers as reported by the CFU. The opportunity cost is the wage for an 8-hour day at the average price of hired labor in the communal lands, Z$0.35/hr, found in the MLARR Communal Lands Farm Survey. The resulting conversion factor is 52 percent. No divergence is applied to the higher-skill category of tractor drivers and mechanics.

In the CA budgets, there are separate listings for adults and children in family and hired labor, plus separate listings for the labor used indirectly in intermediate inputs and in transport. Family workers are valued at the average returns to their labor, and hired workers are valued at their average wages including both cash and the estimated value of in-kind payments. In the 1989

Table A.1
Prices Used for 1989 Harvest-Year PAMs

		Maize	Cotton	Groundnuts	Wheat	Soybeans	Sorghum	Pearl Millet	Finger Millet	Sunflower
Trade Parity at Depots										
Border price received/paid	US$	143	69	756	231	305				
- Domestic marketing costs	US$	38	14	106	32	32				
= Trade parity at depots	US$	105	55	650	199	273				
at end-1989 exchange rate	Z$	233	122	1444	442	607				
x Quality correction factor	%	99.1	93.9	63.8	99.6	100.0				
= Quality-corrected trade parity		231	114	921	440	607				
Coefficient of variation	%	42	19	30	15	24				
Market Prices at Depots										
GMB producer price (Grade A)		215	93	1000	400	435	180/215	250	300	455
LSC: Quality-corrected GMB price		213	87	638	398	435				
CA-Low Pot.:										
Average price received		255		688			260	278	370	455
CA-High Pot.:										
Average price received		213	906	886					370	

Notes: The underlined prices are the final results used in the budgets. All trade prices are 1980–1988 averages except for soybeans, which is a 1975–1988 average. All products are exports, except for maize in 1984 and wheat in all years. GMB prices are for Grade A except soybeans, which is Grade B. Cotton prices are in cents per kilogram. GMB sorghum prices are for red/white varieties. The groundnut correction factor includes shelling as well as quality differences. Sunflower, sorghum, and the millets are not significantly traded.

MLARR survey these were found to be 32 cents and 35 cents per hour respectively. The greater cost of hired labor could reflect a greater intensity of work since payments are often on a piecework rather than an hourly basis. As separate returns to child labor could not be calculated, child hours were arbitrarily assigned a value of half the adult hours.

In CA farming, where there is no market for land and only a very limited market for labor, separating returns to land from returns to labor is an essentially arbitrary exercise. The allocation of returns to one factor or the other has no effect on whole-farm results, and only a small effect on crop rankings (see Part IV for a sensitivity analysis). For this study, labor returns are measured by an unweighted average over all activities and all areas before accounting for land values. The returns to land in the specific activities described by the PAMs are then calculated using the method explained hereafter.

Indirect labor use is figured as a proportion of the value of intermediate inputs, which are broken down into their labor, capital, and tradables components. For transport costs, a survey of road transport firms yielded a breakdown into 17 percent labor, 38 percent capital, and 45 percent tradables (see Table A.6). For other intermediate inputs, the percent tradable is estimated first and shown in the third column of the budgets. Then the remaining costs are divided equally between capital and labor, in the absence of any more reliable method. No item conversion factor is applied to the labor used indirectly.

CAPITAL

In all budgets, capital use is divided into seasonal credit, equipment depreciation, indirect use in inputs and transport, and land use.

Seasonal credit costs, for both LSC and CA budgets, have been applied for an average of 6 months on total variable costs (or equivalently for 12 months on an average of half of TVC). The market interest rate is the current AFC lending rate of 13.9 percent per year.[1] Inflation is taken to be the 1980s average rate of 14 percent, for a real interest rate of zero. The opportunity cost of credit is taken to be a real interest rate of 8 percent per year, for a nominal rate of 23 percent, in the case of LSC farmers and a real interest rate of 10 percent, for a nominal rate of 25 percent, in the case of CA farmers.

Depreciation, for LSC farmers, is taken to be the capital recovery cost of tractor and tillage equipment under the following assumptions:

Annual Capital Costs for Tractor Plowing

	60,000	Tractor (60hp) initial cost
+	10,000	Tillage equipment initial cost

	70,000	Total[2]
-	3,500	NPV of salvage (5 percent of initial value)[3]

	66,500	Net initial cost
x	0.067	Capital Recovery Factor at the market interest rate[4]

	4,433	Annual capital cost
/	4,099	Liters of fuel used per year[5]

	1.08	Capital cost per liter of fuel

The total cost is then allocated to each enterprise proportionately to the liters used in that operation.

At the opportunity cost of 8 percent, the CRF over 15 years is 0.117. Thus, the correction factor (opp. cost/market value) for capital use over this period is 0.117/0.067 = 1.75.[6] Equipment depreciation is also affected by commodity policy, with an import surtax of 5 percent and a sales tax of 12.5 percent. As shown in the tax table, Table A.7, with 80 percent of equipment expenditure affected by the import and sales taxes, the net effect is a correction factor of 0.88. The total correction factor covering the capital subsidy (1.75) and the import taxes (0.88) is (1.75*0.88=) 1.54.

Equipment depreciation in communal areas is figured differently, because almost all capital investments are self-financed, no implicit credit subsidy applies. At a real opportunity cost of capital of 10 percent, the CRF method for the major capital inputs gives annual costs per hectare, as shown in Table A.20.

Indirect capital costs, for both LSC and CA budgets, are figured similarly to indirect labor costs. Capital use is the remaining cost of intermediate inputs after their tradable and labor content is paid, and again no item conversion factor is applied.

Land costs reflect the approximate annual value of using each type of land. But since there is no actual land rental market in Zimbabwe, annual values have been imputed from other data. The particular method used here is to assume that land is the fixed factor that capitalizes farm profits; all average whole-farm returns are attributed to land. For CA land, this method yields average values of Z$10/ha for low-potential areas and Z$150/ha for high-potential areas.

For LSC land, the average-profits method yields land market values of Z$90/ha per season of rainfed summer use, when the value of land under winter irrigation is considered to be five times the value of rainfed land. (The

Table A.2.
Annual Capital Cost for Smallholder Implements

Item	Current Price (P)	Useful Life (n)	Interest Rate (i)	CRF = $\frac{(1+i)^n \cdot i}{(1+i)^n - i}$	Salvage Value (s)	NPV(s) = $s/(1+i)^n$ (S)	Prop. of Ann. Use per ha (u)	Annual Cost per ha = (P-S)*CRF*u
Oxcart	$450	20	10%	0.12	$0	0.00	0.20	10.57
Storage facilities	$50	10	10%	0.16	$0	0.00	0.20	1.63
Cotton sprayer	$100	10	10%	0.16	$0	0.00	0.33	5.37

unirrigated summertime use of irrigable land is charged at the lower rainfed rate.) The proportional difference in value between rainfed and irrigated land was provided by an informal survey of Harare's three major farm valuation firms, who reported appraising cropped land in high-potential areas (NR II) for sales in 1989 at values around Z$1000/ha for rainfed fields and Z$5000/ha for winter-irrigated fields. These purchase-price figures also roughly confirm the accuracy of the Z$90/ha rainfed land rental rate, which would be the annual capital cost of land use at constant real land prices and a real interest rate of 9 percent.

Within high-potential areas, CA land is much more valuable than LSC land because of much higher population densities and more intensive cultivation, yielding higher levels of profitability per hectare. The difference between CA and LSC uses of otherwise similar land is largely due to land tenure rules; if these were relaxed, that difference can be expected to decline. Thus, the national opportunity cost of LSC land is taken to be the implicit market value of CA land, or Z$150/ha for rainfed fields and five times that for fields under winter irrigation.

TRADABLE AND INTERMEDIATE GOODS

The total tradable component of all intermediate goods is given in the last row of the PAM. This is figured as each intermediate good's market-price or opportunity-cost value, times the percentage of that value that can be directly linked to trade opportunities. This "percent tradable" figure generally reflects a breakdown of the input into its component costs, in order to reflect the degree of price transmission between the exchange rate and the cost of the input.

Some virtually nontradable intermediate items have a very small tradables content, estimated to be 10 percent. These items include plowing services in CA budgets, which are charged at actual survey-average rates for hired work, and agricultural lime, insurance, and the mandatory CFU levy in LSC budgets. Ninety percent of the cost of these items is assigned to labor and capital, and no item conversion factor is applied.

Compound (NPK) fertilizers are taken to be 26 percent tradable, accounting for imported ammonia and other ingredients (GOZ 1986, p. 139). Most compound fertilizer costs are allocated to local capital and labor, in the form of locally mined phosphate rock and sulphur, hydroelectric power, and manufacturing costs. Some 3 percent of fertilizer production has recently been exported to neighboring countries, but this has had little impact on local prices. Imports from Europe and South Africa would be available if needed, but landed costs are almost certain to be well above prices for the locally manufactured blend.

Straight nitrogen fertilizer, in contrast, is taken to be 100 percent tradable. It is locally produced in the form of ammonium nitrate (AN), using local electricity and some imported inputs, but it is fully substitutable with imported urea. A trade parity price for AN-equivalent quantities of urea has therefore been calculated directly, as shown in the following calculations. Because trade parity for AN is calculated directly, no conversion factor is used. The conversion factor would have been 363/415 = 0.87, and the Nominal Rate of Protection (NRP) would be (415/363)-1 = 14 percent.

Trade Parity Value of Nitrogenous Fertilizer

	162	US$/mt urea bagged fob Europe (IMF, Int'l. Fin. Stat.)
+	37	US$/mt ocean freight to Beira (FAO, Food Outlook)

=	199	US$/mt urea landed trade parity
/	0.45	US$/Z$ end-1989 exchange rate

=	442	Z$/mt
+	42	Z$/mt Beira-Harare rail freight (NRZ file data)

=	484	Z$/mt urea Harare trade parity
x	0.75	AN/urea nitrogen equivalent (34.5%/46% nitrogen content)

=	363	Z$/mt AN-equivalent trade parity

Seeds, like AN fertilizer, are considered to be 100 percent tradable. Some types of seed are exported, but more important their prices can be expected to be closely linked to the prices of the relevant products, which are highly tradable. In the CA budgets, seed prices are survey averages, and in the LSC budgets seed prices are CFU reference prices.

Chemicals are considered to be 90 percent tradable, with 10 percent of costs allocated to labor and capital in blending, packaging, and marketing the imported ingredients. An item-specific conversion factor of 0.85 is applied, following the tax information in Table A.5. In the CA budgets, chemical costs are reported only in terms of total expenditure, as the survey data did not allow their breakdown by quantities and prices by product as in the LSC budgets.

Packing materials (mostly jute and synthetic sacks and twine) are broken down into tradables, capital, and labor in the same proportions as chemicals. Packing costs are figured by assuming that packing material is lost or destroyed at a rate of 2 percent of delivered number. In addition, a cost of $0.20 per bag and $0.50 per bale is charged, to cover the cost of repairing and marketing used bags. Twine is used at a rate of approximately 5 gms. (0.005 kg) per grain bag, and 25 gms (0.025 kg) per cotton or tobacco bale. Packaging is done as shown in Table A.3.

Table A.3
Crop Packaging Requirements

Product	Packing Unit	Kgs per Bag/Bale	Bags/Bales per mt	Kgs Twine per mt
Grains, peas & beans	Bag	91	11	0.05
Groundnuts (shelled)	Bag	82	12	0.06
Groundnuts (unshelled)	Bag	40	25	0.13
Sunflower seeds	Bag	55	18	0.09
Cotton	Bale	180	6	0.14

Transport costs in the CA budgets are survey averages. For farm output to the point of sale, transport costs are an average of $0.275 per mt-km over a distance of 60 km, making a total of $16.50/mt ($1.50/91kg bag or $3.00 per 180 kg cotton bale). Transport for inputs is more expensive, costing an average of $0.433 per mt-km over the same distance, making a total cost of $26/mt ($1.30/50kg bag). To show parity with marketed items, product transport is assigned to the entire crop, not just the portion sold or actually transported. In the LSC budgets, CFU estimates are used.

Transport costs are broken down into components using the results from an informal survey of major road transporters, shown in Table A.4.[7]

These proportions are also used to calculate the item conversion factor: the fuel excise tax raises transport costs by 2.7 percent and the import surtax plus sales tax on equipment raises costs by 4 percent, for a total effect of 6.7 percent, and a transport correction factor of 0.933 (1-0.067).

Tractor costs, included only in the LSC budgets, are broken down into repairs and maintenance (R&M), fuel, and labor costs using data from private agricultural-sector consultants. R&M is considered 50 percent tradable; the tradable portion is affected by a divergence of +15 percent from commodity policy, for an overall R&M conversion factor of +7.5 percent. Fuel and lubricants are 100 percent tradable and are affected by a special excise duty of 11.8 cents/liter only.

For the LSC wheat budget, irrigation costs are CFU estimates; these are roughly equal to actual electricity and R&M costs for irrigation on the Agricultural Research Trust (ART) farm, which were $60/1000m^3 in 1989.

The specific conversion factor for each intermediate item is calculated in Table A.5.

Table A.4
Composition of Transport Costs

	Average Z$/km	Percent of Total
Labor	0.50	17
R&M-labor	0.32	11
Other labor	0.18	6
Capital	1.09	38
Overhead	0.68	24
Depreciation	0.37	13
Insurance	0.04	1
Tradables	1.30	45
R&M-parts	0.75	26
Fuel	0.39	13
Tires	0.14	5
Oil	0.02	1
Total	2.89	100

Table A.5
Item Correction Factors: Trade and Sales Taxes on Inputs, 1989

	Excise Duty (a)	Surtax (b)	Sales Tax (c)	Total Tax (d)	Tax as % of Retail (e)	% of Item Affected (f)	Avg. Diver. (g)	Item Corr. Factor (h)
				Memo Items				
Tractors and combines	0%	5%	12.5%	18%	15%	80%	12%	0.88
Equipment spares	0%	5%	12.5%	18%	15%	50%	7%	0.93
Fuel	25%	0%	0.0%	25%	20%	100%	20%	0.80
Fertilizers	0%	20%	0.0%	20%	17%	26%	4%	0.96
Chemicals and packaging	0%	20%	0.0%	20%	17%	90%	15%	0.85

Sources: (a,b,c): Commercial Farmers Union, Farmers' Coop.

(d) = (a+b+c)
(e) = 1-(1/(1+d))
(f): author's estimates
(g) = (e*f)
(h) = 1-g

NOTES

1. In practice, the AFC provides only about a third of LSC borrowing. The remainder is borrowed from the private sector, but rates there are not much higher. In 1990 commercial banks were giving overdrafts to LSC farmers at 2.5 percent above the prime rate, which was 9.5 percent until September 1981, then 13 percent until December 1989, and then became 11.5 percent, for a current total rate of 14 percent. In 1990 finance houses were lending on hire-purchase at slightly higher rates: 16.5 percent for "productive" goods and 18 percent for "non-productive" ones. (Before December 1989, hire-purchase rates had been 20 percent for new goods and 23 percent for used ones.) Despite these low rates, set by the reserve bank, funds do seem to be available because of the low demand for investment funds elsewhere in the economy.

2. Data from MLARR, Economics and Markets Branch, Inputs Section files.

3. Estimated by Morris (1988).

4. The Capital Recovery Factor is $CRF = ([(1+i)^n]*i)/([(1+i)^n]-1)$, where i is the real annual interest rate and n is the investment's useful life in years. At zero real interest rates, the formula would be $1/n$, which in this case is $1/15 = 0.067$.

5. CFU estimate, from MLARR survey data.

6. In contrast, the correction factor for seasonal credit over only one year, the same real interest rate of zero and opportunity cost of 8 percent, is only $1.08/1.00 = 1.08$. The difference shows that the transfer (subsidy) component in a cheap long-term loan is much larger than in a cheap short-term loan.

7. These data correspond to trucks with an average load of 22 mt, for a loaded cost of Z$0.131/mt-km. However, backhaulage on agricultural transport is rare. With a load factor of only 50 percent costs double to Z$0.263/mt.

Appendix B

Policy Analysis Matrix Budgets

TABLE B 1
MAIZE- LOW POTENTIAL COMMUNAL AREAS

						Mkt.Val.Opp.Cost Transfers		
NPC	1 10	Returns to:						
EPC	0.74	Management	(Z$/ha)	115.14	229.05	-113.91		
TPC	0.50	Total Var. Costs	(Z$/Z$)	89%	142%	-53%		
PSE	-27.9%	Family Labor	(Z$/hr)	0.59	0.89	-0.30		
SRP	-20.5%	Resource Cost Ratios:		0.67	0.52			

CATEGORY/Item	UNITS	MARKET PRICES ($/unit)	ITEM CONVER. FACTOR	FOR. EXCH. PREMIUM: 50% x PERCENT TRADABLE	OPP. COSTS ($/unit)	QTY. PER HA	MARKET VALUE	OPP.COST VALUE	TRANSFERS
OUTPUT	mt	255.00				1.60	408.00		
Export parity (1980s average)	mt	230.97	1	100%	346.46	1.60	369.56	554.33	-146.33
LABOR							164.93	164.93	
Family Adults	hrs	0.32	1		0.32	327	104.64	104.64	
Children	hrs	0.16	1		0.16	96	1.76	1.76	
Hired Adults	hrs	0.35	1		0.35	11	33.60	33.60	
Children	hrs	0.18	1		0.18	2	1.93	1.93	
Indirect (in inputs)	Z$						13.92	13.92	
Indirect (in transport)	Z$						9.09	9.09	
CAPITAL							72.15	82.45	-10.30
Seasonal loans on 50% of TVC	%of Z$	13.9%	1.08		23.0%	113.03	15.71	26.01	-10.30
Ox-cart depreciation/rental	ha	10.60	1		10.60	1	10.60	10.60	
Storage facility deprec.	ha	1.60	1		1.60	1	1.60	1.60	
Land rental value	ha						10.00	10.00	
Indirect (in inputs)	Z$						13.92	13.92	
Indirect (in transport)	Z$						20.32	20.32	
TRADABLES	Z$						55.78	77.90	-22.12
MEMO ITEMS:							113.03	135.15	-22.12
Plowing services	ha	27.00	1	10%	28.35	1	27.00	28.35	-1.35
Seed	kg	1.12	1	100%	1.68	19	21.28	31.92	-10.64
Fertilizer: D (8-14-7)	mt	416.60	0.96	26%	451.93	0.010	4.17	4.52	-0.35
Fertilizer: AN (34,5% N)	mt	415.40							
Import parity (1989 urea equiv.)		363.00	1	100%	544.50	0.007	2.54	3.81	-1.27
Chemicals (all types)	ha		0.85	90%					
Packing (bags & twine)	ha	0.26	0.85	90%	0.32	18	4.58	5.64	-1.06
Transport - seed	kg	0.03	0.93	45%	0.03	19	0.57	0.65	-0.08
Transport - fertilizer	mt	30.00	0.93	45%	34.18	0.017	0.51	0.58	-0.07
Transport - product	mt	32.74	0.93	45%	37.30	1.60	52.38	59.68	-7.29

TABLE B.2
GROUNDNUTS (UNSHELLED)-LOW POTENTIAL COMMUNAL AREAS

			Mkt.Val.	Opp.Cost	Transfers
NPC	0.75	Returns to:			
EPC	0.48	Management	(Z$/ha) -18.33	298.27	-316.60
TPC	-0.06	Total Var. Costs	(Z$/Z$) -0.19	2.36	-2.56
PSE	-92.0%	Family Labor	(Z$/hr) 0.26	0.76	-0.50
SRP	-45.8%	Resource Cost Ratios:	1.06	0.52	

CATEGORY/Item	UNITS	MARKET PRICES ($/unit)	ITEM CONVER. FACTOR	FOR.EXCH. PREMIUM: 50% x PERCENT TRADABLE	OPP. COSTS ($/unit)	QTY. PER HA.	MARKET VALUE	OPP.COST VALUE	TRANSFERS
OUTPUT	mt	688.00				0.50	344.00		
Export parity (1980s average)	mt	921.00	1	100%	1381.50	0.50	460.50	690.75	-346.75
LABOR							259.72	259.72	
Family Adults	hrs	0.32	1		0.32	560	179.20	179.20	
Children	hrs	0.16	1		0.16	152	5.60	5.60	
Hired Adults	hrs	0.35	1		0.35	35	53.20	53.20	
Children	hrs	0.18	1		0.18	3	6.13	6.13	
Indirect (in inputs)	Z$						12.62	12.62	
Indirect (in transport)	Z$						2.97	2.97	
CAPITAL							53.18	60.86	-7.68
Seasonal loans on 50% of TVC	%of Z$	13.9%	1.08		23.0%	84.29	11.72	19.40	-7.68
Ox-cart depreciation/rental	ha	10.60	1		10.60	1	10.60	10.60	
Storage facility deprec.	ha	1.60	1		1.60	1	1.60	1.60	
Land rental value	ha						10.00	10.00	
Indirect (in inputs)	Z$						12.62	12.62	
Indirect (in transport)	Z$						6.64	6.64	
TRADABLES	Z$						49.43	71.90	-22.47
MEMO ITEMS:							84.29	106.76	-22.47
Plowing services	ha	27.00	1	10%	28.35	1	27.00	28.35	-1.35
Seed	kg	1.04	1	100%	1.56	34	35.36	53.04	-17.68
Fertilizer: D (8-14-7)	mt	416.60	0.96	26%	451.93	0.002	0.83	0.90	-0.07
Fertilizer: AN (34.5% N)	mt	415.40							
Import parity (1989 urea equiv.)	mt	363.00	1	100%	544.50	0.001	0.36	0.54	-0.18
Chemicals (all types)	ha		0.85	90%					
Packing (bags & twine)	ha	0.26	0.85	90%	0.32	13	3.25	4.01	-0.76
Transport - seed	kg	0.03	0.93	45%	0.03	34	1.02	1.16	-0.14
Transport - fertilizer	mt	30.00	0.93	45%	34.18	0.003	0.09	0.10	-0.01
Transport - product	mt	32.74	0.93	45%	37.30	0.50	16.37	18.65	-2.28

TABLE B.3
SUNFLOWER SEEDS- LOW POTENTIAL COMMUNAL AREAS

				Mkt.Val.	Opp.Cost	Transfers
NPC	1.00	Returns to:				
EPC	0.67	Management	(Z$/ha)	-54.47	1.78	-56.25
TPC	-30.68	Total Var. Costs	(Z$/Z$)	-1.00	0.03	-1.03
PSE	-41.2%	Family Labor	(Z$/hr)	0.10	0.29	-0.19
SRP	-27.5%	Resource Cost Ratios:		1.46	0.99	

CATEGORY/Item	UNITS	MARKET PRICES ($/unit)	ITEM CONVER. FACTOR	FOR. EXCH. PREMIUM: 50% x PERCENT TRADABLE	OPP. COSTS ($/unit)	QTY. PER HA.	MARKET VALUE	OPP.COST VALUE	TRANSFERS
OUTPUT	mt	455.00				0.30	136.50		
Opportunity cost	mt	455.00	1	100%	682.50	0.30	136.50	204.75	-68.25
LABOR							128.41	128.41	
Family Adults	hrs	0.32	1		0.32	264	84.48	84.48	
Children	hrs	0.16	1		0.16	78	1.28	1.28	
Hired Adults	hrs	0.35	1		0.35	8	27.30	27.30	
Children	hrs	0.18	1		0.18		1.40	1.40	
Indirect (in inputs)	Z$						12.22	12.22	
Indirect (in transport)	Z$						1.73	1.73	
CAPITAL							44.91	49.25	-4.35
Seasonal loans on 50% of TVC	%of2$	13.9%	1.08		23.0%	47.69	6.63	10.97	-4.35
Ox-cart depreciation/rental	ha	10.60	1		10.60	1	10.60	10.60	
Storage facility deprec.	ha	1.60	1		1.60	1	1.60	1.60	
Land rental value	ha						10.00	10.00	
Indirect (in inputs)	Z$						12.22	12.22	
Indirect (in transport)	Z$						3.86	3.86	
TRADABLES	Z$						17.66	25.32	-7.66

MEMO ITEMS:							47.69	55.34	-7.66
Plowing services	ha	27.00	1	10%	28.35	1	27.00	28.35	-1.35
Seed	kg	0.83	1	100%	1.25	11	9.13	13.70	-4.57
Fertilizer: D (8-14-7)	mt	416.60	0.96	26%	451.93				
Fertilizer: AN (34,5% N)	mt	415.40							
Import parity (1989 urea equiv.)		363.00	1	100%	544.50				
Chemicals (all types)	ha		0.85	90%					
Packing (bags & twine)	ha	0.26	0.85	90%	0.32	5	1.40	1.73	-0.33
Transport - seed	kg	0.03	0.93	45%	0.03	11	0.33	0.38	-0.05
Transport - fertilizer	mt	30.00	0.93	45%	34.18				
Transport - product	mt	32.74	0.93	45%	37.30	0.30	9.82	11.19	-1.37

Appendix B

TABLE B.4
PEARL MILLET-LOW POTENTIAL COMMUNAL AREAS

		Mkt.Val.	Opp.Cost	Transfers
NPC	1.00	Returns to:		
EPC	0.67	Management (Z$/ha)	-159.66	-149.26	-10.40
TPC	1.07	Total Var. Costs (Z$/Z$)	-2.58	-1.88	-0.70
PSE	-18.7%	Family Labor (Z$/hr)	-0.22	-0.19	-0.03
SRP	-12.5%	Resource Cost Ratios:	6.45	4.34

CATEGORY/Item	UNITS	MARKET PRICES ($/unit)	ITEM CONVER. FACTOR	FOR.EXCH. PREMIUM: 50% x PERCENT TRADABLE	OPP. COSTS ($/unit)	QTY. PER HA.	MARKET VALUE	OPP.COST VALUE	TRANSFERS
OUTPUT	mt	278.00				0.20	55.60		
Opportunity cost	mt	278.00	1	100%	417.00	0.20	55.60	83.40	-27.80
LABOR							144.42	144.42	
Family Adults	hrs	0.32	1		0.32	269	86.08	86.08	
Children	hrs	0.16	1		0.16	119	1.60	1.60	
Hired Adults	hrs	0.35	1		0.35	10	41.65	41.65	
Children	hrs	0.18	1		0.18	7	1.75	1.75	
Indirect (in inputs)	Z$						12.18	12.18	
Indirect (in transport)	Z$						1.16	1.16	
CAPITAL							44.55	49.50	-4.96
Seasonal loans on 50% of TVC	%of Z$	13.9%	1.08		23.0%	54.42	7.56	12.52	-4.96
Ox-cart depreciation/rental	ha	10.60	1		10.60	1	10.60	10.60	
Storage facility deprec	ha	1.60	1		1.60	1	1.60	1.60	
Land rental value	ha						10.00	10.00	
Indirect (in inputs)	Z$						12.18	12.18	
Indirect (in transport)	Z$						2.60	2.60	
TRADABLES	Z$						26.30	38.73	-12.44
MEMO ITEMS:							54.42	66.86	-12.44
Plowing services	ha	27.00	1	10%	28.35	1	27.00	28.35	-1.35
Seed	kg	2.00	1	100%	3.00	10	20.00	30.00	-10.00
Fertilizer: D (8-14-7)	mt	416.60	0.96	26%	451.93				
Fertilizer: AN (34.5% N)	mt	415.40							
Import parity (1989 urea equiv.)		363.00	1	100%	544.50				
Chemicals (all types)	ha		0.85	90%					
Packing (bags & twine)	ha	0.26	0.85	90%	0.32	2	0.57	0.70	-0.13
Transport - seed	kg	0.03	0.93	45%	0.03	10	0.30	0.34	-0.04
Transport - fertilizer	mt	30.00	0.93	45%	34.18				
Transport - product	mt	32.74	0.93	45%	37.30	0.20	6.55	7.46	-0.91

TABLE B.5
SORGHUM (ALL TYPES)- LOW POTENTIAL COMMUNAL AREAS

							Mkt.Val.Opp.Cost Transfers		
NPC	1.00	Returns to:							
EPC	0.67	Management				(Z$/ha)	-118.39	-100.86	-17.53
TPC	1.17	Total Var. Costs				(Z$/Z$)	-2.64	-1.89	-0.75
PSE	-33.7%	Family Labor				(Z$/hr)	-0.09	-0.03	-0.06
SRP	-22.5%	Resource Cost Ratios:					3.90	2.63	

CATEGORY/Item	UNITS	MARKET PRICES ($/unit)	ITEM CONVER. FACTOR	FOR. EXCH. PREMIUM: 50% x PERCENT TRADABLE	OPP. COSTS ($/unit)	QTY. PER HA.	MARKET VALUE	OPP.COST VALUE	TRANSFERS
OUTPUT	mt	260.00				0.20	52.00		
Opportunity cost	mt	260.00	1	100%	390.00	0.20	52.00	78.00	-26.00
LABOR							116.75	116.75	
Family Adults	hrs	0.32	1		0.32	280	89.60	89.60	
Children	hrs	0.16	1		0.16	27	2.08	2.08	
Hired Adults	hrs	0.35	1		0.35	13	9.45	9.45	
Children	hrs	0.18	1		0.18		2.28	2.28	
Indirect (in inputs)	Z$						12.18	12.18	
Indirect (in transport)	Z$						1.16	1.16	
CAPITAL							42.45	46.03	-3.58
Seasonal loans on 50% of TVC	%of Z$	13.9%	1.08		23.0%	39.32	5.47	9.05	-3.58
Ox-cart depreciation/rental	ha	10.60	1		10.60	1	10.60	10.60	
Storage facility deprec.	ha	1.60	1		1.60	1	1.60	1.60	
Land rental value	ha						10.00	10.00	
Indirect (in inputs)	Z$						12.18	12.18	
Indirect (in transport)	Z$						2.60	2.60	
TRADABLES	Z$						11.20	16.08	-4.89
MEMO ITEMS:							39.32	44.21	-4.89
Plowing services	ha	27.00	1	10%	28.35	1	27.00	28.35	-1.35
Seed	kg	0.49	1	100%	0.74	10	4.90	7.35	-2.45
Fertilizer: D (8-14-7)	mt	416.60	0.96	26%	451.93				
Fertilizer: AN (34.5% N)	mt	415.40							
Import parity (1989 urea equiv.)	mt	363.00	1	100%	544.50				
Chemicals (all types)	ha		0.85	90%					
Packing (bags & twine)	ha	0.26	0.85	90%	0.32	2	0.57	0.70	-0.13
Transport - seed	kg	0.03	0.93	45%	0.03	10	0.30	0.34	-0.04
Transport - fertilizer	mt	30.00	0.93	45%	34.18				
Transport - product	mt	32.74	0.93	45%	37.30	0.20	6.55	7.46	-0.91

TABLE B.6
FINGER MILLET-LOW POTENTIAL COMMUNAL AREAS

		Mkt.Val.	Opp.Cost	Transfers
NPC	1.00	Returns to:		
EPC	0.67	Management (Z$/ha)	-100.83	-39.26	-61.56
TPC	2.57	Total Var. Costs (Z$/Z$)	-1.76	-0.56	-1.20
PSE	-41.6%	Family Labor (Z$/hr)	0.08	0.23	-0.15
SRP	-27.7%	Resource Cost Ratios:	1.78	1.20	

CATEGORY/Item	UNITS	MARKET PRICES ($/unit)	ITEM CONVER. FACTOR	FOR.EXCH. PREMIUM: 50% x PERCENT TRADABLE	OPP. COSTS ($/unit)	QTY. PER HA.	MARKET VALUE	OPP.COST VALUE	TRANSFERS
OUTPUT	mt	370.00				0.40	148.00		
Opportunity cost	mt	370.00	1	100%	555.00	0.40	148.00	222.00	-74.00
LABOR							183.79	183.79	
Family　Adults	hrs	0.32	1		0.32	374	119.68	119.68	
Children	hrs	0.16	1		0.16	69	12.16	12.16	
Hired　Adults	hrs	0.35	1		0.35	76	24.15	24.15	
Children	hrs	0.18	1		0.18	1	13.30	13.30	
Indirect (in inputs)	Z$						12.21	12.21	
Indirect (in transport)	Z$						2.29	2.29	
CAPITAL							46.53	51.12	-4.59
Seasonal loans on 50% of TVC	%ofZ$	13.9%	1.08		23.0%	50.34	7.00	11.58	-4.59
Ox-cart depreciation/rental	ha	10.60	1		10.60	1	10.60	10.60	
Storage facility deprec.	ha	1.60	1		1.60	1	1.60	1.60	
Land rental value	ha						10.00	10.00	
Indirect (in inputs)	Z$						12.21	12.21	
Indirect (in transport)	Z$						5.12	5.12	
TRADABLES	Z$						18.51	26.36	-7.85
MEMO ITEMS							50.34	58.19	-7.85
Plowing services	ha	27.00	1	10%	28.35	1	27.00	28.35	-1.35
Seed	kg	0.67	1	100%	1.01	13	8.71	13.07	-4.36
Fertilizer　D (8-14-7)	mt	416.60	0.96	26%	451.93				
Fertilizer　AN (34.5% N)	mt	415.40							
Import parity (1989 urea equiv.)		363.00	1	100%	544.50				
Chemicals (all types)	ha		0.85	90%					
Packing (bags & twine)	ha	0.26	0.85	90%	0.32	4	1.14	1.41	-0.27
Transport - seed	kg	0.03	0.93	45%	0.03	13	0.39	0.44	-0.05
Transport - fertilizer	mt	30.00	0.93	45%	34.18				
Transport - product	mt	32.74	0.93	45%	37.30	0.40	13.10	14.92	-1.82

TABLE B.7
COTTON-HIGH POTENTIAL COMMUNAL AREAS

			Mkt.Val.	Opp.Cost	Transfers
NPC	0.79	Returns to:			
EPC	0.53	Management	(Z$/ha) -155.91	194.29	-350.20
TPC	-0.80	Total Var. Costs	(Z$/Z$) -0.67	0.67	-1.34
PSE	-77.4%	Family Labor	(Z$/hr) 0.06	0.65	-0.60
SRP	-40.8%	Resource Cost Ratios:	1.47	0.72	

CATEGORY/Item	UNITS	MARKET PRICES ($/unit)	ITEM CONVER. FACTOR	FOR.EXCH. PREMIUM: 50% x PERCENT TRADABLE	OPP. COSTS ($/unit)	QTY. PER HA.	MARKET VALUE	OPP.COST VALUE	TRANSFERS
OUTPUT	mt	905.00				0.50	452.50		
Opportunity cost	mt	1144.78	1	100%	1717.17	0.50	572.39	858.59	-406.09
LABOR							247.97	247.97	
Family Adults	hrs	0.32	1		0.32	567	181.44	181.44	
Children	hrs	0.16	1		0.16	34	6.72	6.72	
Hired Adults	hrs	0.35	1		0.35	42	11.90	11.90	
Children	hrs	0.18	1		0.18		7.35	7.35	
Indirect (in inputs)	Z$						36.95	36.95	
Indirect (in transport)	Z$						3.60	3.60	
CAPITAL							241.09	259.76	-18.67
Seasonal loans on 50% of TVC	%ofZ$	13.9%	1.08		23.0%	204.92	28.48	47.16	-18.67
Oxcart & sprayer depreciation	ha	16.00	1		16.00	1	16.00	16.00	
Storage facility deprec.	ha	1.60	1		1.60	1	1.60	1.60	
Land rental value	ha						150.00	150.00	
Indirect (in inputs)	Z$						36.95	36.95	
Indirect (in transport)	Z$						8.06	8.06	
TRADABLES	Z$						119.35	156.57	-37.22
MEMO ITEMS:							204.92	242.13	-37.22
Plowing services	ha	30.00	1	10%	31.50	1	30.00	31.50	-1.50
Seed	kg	0.26	1	100%	0.39	37	9.62	14.43	-4.81
Fertilizer: various compounds	mt	510.00	0.96	26%	553.25	0.102	52.02	56.43	-4.41
Fertilizer: AN (34.5% N)	mt	415.40							
Import parity (1989 urea equiv.)		363.00	1	100%	544.50	0.022	7.99	11.98	-3.99
Chemicals (all types)	ha	81.66	0.85	90%	100.65	1	81.66	100.65	-18.99
Packing (bales & twine)	ha	0.81	0.85	90%	1.00	3	2.43	2.99	-0.56
Transport - seed	kg	0.03	0.93	45%	0.03	37	1.11	1.26	-0.15
Transport - fertilizer	mt	30.00	0.93	45%	34.18	0.124	3.72	4.24	-0.52
Transport - product	mt	32.74	0.93	45%	37.30	0.50	16.37	18.65	-2.28

TABLE B.8
FINGER MILLET- HIGH POTENTIAL COMMUNAL AREAS

			Mkt.Val.	Opp.Cost	Transfers
NPC	1.00	Returns to:			
EPC	0.67	Management	(Z$/ha) -148.71	-56.44	-92.27
TPC	2.63	Total Var. Costs	(Z$/Z$) -1.86	-0.57	-1.29
PSE	-41.6%	Family Labor	(Z$/hr) -0.08	0.17	-0.25
SRP	-27.7%	Resource Cost Ratios:	1.77	1.19	

CATEGORY/Item	UNITS	MARKET PRICES ($/unit)	ITEM CONVER. FACTOR	FOR.EXCH. PREMIUM: 50% x PERCENT TRADABLE	OPP. COSTS ($/unit)	QTY. PER HA.	MARKET VALUE	OPP.COST VALUE	TRANSFERS
OUTPUT	mt	370.00				0.60	222.00		
Opportunity cost	mt	370.00	1	100%	555.00	0.60	222.00	333.00	-111.00
LABOR							146.91	146.91	
Family Adults	hrs	0.32	1		0.32	359	114.88	114.88	
Children	hrs	0.16	1		0.16	22	2.88	2.88	
Hired Adults	hrs	0.35	1		0.35	18	7.70	7.70	
Children	hrs	0.18	1		0.18		3.15	3.15	
Indirect (in inputs)	Z$						14.82	14.82	
Indirect (in transport)	Z$						3.48	3.48	
CAPITAL							194.55	200.94	-6.39
Seasonal loans on 50% of TVC	%of Z$	13.9%	1.08		23.0%	70.15	9.75	16.14	-6.39
Ox-cart depreciation/rental	ha	10.60	1		10.60	1	10.60	10.60	
Storage facility deprec.	ha	1.60	1		1.60	1	1.60	1.60	
Land rental value	ha						150.00	150.00	
Indirect (in inputs)	Z$						14.82	14.82	
Indirect (in transport)	Z$						7.78	7.78	
TRADABLES	Z$						29.24	41.58	-12.34
MEMO ITEMS:							70.15	82.49	-12.34
Plowing services	ha	30.00	1	10%	31.50	1	30.00	31.50	-1.50
Seed	kg	0.75	1	100%	1.13	19	14.25	21.38	-7.13
Fertilizer: D (8-14-7)	mt	416.60	0.96	26%	451.93	0.008	3.33	3.62	-0.28
Fertilizer: AN (34.5% N)	mt	415.40							
Import parity (1989 urea equiv.)		363.00	1	100%	544.50	0.001	0.36	0.54	-0.18
Chemicals (all types)	ha		0.85	90%					
Packing (bags & twine)	ha	0.26	0.85	90%	0.32	7	1.72	2.11	-0.40
Transport - seed	kg	0.03	0.93	45%	0.03	19	0.57	0.65	-0.08
Transport - fertilizer	mt	30.00	0.93	45%	34.18	0.009	0.27	0.31	-0.04
Transport - product	mt	32.74	0.93	45%	37.30	0.60	19.64	22.38	-2.74

TABLE B.9
GROUNDNUTS (UNSHELLED)- HIGH POTENTIAL COMMUNAL AREAS

		Mkt.Val.	Opp.Cost	Transfers
NPC	0.96	Returns to:		
EPC	0.63	Management (Z$/ha)	-109.19	51.79	-160.98
TPC	-2.11	Total Var. Costs (Z$/Z$)	-1.00	0.35	-1.36
PSE	-45.4%	Family Labor (Z$/hr)	0.12	0.41	-0.29
SRP	-29.1%	Resource Cost Ratios:	1.37	0.89	

CATEGORY/Item	UNITS	MARKET PRICES ($/unit)	ITEM CONVER. FACTOR	FOR.EXCH. PREMIUM: 50% x PERCENT TRADABLE	OPP. COSTS ($/unit)	QTY. PER HA.	MARKET VALUE	OPP.COST VALUE	TRANSFERS
OUTPUT	mt	886.00				0.40	354.40		
Export parity (1980s average)	mt	921.00	1	100%	1381.50	0.40	368.40	552.60	-198.20
LABOR							208.50	208.50	
Family Adults	hrs	0.32	1		0.32	542	173.44	173.44	
Children	hrs	0.16	1		0.16	39	2.56	2.56	
Hired Adults	hrs	0.35	1		0.35	16	13.65	13.65	
Children	hrs	0.18	1		0.18		2.80	2.80	
Indirect (in inputs)	Z$						13.63	13.63	
Indirect (in transport)	Z$						2.42	2.42	
CAPITAL							194.52	203.24	-8.72
Seasonal loans on 50% of TVC	%of Z$	13.9%	1.08		23.0%	95.65	13.29	22.01	-8.72
Ox-cart depreciation/rental	ha	10.60	1		10.60	1	10.60	10.60	
Storage facility deprec.	ha	1.60	1		1.60	1	1.60	1.60	
Land rental value	ha						150.00	150.00	
Indirect (in inputs)	Z$						13.63	13.63	
Indirect (in transport)	Z$						5.40	5.40	
TRADABLES	Z$						60.57	89.08	-28.50

MEMO ITEMS:							95.65	124.15	-28.50
Plowing services	ha	30.00	1	10%	31.50	1	30.00	31.50	-1.50
Seed	kg	1.32	1	100%	1.98	37	48.84	73.26	-24.42
Fertilizer: D (8-14-7)	mt	416.60	0.96	26%	451.93				
Fertilizer: AN (34.5% N)	mt	415.40							
Import parity (1989 urea equiv.)	mt	363.00	1	100%	544.50				
Chemicals (all types)	ha		0.85	90%		1			
Packing (bags & twine)	ha	0.26	0.85	90%	0.32	10	2.60	3.20	-0.60
Transport - seed	kg	0.03	0.93	45%	0.03	37	1.11	1.26	-0.15
Transport - fertilizer	mt	30.00	0.93	45%	34.18				
Transport - product	mt	32.74	0.93	45%	37.30	0.40	13.10	14.92	-1.82

TABLE B.10
MAIZE-HIGH POTENTIAL COMMUNAL AREAS

					Mkt.Val.	Opp.Cost	Transfers
NPC	0.92	Returns to:					
EPC	0.59	Management	(Z$/ha)		80.94	425.46	-344.53
TPC	0.19	Total Var. Costs	(Z$/Z$)		0.26	1.08	-0.82
PSE	-50.5%	Family Labor	(Z$/hr)		0.53	1.50	-0.96
SRP	-31.1%	Resource Cost Ratios:			0.85	0.53	

CATEGORY/Item	UNITS ($/unit)	MARKET PRICES ($/unit)	ITEM CONVER. FACTOR	FOR.EXCH. PREMIUM: 50% x PERCENT TRADABLE	OPP. COSTS ($/unit)	QTY. PER HA.	MARKET VALUE	OPP.COST VALUE	TRANSFERS
OUTPUT	mt	213.00				3.20	681.60		
Export parity (1980s average)	mt	230.97	1	100%	346.46	3.20	739.11	1108.67	-427.07
LABOR							179.98	179.98	
Family Adults	hrs	0.32	1		0.32	336	107.52	107.52	
Children	hrs	0.16	1		0.16	43	2.08	2.08	
Hired Adults	hrs	0.35	1		0.35	13	15.05	15.05	
Children	hrs	0.18	1		0.18		2.28	2.28	
Indirect (in inputs)	Z$						33.88	33.88	
Indirect (in transport)	Z$						19.17	19.17	
CAPITAL							276.95	301.88	-24.92
Seasonal loans on 50% of TVC	%of Z$	13.9%	1.08		23.0%	273.52	38.02	62.94	-24.92
Ox-cart depreciation/rental	ha	10.60	1		10.60	1	10.60	10.60	
Storage facility deprec.	ha	1.60	1		1.60	1	1.60	1.60	
Land rental value	ha						150.00	150.00	
Indirect (in inputs)	Z$						33.88	33.88	
Indirect (in transport)	Z$						42.86	42.86	
TRADABLES	Z$						143.73	201.35	-57.62
MEMO ITEMS:							273.52	331.14	-57.62
Plowing services	ha	30.00	1	10%	31.50	1	30.00	31.50	-1.50
Seed	kg	0.95	1	100%	1.43	29	27.55	41.33	-13.78
Fertilizer: D (8-14-7)	mt	416.60	0.96	26%	451.93	0.129	53.74	58.30	-4.56
Fertilizer: AN (34,5% N)	mt	415.40							
Import parity (1989 urea equiv.)		363.00	1	100%	544.50	0.109	39.57	59.35	-19.78
Chemicals (all types)	ha	0.73	0.85	90%	0.90	1	0.73	0.90	-0.17
Packing (bags & twine)	ha	0.26	0.85	90%	0.32	35	9.15	11.28	-2.13
Transport - seed	kg	0.03	0.93	45%	0.03	29	0.87	0.99	-0.12
Transport - fertilizer	mt	30.00	0.93	45%	34.18	0.238	7.14	8.13	-0.99
Transport - product	mt	32.74	0.93	45%	37.30	3.20	104.77	119.36	-14.59

TABLE B.11
SUNFLOWER SEEDS- HIGH POTENTIAL COMMUNAL AREAS

							Mkt.Val.	Opp.Cost	Transfers
	NPC	1.00	Returns to:						
	EPC	0.67	Management		(Z$/ha)	-108.93	-18.13	-90.80	
	TPC	6.01	Total Var. Costs		(Z$/Z$)	-1.22	-0.16	-1.06	
	PSE	-39.9%	Family Labor		(Z$/hr)	-0.13	0.24	-0.37	
	SRP	-26.6%	Resource Cost Ratios:			1.57	1.06		

CATEGORY/Item		UNITS	MARKET PRICES ($/unit)	ITEM CONVER. FACTOR	FOR.EXCH. PREMIUM: 50% x PERCENT TRADABLE	OPP. COSTS ($/unit)	QTY. PER HA.	MARKET VALUE	OPP.COST VALUE	TRANSFERS
OUTPUT		mt	455.00				0.50	227.50		
Opportunity cost		mt	455.00	1	100%	682.50	0.50	227.50	341.25	-113.75
LABOR								103.91	103.91	
Family	Adults	hrs	0.32	1		0.32	235	75.20	75.20	
	Children	hrs	0.16	1		0.16	20	1.28	1.28	
Hired	Adults	hrs	0.35	1		0.35	8	7.00	7.00	
	Children	hrs	0.18	1		0.18	2	1.40	1.40	
Indirect (in inputs)		Z$						15.97	15.97	
Indirect (in transport)		Z$						3.06	3.06	
CAPITAL								195.92	203.06	-7.15
Seasonal loans on 50% of TVC		%of Z$	13.9%	1.08		23.0%	78.44	10.90	18.05	-7.15
Ox-cart depreciation/rental		ha	10.60	1		10.60	1	10.60	10.60	
Storage facility deprec.		ha	1.60	1		1.60	1	1.60	1.60	
Land rental value		ha						150.00	150.00	
Indirect (in inputs)		Z$						15.97	15.97	
Indirect (in transport)		Z$						6.85	6.85	
TRADABLES		Z$						36.60	52.40	-15.80
MEMO ITEMS:								78.44	94.25	-15.80
Plowing services		ha	30.00	1	10%	31.50	1	30.00	31.50	-1.50
Seed		kg	0.59	1	100%	0.89	29	17.11	25.67	-8.56
Fertilizer: D (8-14-7)		mt	416.60	0.96	26%	451.93	0.015	6.25	6.78	-0.53
Fertilizer: AN (34.5% N)		mt	415.40							
Import parity (1989 urea equiv.)			363.00	1	100%	544.50	0.011	3.99	5.99	-2.00
Chemicals (all types)		ha	0.73	0.85	90%	0.90	1	0.73	0.90	-0.17
Packing (bags & twine)		ha	0.26	0.85	90%	0.32	9	2.34	2.88	-0.54
Transport - seed		kg	0.03	0.93	45%	0.03	29	0.87	0.99	-0.12
Transport - fertilizer		mt	30.00	0.93	45%	34.18	0.026	0.78	0.89	-0.11
Transport - product		mt	32.74	0.93	45%	37.30	0.50	16.37	18.65	-2.28

TABLE B.12
MAIZE-LSC AREAS (HAND-HARVESTED DRYLAND)

	NPC	0.91	Returns to:			Mkt.Val.	Opp.Cost	Transfers
	EPC	0.53		Management	(Z$/ha)	-38.75	486.41	-525.16
	TPC	-0.08		Variable costs	(Z$/Z$)	-0.05	0.49	-0.53
	PSE	-44%		Resource Cost Ratios:		1.06	0.63	0.42
	SRP	-27%						

| | | | | FOR.EXCH. PREMIUM: | | Yield Factor 1.00 | | | |
| | | MARKET PRICES | ITEM CONVER. | 50% x PERCENT | OPP. COSTS | QTY. PER | MARKET | OPP.COST | |
CATEGORY/Item	UNITS	($/unit)	FACTOR	TRADABLE	($/unit)	HA.	VALUE	VALUE	TRANSFERS
OUTPUT	mt	213.07				5.60	1193.19		
Export parity (1980s average)		233.07	1	100%	349.61	5.60	1305.19	1957.79	-764.60
LABOR							382.14	283.96	98.18
Basic	day/ha	5.44	0.52		2.83	32	174.08	90.52	83.56
Harvest	day/mt	5.44	0.52		2.83	5.60	30.46	15.84	14.62
Tractor (driver & mechanic)	l	0.93	1		0.93	66	61.38	61.38	
Indirect (in inputs & transport)							116.21	116.21	
CAPITAL							359.79	547.80	-188.01
Seasonal loans on 50% of TVC	%ofZ$	13.9%	1.08		23.0%	500.54	69.58	115.18	-45.61
Equipment depreciation	l	1.08	1.54	80%	2.33	66	71.28	153.68	-82.40
Indirect (in inputs & transp.)	Z$						128.93	128.93	
Land rental equivalent	ha						90.00	150.00	-60.00
TRADABLES							490.01	639.62	-149.61
MEMO ITEMS:							735.16	884.77	-149.61
Tractor repair & maintenance	l	2.19	0.93	50%	2.55	66	144.54	168.03	-23.49
Tractor fuel & lubricants	l	0.60	0.80	100%	0.72	66	39.60	47.52	-7.92
Fertilizer (Comp.M 10-10-10)	mt	404.80	0.96	26%	439.13	0.300	121.44	131.74	-10.30
Ammonium Nitrate (34.5% N)	mt	415.40							
Import parity (1989 Urea equiv.)		357.92	1	100%	536.88	0.330	137.08	177.17	-40.09
Seed	kg	1.84	1	100%	2.76	25	46.00	69.00	-23.00
Aldrin (seed treatment)	kg	36.96	0.85	90%	45.55	0.125	4.62	5.69	-1.07
Dual 720 (herbicide)	l	30.17	0.85	90%	37.18	2.0	60.34	74.37	-14.03
Atrazine (herbicide)	l	7.80	0.85	90%	9.61	2.5	19.50	24.03	-4.53
Thiodan 35 (insecticide)	l	14.40	0.85	90%	17.75	0.66	9.50	11.71	-2.21
Dimethoate (insecticide)	l	13.94	0.85	90%	17.18	2.00	27.88	34.36	-6.48
Dipterex 95 (insecticide)	kg	18.95	0.85	90%	23.36	0.06	1.14	1.40	-0.26
Dipterex (gran.)(insect.)	kg	0.90	0.85	90%	1.11	8.00	7.20	8.87	-1.67
Packing (bags & twine)	packs	0.26	0.85	90%	0.32	61.6	16.02	19.74	-3.72
Seed transport	mt	29.03	0.93	45%	33.18	0.03	0.73	0.83	-0.10
Product transport	mt	8.55	0.93	45%	9.77	5.60	47.88	54.72	-6.84
Fertilizer transport	mt	15.80	0.93	45%	18.06	0.88	13.90	15.89	-1.99
Lime	mt	42.00	1	10%	44.10	0.250	10.50	11.03	-0.53
Fertilizer insurance	%ofVal	1.00%	1	10%	1.05%	283	2.83	2.97	-0.14
Product insurance	%ofVal	0.55%	1	10%	0.58%	1193	6.56	6.89	-0.33
CFU levy	%ofVal	1.50%	1	10%	1.58%	1193	17.90	18.79	-0.89

TABLE B.13
GROUNDNUTS (UNSHELLED)-LSC AREAS (HAND-HARVESTED DRYLAND)

					Mkt.Val.Opp.Cost Transfers
NPC	0.69	Returns to:			
EPC	0.40	Management	(Z$/ha)	-41.59	1486.64 -1528.23
TPC	-0.03	Total Var. Costs	(Z$/Z$)	-5.0%	142.5% -147.5%
PSE	-104%	Resource Cost Ratios:		1.04	0.42 0.62
SRP	-48%				

CATEGORY/Item	UNITS	MARKET PRICES ($/unit)	ITEM CONVER. FACTOR	FOR.EXCH. PREMIUM: 50% x PERCENT TRADABLE	OPP. COSTS ($/unit)	QTY. PER HA.	MARKET VALUE	OPP.COST VALUE	TRANSFERS
OUTPUT		638.00				2.30	1467.40		
Export parity (1980s average)		921.05	1	100%	1381.58	2.30	2118.41	3177.62	-1710.22
LABOR							647.94	444.26	203.67
Basic	days	5.44	0.52		2.83	78.00	424.32	220.65	203.67
Tractor driver & mechanic	l	0.93	1		0.93	85	79.05	79.05	
Indirect (in inputs & transport)							144.57	144.57	
CAPITAL							412.61	635.27	-222.66
Seasonal loans on 50% of TVC	%of2$	13.9%	1.08		23.0%	620.47	86.25	142.78	-56.54
Equipment depreciation	l	1.08	1.54	80%	2.33	85	91.80	197.92	-106.12
Indirect (in inputs & transp.)	Z$						144.57	144.57	
Land rental equivalent	ha						90.00	150.00	-60.00
TRADABLES							448.45	611.45	-163.00
MEMO ITEMS:							737.58	900.58	-163.00
Tractor repair & maintenance	l	2.19	0.93	50%	2.55	85	186.15	216.40	-30.25
Tractor fuel & lubricants	l	0.60	0.80	100%	0.72	85	51.00	61.20	-10.20
Fertilizer (Comp.S 7-21-7)	mt	530.80	0.96	26%	575.81	0.250	132.70	143.95	-11.25
Seed	kg	1.61	1	100%	2.42	100	161.00	241.50	-80.50
Dual (herbicide)	l	35.75	0.85	90%	44.06	1.5	53.63	66.09	-12.47
Carbaryl (insecticide)	kg	17.05	0.85	90%	21.01	1.5	25.58	31.52	-5.95
Packing (bags and twine)	packs	0.26	0.85	90%	0.32	57	14.95	18.43	-3.48
Seed transport	mt	29.03	0.93	45%	33.07	0.10	2.90	3.31	-0.40
Product transport	mt	8.55	0.93	45%	9.74	2.30	19.67	22.40	-2.74
Fertilizer transport	mt	15.80	0.93	45%	18.00	0.90	14.22	16.20	-1.98
Lime	mt	42.00	1	10%	44.10	0.250	10.50	11.03	-0.53
Gypsum	mt	83.60	1	10%	87.78	0.400	33.44	35.11	-1.67
Fertilizer insurance	%ofVal	1.00%	1	10%	1.05%	177	1.77	1.85	-0.09
Product insurance	%ofVal	0.55%	1	10%	0.58%	1467	8.07	8.47	-0.40
GFU levy	%ofVal	1.50%	1	10%	1.58%	1467	22.01	23.11	-1.10

TABLE B.14
COTTON (K502)- LSC AREAS (HAND-HARVESTED DRYLAND)

						Mkt.Val.	Opp.Cost	Transfers
NPC	0.76		Returns to:					
EFC	0.42		Management		(Z$/ha)	25.99	1386.42	-1360.43
TPC	0.02		Total Var. Costs		(Z$/Z$)	2.6%	114.3%	-111.7%
PSE	-86%		Resource Cost Ratios:			0.97	0.43	0.55
SRP	-43%							

| | | MARKET | ITEM | FOR.EXCH. PREMIUM: 50% | OPP. | QTY. | | | |
| | | PRICES | CONVER. | x PERCENT | COSTS | PER | MARKET | OPP.COST | |
CATEGORY/Item	UNITS	($/unit)	FACTOR	TRADABLE	($/unit)	HA.	VALUE	VALUE	TRANSFERS
OUTPUT	mt	868.76				1.85	1607.21		
Export parity (1980s average)		1144.78	1	100%	1717.17	1.85		3176.77	-1569.56
LABOR							568.58	399.87	168.71
Basic (pre-harvest)	days	5.44	0.52		2.83	32.00	174.08	90.52	83.56
Tractor (driver & mechanic)	l	0.93	1		0.93	75.00	69.75	69.75	
Picking & packing	kg	0.094	0.52		0.05	1850	173.90	90.43	83.47
Insect scouting		3.50	0.52		1.82	1	3.50	1.82	1.68
Indirect (in inputs & transport)							147.35	147.35	
CAPITAL							426.27	639.98	-213.71
Seasonal loans on 50% of TVC	%of Z$	13.9%	1.08		23.0%	659.29	91.64	151.72	-60.07
Equipment depreciation	l	1.08	1.54	80%	2.33	75	81.00	174.64	-93.64
Indirect (in inputs & transp.)	Z$						163.63	163.63	
Land rental equivalent	ha						90.00	150.00	-60.00
TRADABLES							586.37	750.50	-164.13
MEMO ITEMS:							897.34	1061.48	-164.13
Tractor repair & maintenance	l	2.19	0.93	50%	2.55	75	164.25	190.94	-26.69
Tractor fuel & lubricants	l	0.60	0.80	100%	0.72	75	45.00	54.00	-9.00
Fertilizer (Comp. L 5-18-10)	mt	492.80	0.96	26%	534.59	0.300	147.84	160.38	-12.54
Ammonium Nitrate (34.5% N)	mt	415.40							
Import parity (1989 Urea equiv.)		357.92	1	100%	536.88	0.150	62.31	80.53	-18.22
Seed	kg	0.21	1	100%	0.32	33.5	7.04	10.55	-3.52
Calirus (seed treatment)	kg	105.67	0.85	90%	130.24	0.083	8.80	10.85	-2.05
Brassicol (seed treatment)	kg	19.20	0.85	90%	23.66	3.00	57.60	70.99	-13.39
Trifluralin (herbicide)	l	13.96	0.85	90%	17.21	1.6	22.34	27.53	-5.19
Cotoran (herbicide)	kg	30.01	0.85	90%	36.99	2.5	75.03	92.47	-17.44
Gramoxone (herbicide)	l	19.00	0.85	90%	23.42	1.0	19.00	23.42	-4.42
Bladex (herbicide)	l	15.96	0.85	90%	19.67	1.0	15.96	19.67	-3.71
Thiodan 35 (insecticide)	l	14.40	0.85	90%	17.75	1.43	20.53	25.31	-4.77
Carbaryl 85 (insecticide)	kg	16.72	0.85	90%	20.61	0.71	11.87	14.63	-2.76
Dimethoate 40 (insecticide)	l	13.94	0.85	90%	17.18	0.25	3.49	4.30	-0.81
Agrithin (insecticide)	l	74.85	0.85	90%	92.25	0.95	71.11	87.64	-16.53
Tedion (insecticide)	l	10.60	0.85	90%	13.06	2.40	25.44	31.35	-5.91
Molasses x 9 (wetting agent)	l	0.50	0.85	90%	0.62	2.50	1.25	1.54	-0.29
Cotton Packs (@5.57 packs/mt)	packs	0.50	0.85	90%	0.62	10.30	5.15	6.35	-1.20
Twine (@0,025 kg/pack)	kg	12.20	0.85	90%	15.04	0.26	3.14	3.87	-0.73
Seed transport	mt	29.03	0.933	45%	33.18	0.03	0.97	1.11	-0.14
Product transport	mt	8.55	0.933	45%	9.77	1.85	15.82	18.08	-2.26
Fertilizer transport	mt	15.80	0.933	45%	18.06	0.70	11.06	12.64	-1.58
Aerial spraying (@ 149 ha/hr)	ha	13.03	0.933	45%	14.89	4	52.12	59.57	-7.45
ULV spraying	ha	2.18	0.933	45%	2.49	5	10.90	12.46	-1.56
Lime	mt	42.00	1	10%	44.10	0.250	10.50	11.03	-0.53
Fertilizer insurance	%of Val	1%	1	10%	1%	232	2.32	2.43	-0.12
Product insurance	%of Val	0.25%	1	10%	0.26%	1607	4.02	4.22	-0.20
CFU levy	%of Val	1.4%	1	10%	1.5%	1607	22.50	23.63	-1.13

TABLE B.15
WHEAT-LSC AREAS (COMBINE-HARVESTED IRRIGATED)

							Mkt.Val.	Opp.Cost	Transfers
NPC	0.91		Returns to:						
EPC	0.56		Management		(Z$/ha)	135.66	947.17	-811.50	
TPC	0.14		Total Var. Costs		(Z$/Z$)	9.9%	56.0%	-46.1%	
PSE	-37%		Resource Cost Ratios:			0.91	0.65	0.26	
SRP	-22%								

CATEGORY/Item	UNITS	MARKET PRICES ($/unit)	ITEM CONVER. FACTOR	FOR.EXCH. PREMIUM: 50% x PERCENT TRADABLE	OPP. COSTS ($/unit)	QTY. PER HA.	MARKET VALUE	OPP.COST VALUE	TRANSFERS
OUTPUT	mt	398.24				5.50	2190.32		
Import parity (1980-88 average)		440.00	1	100%	660.00	5.50	2420.00	3630.00	-1439.68
LABOR							412.56	355.12	57.45
Basic	days	5.44	0.52		2.83	22.00	119.68	62.23	57.45
Tractor (driver & mechanic)	l	0.93	1		0.93	55	51.15	51.15	
Indirect (in inputs & transport)							241.73	241.73	
CAPITAL							965.09	1399.59	-434.49
Seasonal loans on 50% of TVC	%of2$	13.9%	1.08		23.0%	722.42	100.42	166.24	-65.83
Equipment depreciation	l	1.08	1.54	80%	2.33	55	59.40	128.07	-68.67
Indirect (in inputs & transp.)	Z$						355.28	355.28	
Land rental equivalent	ha						450.00	750.00	-300.00
TRADABLES							677.00	928.13	-251.13
MEMO ITEMS:							1274.01	1525.14	-251.13
Tractor repair & maintenance	l	2.19	0.93	50%	2.55	55	120.45	140.02	-19.57
Tractor fuel & lubricants	l	0.60	0.8	100%	0.72	55	33.00	39.60	-6.60
Fertilizer (Comp.D 8-14-7)	mt	416.60	0.96	26%	451.93	0.600	249.96	271.16	-21.20
Ammonium Nitrate (34.5% N)	mt	415.40							
Import parity (1989 Urea equiv.)		357.92	1	100%	536.88	0.400	143.17	214.75	-71.58
Seed-Purchased	kg	0.80	1	100%	1.20	90	72.27	108.41	-36.14
Seed-Retained	kg	0.39	1	100%	0.58	40	15.44	23.16	-7.72
Vitavax (seed treatment)	kg	46.47	0.85	90%	57.27	0.08	3.72	4.58	-0.86
Banvel (herbicide)	l	56.00	0.85	90%	69.02	0.25	14.00	17.26	-3.25
MCPA (herbicide)	l	8.69	0.85	90%	10.71	0.75	6.52	8.03	-1.52
Dimethoate (insecticide)	l	13.94	0.85	90%	17.18	0.25	3.49	4.30	-0.81
Metasystox (insecticide)	l	20.25	0.85	90%	24.96	0.40	8.10	9.98	-1.88
Aerial spraying (@149 ha/hr)	ho	13.91	0.93	45%	15.85	1	13.91	15.85	-1.94
Combine hire (@$115/ha+fuel)	ha	124.06	0.93	45%	141.34	1	124.06	141.34	-17.28
Irrigation elect. & mtce.	1000m3	54.73	0.93	45%	62.35	6.5	355.75	405.28	-49.54
Seed transport	mt	29.03	0.93	45%	33.07	0.13	3.77	4.30	-0.53
Product transport	mt	8.55	0.93	45%	9.74	5.50	47.03	53.57	-6.55
Fertilizer transport	mt	15.80	0.93	45%	18.00	0.85	13.43	15.30	-1.87
Lime	mt	42.00	1	10%	44.10	0.250	10.50	11.03	-0.53
Fertilizer insurance	%of Val	1%	1	10%	1%	260	2.60	2.73	-0.13
Product insurance	%of Val	1.075%	1	10%	1.129%	2190	23.55	24.72	-1.18
CFU levy	%of Val	0.425%	1	10%	0.446%	2190	9.31	9.77	-0.47

TABLE B.16
SOYBEANS-LSC AREAS (COMBINE-HARVESTED DRYLAND)

							Mkt.Val.	Opp.Cost	Transfers
NPC	0.72		Returns to:						
EFC	0.39		Management	(Z$/ha)			-47.80	813.33	-861.13
TPC	-0.06		Total Var. Costs	(Z$/Z$)			-6.5%	89.8%	-96.3%
PSE	-66%		Resource Cost Ratios:				1.08	0.48	0.59
SRP	-41%								

			FOR.EXCH. PREMIUM:					
		MARKET	ITEM	50%	OPP.	QTY.		
		PRICES	CONVER.	x PERCENT	COSTS	PER	MARKET	OPP.COST
CATEGORY/Item	UNITS	($/unit)	FACTOR	TRADABLE	($/unit)	HA.	VALUE	VALUE TRANSFERS
OUTPUT	mt	435.00				2.30	1000.50	
Export parity (1975-88 average)		607.00	1	100%	910.50	2.30	1396.10	2094.15 -1093.65
LABOR							290.76	233.31 57.45
Basic	days	5.44	0.52		2.83	22.00	119.68	62.23 57.45
Tractor (driver & mechanic)	l	0.93	1		0.93	50	46.50	46.50
Indirect (in inputs & transp.)	Z$						124.58	124.58
CAPITAL							366.95	527.89 -160.95
Seasonal loans on 50% of TVC	%ofZ$	13.9%	1.08		23.0%	422.77	58.76	97.29 -38.52
Equipment depreciation	l	1.08	1.54	80%	2.33	50	54.00	116.42 -62.42
Indirect (in inputs & transp.)	Z$						164.18	164.18
Land rental equivalent	ha						90.00	150.00 -60.00
TRADABLES							390.60	519.62 -129.02
MEMO ITEMS:							679.36	808.38 -129.02
Tractor repair & maintenance	l	2.19	0.93	50%	2.55	50	109.50	127.29 -17.79
Tractor fuel and lubricants	l	0.60	0.8	100%	0.72	50	30.00	36.00 -6.00
Fertilizer (Comp.D 8-14-7)	mt	416.60	0.96	26%	451.93	0.300	124.98	135.58 -10.60
Seed	kg	0.87	1	100%	1.31	90	78.30	117.45 -39.15
Innoculant	unit	1.50	0.85	90%	1.85	1	1.50	1.85 -0.35
Thiram (seed treatment)	kg	8.13	0.85	90%	10.02	0.2	1.63	2.00 -0.38
Dual 720 (herbicide)	l	30.17	0.85	90%	37.18	1.5	45.26	55.78 -10.52
Sencor (herbicide)	kg	78.73	0.85	90%	97.03	0.6	47.24	58.22 -10.98
Thiodan 35 (insecticide)	l	14.40	0.85	90%	17.75	1.0	14.40	17.75 -3.35
Packing (bags and twine)	packs	0.26	0.85	90%	0.32	25	6.58	8.11 -1.53
Aerial spraying (@149 ha/hr)	ha	13.91	0.93	45%	15.85	1	13.91	15.85 -1.94
Combine hire (@$130/ha+fuel)	ha	139.06	0.93	45%	158.42	1	139.06	158.42 -19.36
Drying (per % moisture removal)		1.78	0.93	45%	2.03	6	10.68	12.17 -1.49
Seed transport	mt	29.03	0.93	45%	33.07	0.09	2.61	2.98 -0.36
Product transport	mt	8.55	0.93	45%	9.74	2.30	19.67	22.40 -2.74
Fertilizer transport	mt	15.80	0.93	45%	18.00	0.55	8.69	9.90 -1.21
Lime	mt	42.00	1	10%	44.10	0.250	10.50	11.03 -0.53
Fertilizer insurance	%ofVal	1%	1	10%	1%	135	1.35	1.42 -0.07
Product insurance	%ofVal	0.35%	1	10%	0.37%	1000	3.50	3.68 -0.18
CFU levy	%ofVal	1%	1	10%	1%	1000	10.01	10.51 -0.50

Appendix C

Selected Tables

TABLE C.1
CROP FORECASTING COMMITTEE FINAL ESTIMATES OF AREAS AND YIELDS, 1987-1989 HARVEST YEARS (TONS PER HECTARE)

AREA PLANTED ('000 ha)	COMMUNAL 1987	'88	'89	LARGE-SCALE 1987	'88	'89	RESETTLEMENT 1987	'88	'89	SMALL-SCALE 1987	'88	'89	NATIONAL TOTAL 1987	'88	'89
Maize (White)	943	1036	920	110	88	80	121	114	110	37	35	38	1211	1273	1148
Maize (Yellow)					27	50								27	50
Sorghum	164	206	151	5	3	4	8	7	7	2	4	3	180	220	165
Pearl Millet	187	237	164	..			3	4	4	1	2	1	191	243	168
Finger Millet	109	120	116	..			7	7	8	3	4	3	120	131	127
Cotton	138	161	153	68	66	56	15	21	17	13	15	12	234	263	237
Groundnuts	177	197	160	5	6	6	10	11	13	10	12	12	202	225	191
Soybeans	2	4	5	55	60	65	1	1	1	..	..	..	59	64	71
Sunflower	73	81	102	6	6	5	2	8	9	6	7	8	87	102	124
Virginia Tobacco				64	59	58							64	59	58
Wheat (winter)				37	40	45							40	40	45

PRODUCTION ('000 mt)	COMMUNAL 1987	'88	'89	LARGE-SCALE 1987	'88	'89	RESETTLEMENT 1987	'88	'89	SMALL-SCALE 1987	'88	'89	NATIONAL TOTAL 1987	'88	'89
Maize (White)	518	1450	1062	440	438	403	109	159	126	26	60	61	1094	2107	1652
Maize (Yellow)					147	279								147	279
Sorghum	38	160	62	12	9	14	3	3	3	1	4	2	53	176	81
Pearl Millet	56	184	90	..			1	2	1	..	1	..	58	187	92
Finger Millet	40	84	44	..			3	4	4	1	3	2	44	91	50
Cotton	83	137	123	154	142	112	14	23	19	9	14	7	260	315	260
Groundnuts	55	106	72	16	18	17	3	5	6	4	6	6	79	135	101
Soybeans	1	3	5	94	117	121	..	..	..	..	..	..	95	120	126
Sunflower	20	47	46	3	7	6	1	6	5	2	5	4	26	65	61
Virginia Tobacco				128	120	130							128	120	130
Wheat (winter)				213	231	257							213	231	257

YIELDS (mt/ha)	COMMUNAL 1987	'88	'89	LARGE-SCALE 1987	'88	'89	RESETTLEMENT 1987	'88	'89	SMALL-SCALE 1987	'88	'89	NATIONAL TOTAL 1987	'88	'89
Maize (White)	0.55	1.40	1.15	4.00	4.97	5.04	0.90	1.40	1.15	0.70	1.70	1.60	0.90	1.66	1.44
Maize (Yellow)					5.43	5.58								5.43	5.58
Sorghum	0.23	0.78	0.41	2.34	3.00	3.24	0.31	0.50	0.43	0.38	0.90	0.69	0.29	0.80	0.49
Pearl Millet	0.30	0.78	0.55	0.51			0.33	0.50	0.40	0.20	0.59	0.26	0.30	0.77	0.54
Finger Millet	0.37	0.70	0.38	0.42			0.37	0.50	0.50	0.30	0.80	0.58	0.37	0.69	0.39
Cotton	0.60	0.85	0.80	2.27	2.14	2.01	0.90	1.10	1.14	0.70	0.90	0.55	1.11	1.20	1.10
Groundnuts	0.31	0.54	0.45	3.21	3.23	2.88	0.30	0.50	0.45	0.42	0.50	0.50	0.39	0.60	0.53
Soybeans	0.35	0.80	0.90	1.70	1.95	1.86	0.36	0.60	0.70	0.29	0.69	1.00	1.61	1.87	1.78
Sunflower	0.28	0.58	0.45	0.50	1.20	1.20	0.40	0.70	0.50	0.29	0.73	0.50	0.30	0.64	0.49
Virginia Tobacco				2.01	2.03	2.25							2.01	2.03	2.25
Wheat (winter)				5.76	5.78	5.70							5.76	5.78	5.70

Source: Calculated from CSO, Crop Forecasting Committee data.

TABLE C.2
EMPLOYMENT AND WAGES IN LARGE-SCALE COMMERCIAL AGRICULTURE AND IN THE WHOLE ECONOMY, 1954-1985

Year	EMPLOYMENT ('000s)			AVERAGE REAL WAGES ('000 1980 Z$)			AVE. AGRICULTURAL WAGES (% of national total)			AGRICULTURAL EMPLOYMENT (% of national total)			MEMO ITEM:
	Agric.	Nonag.	Total	Agric.	Nonag.	Total	Black	Nonblack	Total	Black	Nonblack	Total	C.P.I.
1954	221	396	617	0.37	1.24	0.93	75.0%	99.6%	39.8%	39.4%	4.8%	35.8%	32.4
1955	228	415	643	0.38	1.31	0.98	72.1%	104.5%	38.6%	39.2%	4.3%	35.5%	32.9
1956	231	444	675	0.39	1.33	1.01	70.0%	115.2%	38.3%	37.9%	4.1%	34.2%	34.3
1957	230	470	700	0.39	1.43	1.09	66.4%	88.0%	36.0%	36.5%	5.0%	32.9%	35.4
1958	234	480	714	0.39	1.50	1.13	65.2%	85.3%	34.6%	36.6%	4.7%	32.8%	36.6
1959	235	481	716	0.41	1.50	1.14	63.7%	106.8%	35.8%	36.6%	4.5%	32.8%	37.6
1960	244	485	729	0.41	1.52	1.15	63.1%	112.0%	35.7%	37.5%	4.5%	33.5%	38.5
1961	245	472	717	0.40	1.57	1.17	59.0%	111.3%	34.6%	38.4%	4.5%	34.2%	39.6
1962	248	457	705	0.40	1.65	1.21	55.9%	110.2%	33.2%	39.6%	4.5%	35.2%	40.5
1963	262	434	696	0.43	1.75	1.25	57.4%	93.3%	34.1%	42.3%	5.7%	37.6%	40.8
1964	300	436	736	0.41	1.73	1.19	52.1%	105.0%	34.2%	45.4%	6.8%	40.8%	42.9
1965	295	453	748	0.40	1.75	1.22	49.5%	126.3%	33.1%	44.1%	5.5%	39.4%	43.9
1966	278	457	735	0.39	1.75	1.24	48.0%	108.9%	31.3%	42.4%	5.5%	37.8%	45.3
1967	278	473	751	0.38	1.76	1.25	45.8%	94.4%	30.7%	41.3%	6.5%	37.0%	45.9
1968	288	502	790	0.37	1.78	1.27	44.1%	105.3%	29.1%	40.8%	5.2%	36.5%	47.0
1969	308	527	835	0.36	1.85	1.30	42.7%	86.1%	27.8%	41.1%	6.0%	36.9%	47.2
1970	298	556	854	0.37	1.89	1.36	41.6%	84.8%	27.3%	38.9%	5.8%	34.9%	48.2
1971	311	581	892	0.36	1.97	1.41	40.6%	78.3%	25.8%	39.0%	5.5%	34.9%	49.6
1972	342	611	953	0.36	2.04	1.44	39.8%	79.3%	25.0%	40.0%	5.3%	35.9%	51.1
1973	357	641	998	0.38	2.11	1.49	40.0%	84.0%	25.3%	39.8%	5.2%	35.0%	52.6
1974	366	675	1041	0.39	2.18	1.55	39.5%	85.8%	25.3%	39.0%	5.1%	35.2%	56.1
1975	364	691	1055	0.42	2.24	1.61	38.8%	94.6%	25.8%	38.3%	5.0%	34.5%	61.7
1976	356	683	1039	0.42	2.24	1.62	39.8%	89.0%	26.0%	38.1%	5.0%	34.3%	68.8
1977	348	670	1018	0.42	2.20	1.59	39.5%	88.5%	26.2%	38.0%	5.1%	34.2%	77.1
1978	341	645	986	0.42	2.22	1.60			26.0%			34.6%	84.6
1979	335	650	985	0.43	2.19	1.59			27.0%			34.0%	95.8
1980	327	683	1010	0.46	2.53	1.86			24.6%			32.4%	100.0
1981	294	743	1037	0.66	2.47	1.96			33.6%			28.4%	113.1
1982	274	772	1046	0.73	2.76	2.23			32.9%			26.2%	125.2
1983	264	770	1033	0.69	2.44	1.99			34.6%			25.5%	154.1
1984	271	765	1036	0.64	2.23	1.81			35.0%			26.2%	185.2
1985	275	787	1062										

Notes: Real wages are deflated by low-income CPI, 1980=100. 1985 employment data are through September only.
Source: Author's calculations, from CSO Quarterly and Monthly Digest of Statistics (various issues).

TABLE C.3
LONG-RUN ESTIMATES OF THE TOTAL LABOR FORCE AND EMPLOYMENT

CURRENT-TREND CASE (Nonfarm jobs grow at 2.3% annually)	CENSUS DATA 1982	PROJECTIONS										
		1990	2000	2010	2020	2030	2040	2050	2060	2080	2090	2100
Total workers (millions)	2.5	3.4	5.1	6.8	8.3	9.6	10.6	11.7	13.0	14.3	15.8	17.5
Farm workers (millions)	1.6	2.4	3.7	5.1	6.2	7.0	7.4	7.6	7.9	7.9	7.8	7.5
Nonfarm workers (millions)	0.9	1.1	1.4	1.7	2.1	2.7	3.4	4.2	5.3	6.7	8.4	10.5
Growth in total workers (%)	4.0%	4.0%	3.0%	2.0%	1.5%	1.0%	1.0%	1.0%	1.0%	1.0%	1.0%	1.0%
Growth in nonfarm jobs (%)	2.3%	2.3%	2.3%	2.3%	2.3%	2.3%	2.3%	2.3%	2.3%	2.3%	2.3%	2.3%
Growth in farm workers (%)	5.0%	4.8%	3.2%	1.9%	1.2%	0.5%	0.4%	0.3%	0.1%	-0.1%	-0.4%	-0.9%
Prop. of workers in agric.(%)	64%	69%	74%	76%	75%	73%	69%	65%	61%	55%	49%	43%

FAST-GROWTH CASE (Nonfarm jobs grow at 4% annually)	CENSUS DATA 1982	PROJECTIONS						
		1990	2000	2010	2020	2030	2040	2050
Total workers (millions)	2.5	3.4	5.1	6.8	8.3	9.6	10.6	11.7
Farm workers (millions)	1.6	2.4	3.5	4.5	4.9	4.7	3.7	2.2
Nonfarm workers (millions)	0.9	1.1	1.6	2.4	3.5	5.2	7.7	11.4
Growth in total workers (%)	4.0%	4.0%	3.0%	2.0%	1.5%	1.0%	1.0%	1.0%
Growth in nonfarm jobs (%)	2.3%	4.0%	4.0%	4.0%	4.0%	4.0%	4.0%	4.0%
Growth in farm workers (%)	5.0%	4.0%	2.5%	0.9%	-0.3%	-2.3%	-5.4%	-15.6%
Prop. of workers in agric.(%)	64%	69%	69%	66%	59%	49%	35%	18%

Sources: Projections for the future labor force are taken from CSO (1986) Population Projections of Zimbabwe: 1982 to 2032. Nonfarm job growth is assumed to be 4% for the optimistic case and 2.3% (actual growth rate of non-agricultural jobs between 1980 and 1985) for the current-trend case.

Actual census data are taken from CSO (1985), Main Demographic Features of the Population of Zimbabwe: An Advance Report Based on a Ten Percent Sample, and CSO, Monthly Bulletin of Statistics. Initial total labor force is the total population (7.5 m.), minus children under 15 (3.6 m.), minus students (0.4 m.), homemakers (0.8 m.), income recipients and other economically inactive (0.2 m.). Initial farm labor force includes communal farmers (1.1 million) plus unemployed (0.3 million) plus those employed on commercial farms (0.3 million).

TABLE C.4
ESTIMATED TOTAL PRODUCT MARKET SUBSIDIES AND MARKETING BOARD LOSSES, 1966-1989 (Z$ MILLIONS)

Fiscal Year Ending	Maize	Wheat	Sorgh.	Oils	G'nut	Soy	Other	Grains Total	Cotton	Beef	Dairy	Tobac.	Total (Curr. Z$)	Total (1980 Z$)	Memo Item: CPI	Tot. Gvt. Exp.	Subsidies as a % of Gvt.Exp.
1966	0.4		..					0.4			..	0.1	0.5	1.0	45.3	152	0.3%
1967		..	..					..		0.7	..		0.7	1.5	45.9	164	0.4%
1968	2.9	0.1					2.7	5.8		0.1	..	16.7	22.6	48.0	47.0	188	12.0%
1969		0.2						0.2			..	10.0	10.3	21.8	47.2	225	4.6%
1970		0.3		0.2				0.5	1.6		..	9.0	11.1	23.0	48.2	214	5.2%
1971	0.9	0.1		0.2				1.2			..	16.0	17.2	34.7	49.6	238	7.2%
1972		..		0.2				0.2			..	19.0	19.2	37.6	51.1	256	7.5%
1973				0.2				0.2			..	20.0	20.2	38.4	52.6	366	5.5%
1974											..	14.7	14.8	26.3	56.1	474	3.1%
1975							1.3	1.3			..	9.8	11.2	18.2	61.7	547	2.0%
1976	0.3	2.2					0.3	2.8	..		1.9	3.3	8.0	11.7	68.8	608	1.3%
1977	0.6	2.0				0.5	0.6	3.7	6.3		..	11.7	21.7	28.1	77.1	738	2.9%
1978	0.4	2.8					0.4	3.6	11.3		1.9	6.9	23.7	28.0	84.6	882	2.7%
1979	12.8	3.7				1.5		18.0	5.0	20.5	3.7		47.2	49.3	95.8	984	4.8%
1980	5.7	4.2				1.4		11.3	1.4	12.9	2.1		27.7	27.7	100.0	1226	2.3%
1981	24.1	5.6		4.8		1.9		36.4		9.6	4.5		50.5	44.7	113.1	1628	3.1%
1982	85.2	17.8	0.5	6.2	0.5		2.1	112.7	-0.9	50.9	18.3		181.0	144.6	125.2	2122	8.5%
1983	95.6	12.1	0.7		0.6		5.7	114.7	17.8	46.4	35.7		214.6	139.3	154.1	2936	7.3%
1984	45.0	10.2	1.9				3.6	60.7	-4.3	45.3	38.7		140.4	75.8	185.2	3053	4.6%
1985	64.7	4.4			0.2	-0.5	0.5	69.3	-56.8	45.8	44.0		102.3	50.9	200.9	3389	3.0%
1986	63.8	5.8	1.6		0.4		1.3	72.9	14.3	33.4	55.6		176.2	76.7	229.7	3875	4.5%
1987	57.3	14.3	5.4		0.6		-0.2	77.4	53.9	28.7	49.3		209.3	81.0	258.3	4574	4.6%
1988	58.5	2.9	2.4		0.8		-0.3	64.3	35.4	37.2	51.3		188.2	68.1	276.3	5390	3.5%
1989	12.9	27.5	1.8		0.8		-1.8	41.2	26.1	50.4	52.3		170.0	54.3	313.0	6351	2.7%

Notes: Data include payments to processors through the Ministry of Trade and Commerce as well as deficits of marketing parastatals and other payments made directly to producers. Subsidies on inputs (particularly credit, through AFC losses), losses of production parastatals (particularly ARDA/ADA), and public expenditures on infrastructure, research, extension, veterinary services, and drought relief programs are not included.
Source: Calculated from MLARR file data and Marketing Board annual reports. Fiscal years generally end June 30th.

TABLE C.5
CALCULATION OF NOMINAL PROTECTION COEFFICIENTS FOR SELECTED CROPS, 1966-1988 HARVEST YEARS
(Z$/MT UNLESS NOTED)

		Period averages				
		1966-69	1970-74	1975-79	1980-84	1985-88
M A I Z E						
Border price at depot	(a)		63.06	73.08	152.89	219.30
Domestic oper. costs	(b)	8.04	10.10	15.19	30.05	70.38
Trade parity at depot	(c=a-b)		52.70	57.89	140.53	148.92
Prod. price at depot	(d)	30.35	33.08	49.30	117.00	183.75
Selling price at depot	(e)	43.02	43.20	55.12	139.40	227.75
NPC - Producer	(d/c)		0.67	0.85	1.15	1.46
NPC - Consumer	(e/c)		0.90	0.96	1.36	1.81
C O T T O N (cents/kg)						
Lint export price (fob)	(a)	46.47	66.62	109.85	173.42	238.10
Export costs	(b)	3.27	3.94	9.96	18.39	31.83
Lint exp. price at dep.	(c=a-b)	43.20	62.68	99.89	155.03	206.27
Seed cotton equiv.	(d=c*.35)	15.12	21.94	34.96	54.26	72.19
Domestic oper. costs	(e)	11.88	4.83	5.08	11.93	13.78
Lint parity at depot	(f=d-e)	3.25	17.11	29.89	42.33	58.41
Seed revenue at depot	(g)	3.77	4.36	5.75	11.12	20.14
Crop parity at depot	(h=f+g)	7.01	21.46	35.64	53.45	78.55
Prod. price at depot	(i)	15.27	20.88	32.93	47.50	76.75
Dom. Selling price-lint	(j)	43.33	68.15	97.42	129.09	164.83
NPC-Prod. (seed cotton)	(i/h)	2.53	1.16	0.92	0.93	1.00
NPC-Cons. (cotton lint)	(j/c)	1.07	1.09	0.97	0.86	0.82
G R O U N D N U T S (S H E L L E D)						
Border price at depot	(a)		229.38	438.74	722.96	1053.94
Domestic oper. costs	(b)		6.58	20.93	85.56	197.61
Trade parity at depot	(c=a-b)		222.80	417.81	637.40	856.32
Prod. price at depot	(d)	122.63	170.24	292.75	442.00	850.00
Selling price at depot	(e)	76.46	112.72	245.80	394.00	822.48
NPC - Producer	(d/c)		0.94	0.70	0.71	1.02
NPC - Consumer	(e/c)		0.62	0.59	0.63	0.99
S O R G H U M (R E D)						
Border price at depot	(a)		58.59	76.09	117.90	203.67
Domestic oper. costs	(b)	7.59	10.28	14.67	30.72	133.63
Trade parity at depot	(c=a-b)		47.63	61.42	92.86	70.04
Prod. price at depot	(d)	33.06	40.24	66.31	119.00	147.50
Selling price at depot	(e)		54.92	77.21	132.60	247.62
NPC - Producer	(d/c)		1.02	1.28	1.19	2.58
NPC - Consumer	(e/c)		1.33	1.53	1.26	4.68
W H E A T						
Border price at depot	(a)		86.38	117.29	219.82	343.79
Domestic oper. costs	(b)		12.18	13.80	24.65	59.70
Trade parity at depot	(c=a-b)		74.20	103.49	195.17	284.09
Prod. price at depot	(d)	70.80	73.00	115.80	192.00	320.00
Selling price at depot	(e)		78.00	105.39	196.80	383.20
NPC - Producer	(d/c)		0.98	1.12	0.98	1.13
NPC - Consumer	(e/c)		1.05	1.02	1.01	1.35
S O Y B E A N S						
Border price at depot	(a)		135.83	155.29	216.57	754.43
Domestic oper. costs	(b)	8.33	23.16	16.78	32.11	52.21
Trade parity at depot	(c=a-b)		104.04	138.51	190.52	698.48
Prod. price at depot	(d)	83.88	86.44	124.06	215.40	366.25
Selling price at depot	(e)	90.20	79.58	110.95	230.00	433.09
NPC - Producer	(d/c)		0.97	0.91	0.94	0.58
NPC - Consumer	(e/c)		0.93	0.83	0.95	0.69
B E E F (cents/kg)						
Border price at depot	(a)	37.75	44.60	47.80	90.20	506.33
Domestic oper costs	(b)	5.41	5.35	12.42	46.32	102.93
Trade parity at depot	(c=a-b)	32.59	39.25	35.38	43.88	403.40
Prod. price at depot	(d)	35.41	43.71	60.32	118.34	189.84
Selling price at depot	(e)	32.59	36.35	50.10	103.94	180.13
NPC - Producer	(d/c)	1.10	1.14	1.79	2.76	0.72
NPC - Consumer	(e/c)	1.02	0.97	1.50	2.39	0.72
T O B A C C O (flue-cured, cents/kg)						
Producer price (Harare auction)		47.35	54.19	78.42	165.14	298.32

Source: Adapted from data in Takavarasha and Rukovo (forthcoming), from GMB, CMB and TMB files.
Notes: Producer and selling prices are for Grade A, except soybeans which are Grade B. Border and domestic prices are average realizations (unit values). Trading costs are deducted from export revenues, added to import costs. Border prices are generally cif or fob Harare. Domestic operating costs include all inter-depot transport and storage costs, including interest. Sorghum is both red and white, although red sorghum dominates GMB intake and sales. For 1988 and 1989, prices given are for red sorghum only. White sorghum producer prices were kept equal to maize.

TABLE C.6
LSC AND CA LAND USE INTENSITY BY NATURAL REGION, 1989 HARVEST YEAR

		i	ii	iii	iv	v	National
Total land	('000 ha)	700	6,160	7,200	14,550	10,450	39,060
LSC land area	('000 ha)	202	3,687	2,405	2,429	2,490	11,213
CSO estimates:							
No. of farms	no.	117	2,664	954	731	194	4,660
Average farm size	(ha/farm)	1,726	1,384	2,521	3,323	12,835	2,406
Cropped area	('000 ha)	12	379	48	9	52	501
Cropped area/farm	(ha/farm)	100	142	51	12	270	107
Cropped area/total area	(%)	6%	10%	2%	0%	2%	4%
CA land area	('000 ha)	95	1,477	2,808	7,691	4,345	16,416
CSO estimates:							
No. of farms (est.)	(no.)	12,250	111,750	135,125	268,000	123,375	650,500
Average farm size	(ha/farm)	8	13	21	29	35	25
Agritex estimates:							
Cropped area	('000 ha)	22	529	508	1,703	398	3,160
Cropped area/farm	(ha/farm)	2	5	4	6	3	5
Cropped area/total area	(%)	23%	36%	18%	22%	9%	19%
Revised estimate (CSO & MLARR data):							
Cropped area/total area	(%)	41%	24%	17%	13%	11%	14%
Memo items:							
LSC irrigated area	('000 ha)	7	99	16	5	51	179
LSC irrig. area/crop area	(%)	63%	26%	32%	57%	98%	36%
CA population	(est. '000s)	98	894	1081	2144	987	5,204
CA fallow area	('000 ha)	4	216	160	517	155	1,051
CA cropped+fallow	('000 ha)	25	745	668	2,220	554	4,212
Fallow (% of cropped+fallow)		14%	29%	24%	23%	28%	25%

Sources and notes: LSC data are calculated from FAO/Harare (1990), based on CSO files.
CA data are calculated from Masters (1990) based on CSO and Agritex estimates. Numbers
of CA farms are based on 1989 population estimates, at an average of 8 residents per
farming unit (Chapter 6, Table 6.1 from MLARR 1990 data). CA cropped area is based
on the Agritex Grid Point Survey, and are averages for the 1986-1989 harvest years.
These are likely to somewhat overestimate cropped land, as suggested by the overly-high
estimate of cropped land per farm in regions ii and iv. The revised CA estimate is
based on CSO population figures, converted to farming units at 8 residents per unit,
and applying MLARR (1990) cropping rates of 3.2 ha/farm in NRs I and II, 3.5 ha/farm in
NR III, and 3.7 ha/farm in NRs IV and V. The resulting national estimate of 14% planted
is still somewhat higher than the CSO crop forecasting committee estimate of 11%, which
is probably an underestimate.

TABLE C.7
REAL GOVERNMENT EXPENDITURE ON AGRICULTURE, 1966-1967 TO 1988-1989 FISCAL YEARS
(1980 Z$ '000S, DEFLATED BY LOW-INCOME CPI)

Fiscal Year Ending	Total Govt. Expen.	Total Expen. on Ag.	Of which:				Expen. on Agric. / Tot. Exp. (%)	Expen./Total Agric. Exp. (%)				MEMO ITEM:
			Research	Extension	Veterinary Services	Admin.+ Subsidies		Rsrch.	Exten.	Vet.	Other	CPI
1967	160,674	15,417	1,678	3,071	2,109	8,559	10%	10.9%	19.9%	13.7%	55.5%	46
1968	178,756	70,400	1,916	3,288	2,148	63,048	39%	2.7%	4.7%	3.1%	89.6%	47
1969	398,309	75,855	4,363	7,132	1,721	59,639	19%	5.8%	9.4%	6.2%	78.6%	47
1970	419,058	65,451	4,697	3,688	4,855	52,210	16%	7.2%	5.6%	7.4%	79.8%	48
1971	430,803	98,812	5,111	3,741	5,008	84,951	23%	5.2%	3.8%	5.1%	86.0%	50
1972	492,012	98,627	5,477	4,078	5,471	83,600	20%	5.6%	4.1%	5.5%	84.8%	51
1973	530,927	103,296	6,178	4,062	6,435	86,621	19%	6.0%	3.9%	6.2%	83.9%	53
1974	622,182	117,279	5,942	3,884	6,798	100,656	19%	5.1%	3.3%	5.8%	85.8%	56
1975	672,222	68,242	6,297	4,007	6,014	51,924	10%	9.2%	5.9%	8.8%	76.1%	62
1976	662,781	39,193	6,138	3,934	6,671	22,451	6%	15.7%	10.0%	17.0%	57.3%	69
1977	766,383	62,887	5,895	3,762	7,304	45,927	8%	9.4%	6.0%	11.6%	73.0%	77
1978	880,452	124,734	5,491	3,476	5,102	110,665	14%	4.4%	2.8%	4.1%	88.7%	85
1979	898,013	112,288	5,559	3,494	5,899	97,335	13%	5.0%	3.1%	5.3%	86.7%	96
1980	1,027,229	89,851	5,930	3,734	6,082	74,105	9%	6.6%	4.2%	6.8%	82.5%	100
1981	1,062,990	77,850	7,045	3,610	7,763	59,431	7%	9.0%	4.6%	10.0%	76.3%	113
1982	1,254,971	101,468	7,197	7,958	13,719	72,593	8%	7.1%	7.8%	13.5%	71.5%	125
1983	1,305,679	129,336	5,159	9,655	12,259	102,263	10%	4.0%	7.5%	9.5%	79.1%	154
1984	1,313,163	168,687	4,949	9,132	11,480	143,126	13%	2.9%	5.4%	6.8%	84.8%	185
1985	1,314,714	189,978	5,343	10,260	12,190	162,185	14%	2.8%	5.4%	6.4%	85.4%	201
1986	1,361,133	180,280	6,035	11,330	12,061	150,853	13%	3.3%	6.3%	6.7%	83.7%	230
1987	1,479,716	183,446	5,780	11,576	13,010	153,080	12%	3.2%	6.3%	7.1%	83.4%	258
1988	1,277,889	206,644	5,867	12,037	12,974	175,767	16%	2.8%	5.8%	6.3%	85.1%	277
1989	1,416,246	164,607	6,331	12,348	13,569	132,359	12%	3.8%	7.5%	8.2%	80.4%	313

Source: Calculated from CSO, Quarterly Digest of Statistics (1966-1987 data) and MLARR file data (1988-1989).

TABLE C.8
CROPPED AREA AND INPUT USE ESTIMATES, 1956-1990 HARVEST YEARS

HARVEST YEAR	CROP AREA ('000 ha) LSC	CA	FERTILIZER USE ('000 mt) LSC	Small-holder	Of which: CA	RA	SSC	Hybrid Maize Seed (Smhldr.)	FERTILIZER USE (mt/ha) LSC	CA
1956	343		91						0.27	
1957	335		102						0.30	
1958	345		104						0.30	
1959	367		117						0.33	
1960	378		120						0.32	
1961	417		134						0.32	
1962	406		143						0.35	
1963	399		145						0.36	
1964	431		170						0.40	
1965	448	937	182						0.41	
1966	491	1265	192						0.39	
1967	474	1477	214						0.45	
1968	536	1173	203						0.38	
1969	555	1467	236						0.43	
1970	547	1331	236						0.43	
1971	553	1404	288						0.52	
1972	595	1415	313						0.53	
1973	605	1147	381						0.63	
1974	614	1394	380						0.62	
1975	591	1856	425	24				2.35	0.72	0.013
1976	566	1931	315	19				3.95	0.56	0.010
1977	575	1673	342	20				2.70	0.59	0.012
1978	564	1393	359	25				3.70	0.64	0.018
1979	542	1330	332	25				4.25	0.61	0.019
1980	575	1650	328	27				4.30	0.57	0.016
1981	547	1879	366	90				10.60	0.71	0.048
1982	538	1911	436	96				15.10	0.81	0.050
1983	500	1895	365	98				18.20	0.73	0.052
1984	480	1856	357	106				18.30	0.74	0.057
1985	483	1797	274	128				18.90	0.57	0.071
1986	495	1818	382	124				24.60	0.77	0.068
1987	431	1718	338	124	80	33	12	21.40	0.78	0.072
1988	443	1957	311	111	75	24	12	22.70	0.70	0.057
1989		1664	349	110	73	23	14	25.30		0.066
1990			348	111	76	22	13			

Sources: Cropped area estimates are calculated from Muir-Leresche (1984), Weinmann (1972, 1975), and CSO file data. Fertilizer and seed use estimates are calculated from Rohrbach (1988) and file data from ZFC and Seed Coop.

TABLE C.9
FERTILIZER PRICES, SMALLHOLDER CREDIT, AND SMALLHOLDER FERTILIZER USE, 1976-1990

Hvst. Year	Fert. Price (Z$/mt)	Maize Price (Z$/mt)	Fert./ Maize Ratio	Smallholder Fertilizer Use (mmt)	Value (Z$m.)	Smallholder AFC Lending (Z$ m.)	Of which: CA	SSC	RA
1976	109.4	48	2.3	0.02	2.1				
1977	107.9	52	2.1	0.02	2.2				
1978	117.7	53	2.2	0.03	2.9				
1979	126.5	61	2.1	0.03	3.2				
1980	134.9	85	1.6	0.03	3.6	1.7		1.7	
1981	161.1	120	1.3	0.09	14.5	7.9	4.2	3.7	
1982	177.6	120	1.5	0.10	17.0	15.2	10.1	4.6	0.5
1983	198.1	120	1.7	0.10	19.4	19.2	13.2	4.5	1.5
1984	198.1	140	1.4	0.11	21.0	42.1	23.4	8.1	10.6
1985	339.1	180	1.9	0.13	43.4	51.4	32.0	8.7	10.7
1986	380.8	180	2.1	0.12	47.2	58.9	38.9	11.5	8.5
1987	380.8	180	2.1	0.12	47.3	78.2	60.0	9.6	8.6
1988	416.0	195	2.1	0.11	46.3	63.0	49.4	6.8	6.8
1989	416.0	215	1.9	0.11	45.7	52.5	41.3	5.3	5.9
1990	447.2	225	2.0	0.11	49.6				

Notes: The price of fertilizer is for a blend of half Compound D (8-14-7) and
Ammonium Nitrate (34.5% N). The maize price is for Grade A.
Sources: Calculated from ZFC, GMB and AFC file data.

TABLE C.10
CALCULATION OF SMALLHOLDER AND LSC PRODUCER PRICE INDEXES FOR MAJOR CONTROLLED CROPS, 1966-1989

| | AVERAGE PRICE PAID BY MARKETING BOARD (Z$/mt) | | | | | | PRODUCER PRICE INDEX (1980=100) | | | | | | Memo: Low-income CPI |
| | | | | | | | CURRENT Z$ | | | DEFLATED BY CPI | | | |
Harvest Year	Maize	Cotton	Wheat	Soy-beans	G'nuts (Unsh.)	Sorgh.	Small	LSC	Nat'l.	Small	LSC	Nat'l.	
1966	32.3	137.5	65.9	nc	110.3	34.4	37.5	39.3	38.6	82.8	86.7	85.1	45.3
1967	32.6	150.0	74.1	nc	116.4	31.2	40.4	42.3	41.5	87.9	92.1	90.4	45.9
1968	34.8	152.5	74.1	81.6	134.8	30.6	41.5	43.6	42.7	88.2	92.8	90.9	47.0
1969	33.6	142.5	69.1	86.3	134.8	33.5	39.1	41.7	40.6	82.8	88.2	86.0	47.2
1970	39.2	147.5	72.3	85.7	134.8	34.5	41.4	43.9	42.9	85.8	91.2	89.0	48.2
1971	34.3	157.5	72.4	87.8	134.8	40.2	42.4	44.4	43.6	85.6	89.6	88.0	49.6
1972	29.6	167.5	71.3	76.8	158.6	44.0	43.7	44.5	44.1	85.5	87.0	86.4	51.1
1973	39.7	242.5	63.1	113.5	188.6	44.2	61.8	59.2	60.3	117.5	112.5	114.5	52.6
1974	39.3	262.5	77.3	124.1	259.0	38.4	66.6	64.8	65.5	118.6	115.6	116.8	56.1
1975	41.6	217.5	109.4	103.2	219.0	40.6	57.6	60.3	59.2	93.4	97.8	96.0	61.7
1976	47.3	315.0	120.1	102.9	254.0	50.9	79.7	77.3	78.3	115.9	112.4	113.8	68.8
1977	51.7	312.5	121.4	129.7	295.0	68.8	80.6	80.2	80.3	104.5	104.0	104.2	77.1
1978	52.0	305.0	108.1	139.5	278.0	69.6	78.8	78.2	78.4	93.1	92.4	92.7	84.6
1979	60.3	343.5	114.6	146.3	360.0	75.7	89.4	87.8	88.4	93.3	91.6	92.3	95.8
1980	89.0	362.8	134.7	159.6	362.0	97.8	100.0	100.0	100.0	100.0	100.0	100.0	100.0
1981	119.1	380.0	173.4	169.5	398.5	104.7	110.8	114.2	112.8	98.0	101.0	99.7	113.1
1982	119.6	497.0	186.8	199.1	426.2	105.2	135.9	134.5	135.1	108.5	107.4	107.9	125.2
1983	119.6	493.0	219.7	256.9	451.7	109.0	135.6	140.6	138.5	88.0	91.2	89.9	154.1
1984	152.1	550.0	249.0	285.9	506.9	133.5	155.4	161.6	159.1	83.9	87.2	85.9	185.2
1985	178.9	646.0	283.7	319.0	706.3	171.8	183.3	189.7	187.1	91.3	94.4	93.1	200.9
1986	177.9	722.0	298.8	336.4	673.0	173.1	199.0	202.4	201.0	86.6	88.1	87.5	229.7
1987	179.4	740.0	329.3	382.9	931.0	145.5	205.2	214.0	210.4	79.4	82.9	81.5	258.3
1988	193.2	788.0	362.1	416.4	986.0	156.8	219.1	229.9	225.5	79.3	83.2	81.6	276.3
1989	213.0	857.5	396.8	431.3	986.0	217.1	238.6	249.1	244.8	76.2	79.6	78.2	313.0

Notes: Prior to 1968 soybeans were not controlled; the index for those years is calculated without soybeans, and linked to later years. Crop weights are based on 1981-88 shares of total formal market value for the crops listed:

	Maize	Cotton	Wheat	Soybn.	G'nut	Sorgh.
Smallholder	48.4%	46.8%	2.2%	0.2%	1.6%	0.8%
LSC	42.1%	26.6%	17.9%	9.8%	2.4%	1.2%
National	44.4%	33.9%	12.2%	6.3%	2.1%	1.1%

Source: Calculated from data in Muir-Leresche (1984) for 1980 and earlier, and GMB and CMB Annual Reports for 1981 and later.

Appendix D

Chronology of Historical Events

13th-14th Century: Shona-speaking kingdom builds Great Zimbabwe, which is preceded and succeeded by a series of other states.

Mid-19th Century: After the Mfecane migration from South Africa, totalling about 20,000 people, Ndebele-speaking states are established in Southwestern Zimbabwe (see Beach 1984, p. 6). Shona-speaking states in the North and Northeast total about 500,000 people (see Mosley 1983, p. 72; and Beach 1984, p. 44). Small numbers of white traders, mineral prospectors, and missionaries settle in Zimbabwe under individual agreements with local leaders.

1889: The British South Africa Company (BSAC) receives a Royal Charter to administer the territory, sanctioned by the disputed Rudd Concession of 1898 between agents of Cecil Rhodes and Lobengula, the Ndebele leader.

1890: The BSAC Pioneer Column invades Zimbabwe, founding Fort Salisbury (now Harare). Territory is administered directly by the BSAC, under a partly elected legislative council. Land Commission supervises the alienation of land to individual settlers and companies; by 1899 title to 6.3 million hectares is granted.

1894: BSAC Order-in-Council initiates creation of Native Reserves, with boundaries to be specified by local BSAC Native Commissioners.

1896–1897: The first Chimurenga (liberation war), in which Ndebele and Shona military resistance is crushed by the BSA Police.

1902: Railway is completed linking Zimbabwe with South Africa (via Bulawayo and Gaborone) and the sea (via Mutare to the port of Beira).

1903: Rhodesian Native Labour Board is founded, to recruit workers from Mozambique and Malawi on temporary contracts.

1904: Settler population estimated at 12,000.

1911: Settler population estimated at 24,000.

1914: Native Reserves Commission finalizes reserves boundaries; total area is 8.6 million hectares. BSAC Charter expires; settler population votes to renew the charter for ten years.

1922: Settler population votes to establish self-government as a British colony, rather than unite with South Africa.

1925: Land Commission under Sir Morris Carter recommends creation of African Purchase Areas to supplement reserves.

1930: Land Apportionment Act officially establishes racial segregation in land tenure, with 50.8% of land reserved for freehold ownership by whites (some of which as yet unassigned), 22.4% in Native Reserves, 7.8% in African Purchase Areas, and 19% in Forest and Crown Lands.

1931: Maize Control Act introduces government monopoly on urban and export maize sales, to raise local prices above export levels. Local-market quotas are allocated preferentially to white farmers.

1934: Industrial Conciliation Act and subsequent amendments strengthens whites-only unions against African competition.

1936: Native Registration Act reduces African mobility and job search opportunities.

1948: Land Commission under the Hon. Max Danzinger proposes reallocation of some unassigned land to supplement the Reserves as Special Native Areas.

1950: Land Apportionment Act is amended to include some Special Native Areas; boundaries are revised again repeatedly.

1951: Land Husbandry Act attempts to restrict grazing rights and enforce soil conservation measures in Native Reserves; after popular opposition the Act is suspended in 1960.

1953–1963: Federation of Rhodesia and Nyasaland unites Southern Rhodesia (Zimbabwe) with Northern Rhodesia (Zambia) and Nyasaland (Malawi).

1963: Federation breaks up as Zambia and Malawi become independent; Rhodesian Front is elected to power.

1965: Rhodesian Front government makes Unilateral Declaration of Independence (UDI) from Britain; UN-mandated trade sanctions are imposed in response. The economy stalls, then grows sharply with 7.6% annual growth in real income between 1967 and 1974, then stalls again, falling almost to pre-UDI levels.

1966: First military contact between Nationalist forces and the Rhodesian army; the second Chimurenga begins.

1969: Land Tenure Act replaces Land Apportionment Act, renaming some categories and redrawing some boundaries; the resulting distribution of land is 40% European freehold, 41% Tribal Trust Lands, 3.8% African Purchase Areas, and 14.8% National Parks, forests, and game reserves.

1978: Internal settlement between the Rhodesian Front and several Nationalist leaders fails to end the war.

1979: British-sponsored Lancaster House Conference ends in cease-fire and British-supervised elections.

1980: (18 April) Independence; Mugabe government is installed. Major initiatives include minimum wage legislation and a large resettlement program onto previously white-owned lands.

Appendix E

Maps

Map 1. Natural Regions and Survey Sites

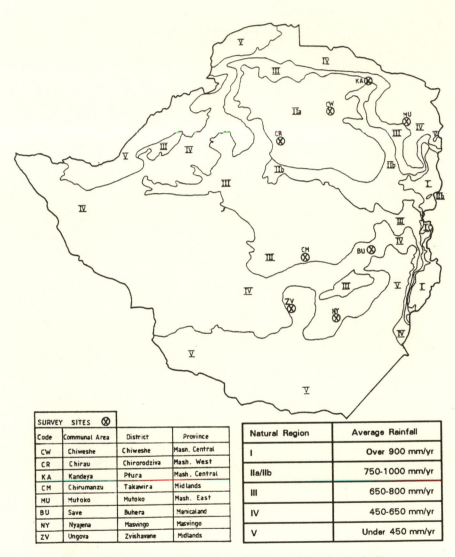

SURVEY SITES ⊗			
Code	Communal Area	District	Province
CW	Chiweshe	Chiweshe	Masn. Central
CR	Chirau	Chirorodziva	Mash. West
KA	Kandeya	Pfura	Mash. Central
CM	Chirumanzu	Takawira	Midlands
MU	Mutoko	Mutoko	Mash. East
BU	Save	Buhera	Manicaland
NY	Nyajena	Masvingo	Masvingo
ZV	Ungova	Zvishavane	Midlands

Natural Region	Average Rainfall
I	Over 900 mm/yr
IIa/IIb	750-1000 mm/yr
III	650-800 mm/yr
IV	450-650 mm/yr
V	Under 450 mm/yr

Source: Government of Zimbabwe, Ministry of Lands, Agriculture
and Rural Resettlement, Cartographic Section

Map 2. Main Roads and Land Tenure Classification

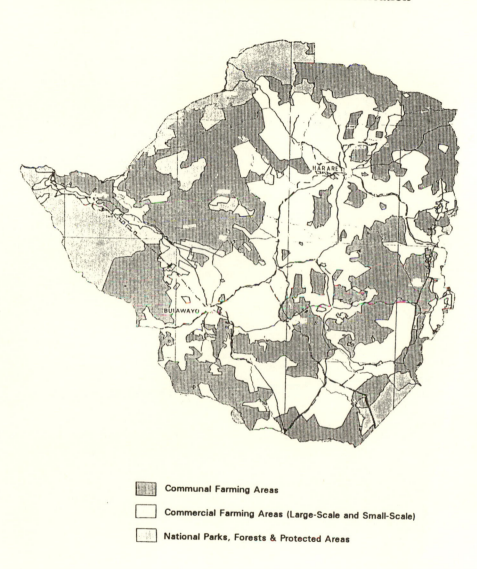

▨ Communal Farming Areas

☐ Commercial Farming Areas (Large-Scale and Small-Scale)

▨ National Parks, Forests & Protected Areas

Source: Government of Zimbabwe, Department of the Surveyor-General

References

GENERAL WORKS

Ahmed, R., and N. Rustagi. (1987). "Marketing and Price Incentives in African and Asian Countries: A Comparison," in D. Elz, ed., *Agricultural Marketing Strategy and Pricing Policy*. Washington, DC: World Bank.

Balassa, Bela. (1964). "The Purchasing Power Parity Doctrine: A Reappraisal." *Journal of Political Economy* 72(6): 584-596.

_____. (1965). "Tariff Protection in Industrial Countries: An Evaluation." *Journal of Political Economy* 73(6): 573-594.

Balassa, Bela and Associates. (1971). *The Structure of Protection in Developing Countries*. Baltimore: Johns Hopkins University Press.

Bale, M. D., and E. Lutz. (1981). "Price Distortions in Agriculture: An International Comparison." *American Journal of Agricultural Economics* 63(1): 8-22.

Barber, C. L. (1955). "Canadian Tariff Policy." *Canadian Journal of Economics and Political Science* 21: 513-530.

Bates, Robert H. (1981). *Markets and States in Tropical Africa*. Cambridge: Cambridge University Press.

Berry, R. Albert, and William R. Cline. (1979). *Agrarian Structure and Productivity in Developing Countries*. Baltimore: Johns Hopkins University Press.

Bhagwati, Jagdish. (1978). *The Anatomy and Consequences of Exchange Control Regimes*. Cambridge, MA: Ballinger.

Bhagwati, Jagdish, and T. N. Srinivasan. (1973). "The General Equilibrium Theory of Effective Protection and Resource Allocation." *Journal of International Economics* 3(3): 259-282.

Bhagwati, Jagdish, and H. Wan, Jr. (1979). "The 'Stationarity' of Shadow Prices of Factors in Project Evaluation." *American Economic Review* 69(3): 261-273.

Binswanger, Hans P., and Miranda Elgin. (1989). "What Are the Prospects for Land Reform?" In Allen Maunder and Alberto Valdes, eds., *Agriculture in an Interdependent World*. Proceedings of the 20th International Conference of Agricultural Economics, Buenos Aires. Oxford: Queen Elizabeth House.

Birkhaeuser, Dean, Robert E. Evenson, and Gershon Feder. (1989). "The Economic Impact of Agricultural Extension: A Review." Discussion Paper No. 567. New Haven: Economic Growth Center, Yale University.

Braverman, A., J. S. Hammer, and A. Gron. (1987). "Multimarket Analysis of Agricultural Price Policies in an Operational Context: The Case of Cyprus." *World Bank Economic Review* 1(2): 337-356.

Brown, M. L. (1979). *Farm Budgets: From Farm Income Analysis to Agricultural Project Analysis*. Baltimore, MD: Johns Hopkins University Press.

Bruno, Michael. (1972). "Domestic Resource Cost and Effective Protection: Clarification and Synthesis." *Journal of Political Economy* 80(1): 16-33.

_____. (1976). "The Two-Sector Open Economy and the Real Exchange Rate." *American Economic Review* 66(4): 566-577.

Byerlee, Derek. (1989). "Bread and Butter Issues in Ecuadorean Food Policy: A Comparative Advantage Approach." *World Development* 17(10): 1585-96.

Chenery, Hollis B. (1961). "Comparative Advantage and Development Policy." *American Economic Review* 51(1): 18-51.

Clarete, Ramon L., and John Whalley. (1988). "Interactions between Trade Policies and Domestic Distortions in a Small, Open Developing Country." *Journal of International Economics* 24: 345-358.

Clay, Edward, and Charlotte Benson. (1990). "Aid for Food: Acquisition of Commodities in Developing Countries for Food Aid in the 1980s." *Food Policy* 15(1): 27-43.

Coes, Donald V. (1989). "Real Exchange Rates: Definition, Measurement and Trends in France, West Germany, Italy and the United Kingdom." In Donald R. Hodgman and Geoffrey E. Wood, eds., *Macroeconomic Policy and Economic Interdependence*. London: Macmillan.

Corden, W. Max. (1960). "The Geometric Representation of Policies to Attain Internal and External Balance." *Review of Economic Studies* 28: 1-22.

_____. (1966). "The Structure of a Tariff System and the Effective Protection Rate." *Journal of Political Economy* 74: 221-237.

_____. (1971). *The Theory of Protection*. Oxford: Clarendon.

_____. (1974). *Trade Policy and Economic Welfare*. Oxford: Clarendon.

_____. (1984a). "Booming Sector and Dutch Disease Economics: Survey and Consolidation." *Oxford Economic Papers*, New Series 36(3): 359-380.

_____. (1984b). "The Normative Theory of International Trade." In Ronald W. Jones and Peter B. Kenen, eds., *Handbook of International Economics, vol. 1*. Amsterdam: Elsevier.

Dasgupta, Partha. (1972). "A Comparative Analysis of the UNIDO *Guidelines* and the OECD *Manual*." *Bulletin of the Oxford University Institute of Economics and Statistics* 34(1): 33-52.

Dasgupta, Partha, Stephen Marglin, and Amartya Sen. (1972). *UNIDO Guidelines for Project Evaluations*. New York: United Nations.

Delgado, Christopher L., and John W. Mellor. (1984). "A Structural View of Policy Issues in African Agricultural Development." *American Journal of Agricultural Economics* 66(5): 665-670.

Dervis, Kemal, Jaime de Melo, and Sherman Robinson. (1982). *General Equilibrium Models for Development Policy.* Cambridge: Cambridge University Press.

Devarajan, S., J. D. Lewis, and S. Robinson. (1986). "A Bibliography of Computable General Equilibrium Models Applied to Developing Countries." Working Paper No. 400. Berkeley, CA: Giannini Foundation of Agricultural Economics.

Dornbusch, Rudiger. (1974). "Tariffs and Non-traded Goods." *Journal of International Economics* 4: 177-85.

Echevarria, Ruben G. (1990). *Methods for Diagnosing Research System Constraints and Assessing the Impact of Agricultural Research.* Vol. II, "Assessing the Impact of Agricultural Research." The Hague: ISNAR.

Edwards, Sebastian. (1989). *Real Exchange Rates, Devaluation and Adjustment: Exchange Rate Policy in Developing Countries.* Cambridge, MA: MIT Press.

Eicher, Carl K. (1984). "International Technology Transfer and the African Farmer: Theory and Practice." Working Paper No. 3/84. Harare: University of Zimbabwe, Department of Land Management.

Ethier, Wilfred. (1972). "Input Substitution and the Concept of the Effective Rate of Protection." *Journal of Political Economy* 80(1): 34-47.

Food and Agriculture Organization of the United Nations (FAO). (1982). *Food Balance Sheets 1979-81.* Rome: FAO.

——————. (various years). *Trade Yearbook, Production Yearbook, Monthly Bulletin of Statistics,* and *Food Outlook.* Rome: FAO.

Frenkel, Jacob A. (1978). "Purchasing Power Parity: Doctrinal Perspectives and Evidence from the 1920s." *Journal of International Economics* 8(2): 169-191.

Gardner, Bruce. (1989). "Recent Studies of Agricultural Trade Liberalization." In Allen Maunder and Alberto Valdes, eds., *Agriculture in an Interdependent World.* Proceedings of the 20th International Conference of Agricultural Economics, Buenos Aires. Oxford: Queen Elizabeth House.

Haggblade, Steven, Peter Hazell and James Brown. (1987). "Farm/Nonfarm Linkages in Rural Sub-Saharan Africa: Empirical Evidence and Policy Implications." AGRAP Economics Discussion Papers No. 2. Washington, DC: World Bank, Agricultural Policies Division, Agriculture and Rural Development Department.

Harberger, Arnold C. (1969). "Professor Arrow on the Social Discount Rate." In G. G. Somers and W. D. Wood, eds., *Cost-Benefit Analysis of Manpower Policies*. Kingston, Ontario: Queen's University. Reprinted in A. C. Harberger (1972), *Project Evaluation*. Chicago: Markham.

——————. (1971). "Three Basic Postulates for Applied Welfare Economics: An Interpretive Essay." *Journal of Economic Literature* 9: 785-797.

Hazell, Peter B. R. and Roger D. Norton. (1986). *Mathematical Programming for Economic Analysis in Agriculture*. New York: Macmillan.

Helpman, Elhanan. (1990). "The Noncompetitive Theory of International Trade and Trade Policy." In Stanley Fischer and Dennis de Tray, eds., *Proceedings of the World Bank Annual Conference on Development Economics*, Supplement to the *World Bank Economic Review*. Washington, DC: World Bank.

Herrmann, Roland, Patricia Schenck, and Manfred Wiebelt. (1990). "On the Measurement of Agricultural Price Protection: How Price Uncertainty and Limited Substitution Matter." Working Paper No. 414. Kiel: Kiel Institute of World Economics.

International Monetary Fund (IMF). (1987). *International Financial Statistics*. Washington, DC: IMF.

Jabara, Cathy L., and Nancy E. Schwartz. (1987). "Flexible Exchange Rates and Commodity Price Changes: The Case of Japan." *American Journal of Agricultural Economics* 69(3): 580-590.

Jabara, Cathy L., and Robert L. Thompson. (1980). "Agricultural Comparative Advantage under International Price Uncertainty: The Case of Senegal." *American Journal of Agricultural Economics* 62(2): 188-198.

Johnson, Harry G. (1965). "The Theory of Tariff Structure, with Special Reference to World Trade and Development." In H. G. Johnson and P. B. Kenen, eds., *Trade and Development*. Geneva: Librairie Droz.

Johnston, Bruce F., and Peter Kilby. (1975). *Agriculture and Structural Transformation: Economic Strategies in Late-Developing Countries*. New York: Oxford University Press.

Johnston, Bruce F., and Thomas P. Tomich. (1985). "Agricultural Strategies and Agrarian Structure." *Asian Development Review* 3(2): 1-37.

Jones, William O. (1987). "Food-Crop Marketing Boards in Tropical Africa." *Journal of Modern African Studies* 25(3): 375-402.

Joshi, Vijay. (1972). "Rationale and Relevance of the Little-Mirrlees Criterion." *Bulletin of the Oxford University Institute of Economics and Statistics* 34(1): 3-32.

Josling, Tim, and Stefan Tangermann. (1989). "Measuring Levels of Protection in Agriculture: A Survey of Methods and Approaches." In Allen Maunder and Alberto Valdes, eds., *Agriculture in an Interdependent World*. Proceedings of the 20th International Conference of Agricultural Economics, Buenos Aires. Oxford: Queen Elizabeth House.

Krueger, Anne O. (1966). "Some Economic Costs of Exchange Control: The Turkish Case." *Journal of Political Economy* 74(5): 466-480.

_____. (1972). "Evaluating Restrictionist Trade Regimes: Theory and Measurement." *Journal of Political Economy* 80(1): 48-62.

_____. (1978). *Liberalization Attempts and Consequences*. Cambridge, MA: Ballinger.

Krueger, Anne O., Maurice Schiff, and Alberto Valdes. (1988). "Agricultural Incentives in Developing Countries: Measuring the Effects of Sectoral and Economywide Policies." *World Bank Economic Review* 2(3): 255-71.

Lipsey, R.G., and K. Lancaster. (1956). "The General Theory of Second-Best." *Review of Economic Studies* 24: 11-32.

Little, Ian M. D., and James A. Mirrlees. (1969). *Manual of Industrial Project Analysis in Developing Countries, vol. 2*. Paris: OECD. Revised and republished in 1974 as *Project Appraisal and Planning for Developing Countries*. New York: Basic Books.

Little, Ian M. D., Tibor Scitovsky, and Maurice Scott. (1970). *Industry and Trade in Some Developing Countries: A Comparative Study*. New York: Oxford University Press.

McIntire, John, and Christopher L. Delgado. (1985). "Statistical Significance of Indicators of Efficiency and Incentives: Examples from West African Agriculture." *American Journal of Agricultural Economics* 67(4): 733-738.

McKinnon, Ronald I. (1979). "Foreign Trade Regimes and Economic Development: A Review Article." *Journal of International Economics* 9(3): 429-452.

Miracle, Marvin P. (1966). *Maize in Tropical Africa*. Madison: University of Wisconsin Press.

Monke, Eric A., and Scott R. Pearson. (1989). *The Policy Analysis Matrix for Agricultural Development*. Ithaca, NY: Cornell University Press.

Mundlak, Yair, Domingo Cavallo, and Roberto Domenech. (1989). "Agriculture and Economic Growth in Argentina, 1913-1984." Research Report 76. Washington, DC: International Food Policy Research Institute (IFPRI).

Musgrave, R.A. (1969). "Cost-Benefit Analysis and the Theory of Public Finance." *Journal of Economic Literature* 7(3): 797-806.

Nelson, Gerald C. and Martin Panggabean (1991). "The Costs of Indonesian Sugar Policy: A Policy Analysis Matrix Approach." *American Journal of Agricultural Economics* 73(3): 703-712.

Officer, Lawrence H. (1976). "The Purchasing-Power-Parity Theory of Exchange Rates: A Review Article." *IMF Staff Papers* 23(1): 1-60.

Palma, Gabriel. (1978). "Dependency: A Formal Theory of Underdevelopment or a Methodology for the Analysis of Concrete Situations of Underdevelopment?" *World Development* 6: 881-924.

Pasour, E. C., Jr. (1980). "Cost of Production: A Defensible Basis for Agricultural Price Supports?" *American Journal of Agricultural Economics* (May): 244-248.

Pearson, Scott R. (1976). "Net Social Profitability, Domestic Resource Costs and Effective Protection." *Journal of Development Studies* 12(4): 321-333.

Pearson, Scott R., and Ronald K. Meyer. (1974). "Comparative Advantage among African Coffee Producers." *American Journal of Agricultural Economics* 56(2): 310-313.

Pearson, Scott R., J. D. Stryker, and C. P. Humphreys. (1981). *Rice in West Africa: Policy and Economics*. Ithaca, NY: Cornell University Press.

Pearson, Scott R., Francisco Avilez, Jeffery W. Bentley, Timothy J. Finan, Roger Fox, Timothy Josling, Mark Langworthy, Eric Monke and Stefan Tangermann (1987). *Portuguese Agriculture in Transition*. Ithaca, NY: Cornell University Press.

Peterson, Willis L. (1979). "International Farm Prices and the Social Cost of Cheap Food Policies." *American Journal of Agricultural Economics* 61(1): 12-21.

Roumasset, James, and Suthad Setboonsarng. (1988). "Second-Best Agricultural Policy: Getting the Price of Thai Rice Right." *Journal of Development Economics* 28: 323-340.

Salter, W.E.G. (1959). "Internal and External Balance: The Role of Price and Expenditure Effects." *Economic Record* 35(71): 226-238.

Samuelson, Paul A. (1962). "The Gains from Trade Once Again." *Economic Journal* 72(288): 820-829.

Scandizzo, Pasquale L., and Colin Bruce. (1980). "Methodologies for Measuring Agricultural Price Intervention Effects." Staff Working Paper No. 394. Washington, DC: World Bank.

Schafer, Hartwig. (1989). "Real Exchange Rates and Economic Performance: The Case of Sub-Saharan Africa." Unpublished Ph.D. dissertation. Raleigh, NC: North Carolina State University, Department of Economics and Business.

Schultz, T. W., ed. (1978). *Distortions of Agricultural Incentives*. Bloomington, IN: Indiana University Press.

Sen, A. K. (1972). "Control Areas and Accounting Prices: An Approach to Economic Evaluation." *Economic Journal* 82: 486-501.

Singh, Inderjit, Lyn Squire, and James Kirchner. (1985). "Agricultural Pricing and Marketing Policies in an African Context: A Framework for Analysis." Staff Working Paper 743. Washington, DC: World Bank.

Sjaastad, Larry A. (1980). "Commercial Policy, True Tariffs, and Relative Prices." In John Black and Brian Hindley, eds., *Current Issues in Commercial Policy and Diplomacy*. New York: St. Martin's Press.

Smith, Adam (1776, 1937), *An Inquiry into the Nature and Causes of the Wealth of Nations*. New York: Random House.

Squire, Lyn, and Herman van der Tak. (1975). *Economic Analysis of Projects*. Baltimore: Johns Hopkins University Press.

Srinivasan, T. N., and Jagdish N. Bhagwati. (1978). "Shadow Prices for Project Selection in the Presence of Distortions: Effective Rates of Protection and Domestic Resource Costs." *Journal of Political Economy* 86(1): 97-114.

Swan, W. (1960). "Economic Control in a Dependent Economy." *Economic Record* 36(73): 51-66.

Thorbecke, Eric. (1990). Review of Eric A. Monke and Scott R. Pearson (1989), *The Policy Analysis Matrix for Agricultural Development*. In *American Journal of Agricultural Economics* 72(2): 511-512.

Tower, Edward. (1984). "Effective Protection, Domestic Resource Costs and Shadow Prices." Staff Working Paper 664. Washington, DC: World Bank.

Unnevehr, Laurian J. (1986). "Changing Comparative Advantage in Philippine Rice Production, 1966-1982." *Food Research Institute Studies* 20(1): 43-71.

Valdes, Alberto. (1986). "Exchange Rates and Trade Policy: Help or Hindrance to Agricultural Growth?" In Allen Maunder and Ulf Renborg, eds., *Agriculture in a Turbulent World Economy*. Proceedings of the Nineteenth International Conference of Agricultural Economists. Oxford: Gower.

Warr, Peter G. (1976). "Benefit-Cost Analysis with Market Distortions: An Indonesian Case Study." *Food Research Institute Studies* 15(1): 1-23.

_____. (1977). "On the Shadow Pricing of Traded Commodities." *Journal of Political Economy* 85(4): 865-872.

_____. (1982). "Shadow Pricing Rules for Nontraded Commodities." *Oxford Economic Papers* 34(2): 305-325.

_____. (1983). "The Domestic Resource Cost as an Investment Criterion." *Oxford Economic Papers* 35(2): 302-306.

Wood, Adrian. (1988). "Global Trends in Real Exchange Rates, 1960-1984." World Bank Discussion Papers No. 35. Washington, DC: World Bank.

World Bank. (1988). *Price Prospects for the Major Primary Commodities.* Three volumes. Washington, DC: World Bank, International Economics Department, International Commodity Markets Division.

_____. (various years). *World Tables.* Washington, DC: World Bank.

_____. (various years). *World Development Report.* Washington, DC: World Bank.

Wrigley, Gordon. (1982). *Tropical Agriculture: The Development of Production* (fourth ed.). London: Longman.

ZIMBABWE

Agricultural Finance Corporation. (various years). *Annual Report.* Harare: Agricultural Finance Corporation.

Agricultural Marketing Authority. (1989). "Groundnut Review Committee Report." Harare: AMA.

_____. (various years). *Annual Economic Review of the Agricultural Industry.* Harare: AMA.

Agritex. (1983). "Wedza Baseline Study: Summary and Analysis." Harare: Ministry of Lands, Agriculture and Rural Resettlement, Department of Agricultural, Technical and Extension Services (Agritex).

Agronomy Institute (various years), *Annual Report.* Harare: Ministry of Lands, Agriculture and Rural Resettlement, Department of Research and Specialist Services (DR&SS).

Bannerman, J. H. (1982). "The Land Apportionment Act: A Paper Tiger?" *Zimbabwe Agricultural Journal* 79(3): 101-106.

Beach, D. N. (1984). *Zimbabwe before 1900*. Gweru: Mambo Press.

Billing, K. J. (1985). *Zimbabwe and the CGIAR Centers: A Study of Their Collaboration in Agricultural Research*. CGIAR Study Paper No. 6. Washington, DC: World Bank.

Blackie, Malcolm J. (1986). "Restructuring Marketing Systems for Small-holders: Cases in Zimbabwe" In J. W. Mellor, C. L. Delgado and M. J. Blackie, eds., *Accelerating Food Production in Sub-Saharan Africa*. Baltimore: Johns Hopkins University Press.

Bratton, Michael. (1986). "Financing Smallholder Production: A Comparison of Individual and Group Credit Schemes in Zimbabwe." *Public Administration and Development* 6: 115-132.

Bratton, Michael, and Kate Truscott. (1985). "Fertilizer Packages, Maize Yields and Economic Returns." *Zimbabwe Agricultural Journal* 82(1): 1-8.

Buccola, Stephen T., and Chrispen Sukume. (1988). "Optimal Grain Pricing and Storage Policies in Controlled Agricultural Economies: Application to Zimbabwe." *World Development* 16(3): 361-371.

Cargill Technical Services. (1989). "Study to Establish the Feasibility of a Bulk Grain Terminal at Beira." Harare: USAID.

Central Statistical Office (CSO). (1984). *1982 Population Census: A Preliminary Assessment*. Harare: Central Statistical Office.

_____. (1985). *Main Demographic Features of the Population of Zimbabwe: An Advance Report Based on a Ten Percent Sample*. Harare: CSO.

_____. (1986a). *Agriculture and Livestock Survey: Communal Lands, 1985/86*. Zimbabwe National Household Survey Capability Program Report No. AL3. Harare: CSO.

_____. (1986b). *Population Projections of Zimbabwe: 1982-2032*. Harare: Central Statistical Office.

_____. (1988). *The Economy of Households in Zimbabwe 1985: Main Preliminary Results from the Income, Consumption and Expenditure Survey 1984/85*. Harare: CSO.

_____. (1989). *Demographic and Health Survey 1988*. Harare: CSO.

_____. (various years). *Quarterly Digest of Statistics* and *Monthly Digest of Statistics*. Harare: CSO.

Chavunduka, G. L., et al. (1982). *Report of the Commission of Inquiry into the Agricultural Industry*. Harare: Zimbabwe Government Printing Office.

Chigume, Solomon, and Thomas S. Jayne. (1990). "Do Underdeveloped Rural Grain Markets Constrain Cash Crop Production? Evidence from Zimbabwe." Paper presented at the Sixth Annual Conference on Food Security Research in Southern Africa, 13 November 1990. Harare: University of Zimbabwe, Department of Agricultural Economics and Extension, Food Security Research Project.

Child, Brian, Kay Muir, and Malcolm Blackie. (1985). "An Improved Maize Marketing System for African Countries: The Case of Zimbabwe." *Food Policy* 10(4): 365-373.

Chipika, Stephen. (1988). "An Evaluation of the Coordinated Agricultural and Rural Development Pilot Crop Project in Gutu District." Harare: Ministry of Lands, Agriculture and Rural Development, Agritex Monitoring and Evaluation Unit.

Chivinga, Augustine O. (1984). "The Role of Herbicide Technology on the Small-Scale Farms on Zimbabwe." *Zimbabwe Agricultural Journal* 81(3): 97-102.

Chr. Michelsen Institute. (1986). "SADCC Intra-Regional Trade Study." Report Prepared for the SADCC Secretariat, Gaborone. Bergen, Norway: Chr. Michelsen Institute.

Cliffe, Lionel. (1986). "Policy Options for Agrarian Reform in Zimbabwe: A Technical Appraisal." Harare: FAO.

Collinson, Michael. (1986). "Eastern and Southern Africa." In John W. Mellor, Christopher L. Delgado, and Malcolm J. Blackie, eds. *Accelerating Food Production in Sub-Saharan Africa*. Baltimore: Johns Hopkins University Press.

Cotton Marketing Board (CMB). (various years). *Annual Report*. Harare: CMB.

Cousins, Ben. (1987). "A Survey of Current Grazing Schemes in the Communal Lands of Zimbabwe." Harare: University of Zimbabwe, Center for Applied Social Sciences (CASS).

_____, ed. (1989). *People, Land and Livestock*. Proceedings of a Workshop on the Socio-Economic Dimensions of Livestock Production in the Communal Lands of Zimbabwe, 12-14 September 1988. Harare: CASS/GTZ.

Crop Breeding Institute. (various years). *Annual Report*. Harare: Department of Research and Specialist Services, Ministry of Lands, Agriculture and Rural Resettlement.

Dailami, Mansour, and Michael Walton. (1989). "Private Investment, Government Policy and Foreign Capital in Zimbabwe." PPR Working Paper No. WPS 248. Washington, DC: The World Bank, Country Economics Department.

Department of Physical Planning. (various years). *Annual Review*. Harare: Ministry of Local Government, Rural and Urban Development, Department of Physical Planning.

Dunlop, H. (1971). *The Development of European Agriculture in Rhodesia, 1945-1965*. Department of Economics Occasional Paper No. 5. Salisbury: University of Rhodesia.

Eurostat. (1990). *Zimbabwe Statistical Review*. Luxembourg: Statistical Office of the European Community (Eurostat).

Food and Agriculture Organization/Harare. (1990). *Irrigation Subsector Review and Development Strategy*. Draft Technical Report No. TCP/ZIM/8955. Harare: Food and Agriculture Organization of the United Nations.

Friis-Hansen, Esbern. (1991). "The Role of the Seed." Unpublished research report. Copenhagen: Center for Development Research.

Friis-Hansen, Esbern, and Roger Mpande. (1990). "Review of Government Plant Breeding in Zimbabwe, with Reference to Its Use by Communal Farmers." Paper presented at the Agricultural Extension Workshop, 18 January 1990. Harare: Zimbabwe Institute of Development Studies (ZIDS).

Gasper, Des R. (1990). "What Happened to the Land Question in Zimbabwe? Rural Reform in the 1980s." Working Paper Series No. 91. The Hague: Institute of Social Studies.

Giga, D. P. (1987). "Viable Grain Storage for Small Farmers in Zimbabwe." In Agritex and R&SS, *Cropping in the Semi-Arid Areas of Zimbabwe.* Proceedings of a workshop held in Harare, 24-28 August 1987. Harare: GTZ.

Giga, D. P., and Y. Katerere. (1986). "Rural Grain Storage in Zimbabwe: Problems, Loss Assessment and Prevention." Harare: ENDA/Zimbabwe and University of Zimbabwe, Department of Crop Science.

Giga, D. P., and T. Rukuni. (1989). "Postharvest Losses and Their Prevention: Research Strategies for SADCC." *SADCC/PFIAU Post-Production Systems Newsletter*, 11:26-36 (Harare: Post-Production Food Industry Advisory Unit).

Gomez, Manel I. (1988). "A Resource Inventory of Indigenous and Traditional Foods in Zimbabwe." *Zambezia* 15(1): 53-73 (Harare: University of Zimbabwe).

Government of Zimbabwe (GOZ). (1981). *Growth with Equity: An Economic Policy Statement*. Harare: Government Printers.

_____. (1982). *Transitional National Development Plan, 1982/83-1984/85*. Harare: Government Printers.

_____. (1986a). *First Five Year National Development Plan, 1986-1990*. Harare: Government Printers.

_____. (1986b). *Socio-Economic Review of Zimbabwe, 1980-1985*. Harare: Government Printers.

_____. (1989). *The Promotion of Investment: Policy and Regulations*. Harare: Government Printers.

_____. (1990). *Economic Policy Statement: Macroeconomic Adjustment and Trade Liberalization*. Budget statement presented to the Parliament of Zimbabwe, July 26. Reprinted from *Parliamentary Debates* 17(26). Harare: Government Printers.

Grain Marketing Board (GMB). (various years). *Report and Accounts*. Harare: GMB.

Grant, Penelope M. (1981). "The Fertilization of Sandy Soils in Peasant Agriculture." *Zimbabwe Agricultural Journal* 78(5): 169-175.

Gustaffson, Allan B. (1987). "Economywide Implications of Resettlement in Zimbabwe." Unpublished Ph.D. dissertation. Stanford, CA: Stanford University, Food Research Institute.

Hall, Susan. (1987), "The Preferential Trade Area for Eastern and Southern African States: Strategy, Progress and Problems." Working Paper No. 453. Nairobi: Institute for Development Studies.

Hawkins, Anthony M., et al. (1988). *Formal Sector Employment Demand Conditions in Zimbabwe*. Harare: University of Zimbabwe Publications.

Hazlewood, Arthur. (1985). "Kenyan Land-Transfer Programmes and their Relevance for Zimbabwe." *Journal of Modern African Studies* 23(3): 445-461.

Hedden-Dunkhorst, Bettina. (1990). "The Role of Small Grains in Semi-Arid Smallholder Farming Systems in Zimbabwe: Preliminary Findings." Bulawayo: SADCC/ICRISAT.

Heidhues, Franz, and Frank Thalheimer. (1986). "Agricultural Production and Marketing in the Communal Areas of Zimbabwe since Independence." Frankfurt: Kreditanstalt fur Wiederaufbau (KfW).

Helmsing, A.H.J. (1987). "Nonagricultural Enterprises in the Communal Lands of Zimbabwe: Preliminary Results of a Survey." Occasional Paper No. 10. Harare: University of Zimbabwe, Department of Rural and Urban Planning.

Herbst, Jeffrey. (1990). *State Politics in Zimbabwe*. Harare: University of Zimbabwe Publications and Berkeley, CA: University of California Press.

Hodder-Williams, Richard. (1983). *White Farmers in Rhodesia, 1890-1965: A History of the Marandellas District*. London: Macmillan.

Hussein, Janet. (1987). "Agroclimatological Analysis of Growing Season in Natural Regions III, IV and V of Zimbabwe." In Agritex and R&SS (1987), *Cropping in the Semi-Arid Areas of Zimbabwe*. Proceedings of a workshop held in Harare, 24-28 August 1987. Harare: GTZ.

Iliffe, John. (1990). *Famine in Zimbabwe, 1890-1960*. Gweru: Mambo Press.

Jackson, J. C., and P. Collier. (1988). "Incomes, Poverty and Food Security in the Communal Lands of Zimbabwe." Occasional Paper No. 11. Harare: University of Zimbabwe, Department of Rural and Urban Planning.

Japanese International Cooperation Agency (JICA). (1989). "Feasibility Study Report on the Establishment of an Ammonia Plant in the Republic of Zimbabwe." Harare: JICA.

Jayne, Thomas L., Munhamo Chisvo, Bettina Hedden-Dunkhorst, and Solomon Chigume. (1990). "Unravelling Zimbabwe's Food Insecurity Paradox: Implications for Grain Marketing Reform." In T. S. Jayne, J. B. Wyckoff, and M. Rukuni, eds., *Integrating Food, Nutrition and Agricultural Policy in Zimbabwe*. Proceedings of a workshop on Food and Nutrition Policy, 16-18 July 1990. Harare: University of Zimbabwe, Department of Agricultural Economics and Extension, Food Security Research Project.

Johnson, R.W.M. (1964). "African Agricultural Development in Southern Rhodesia: 1945-1960." *Food Research Institute Studies* 4(2): 165-223.

Kennan, P. B. (1980). "Agricultural Extension in Zimbabwe, 1950-1980." *Zimbabwe Science News* 14(8): 183-186.

Kingsbury, David S. (1989). "Agricultural Pricing Policy and Trade in Several SADCC Countries: Preliminary Results." In Godfrey Mudimu and Richard H. Bernsten, eds., *Household and National Food Security in Southern Africa*. Proceedings of the Fourth Annual Conference on Food Security Research in Southern Africa, 31 October-3 November 1988. Harare: University of Zimbabwe, Department of Agricultural Economics and Extension, Food Security Research Project.

Kinsey, Bill H. (1983). "Emerging Policy Issues in Zimbabwe's Land Resettlement Programmes." *Development Policy Review* 1(2): 163-96.

Koester, Ulrich. (1986). *Regional Cooperation to Improve Food Security in Southern and Eastern African Countries*. Research Report No. 53. Washington, DC: International Food Policy Research Institute (IFPRI).

LeRoux, A. A. (1969). "African Agriculture in Rhodesia." *Rhodesian Agricultural Journal* 66: 83-89.

Lewis, Stephen R. (1987). "Economic Realities in Southern Africa (or, One Hundred Million Futures)." Research Memorandum No. 107. Williamstown, MA: Williams College, Center for Development Economics.

Mandaza, Ibbo, ed. (1986). *Zimbabwe: The Political Economy of Transition 1980-1986*. Dakar: CODESRIA.

Martin, Roger. (1988). *Southern Africa: The Price of Apartheid*. EIU Special Report No. 1130. London: Economist Intelligence Unit.

Mason, E. (1990). "The Nutrition Situation: Current Strategies and Plans—Consequences of Malnutrition." In T. S. Jayne, J. B. Wyckoff and M. Rukuni, eds., *Integrating Food, Nutrition and Agricultural Policy in Zimbabwe*. Proceedings of a workshop on Food and Nutrition Policy, 16-18 July 1990. Harare: University of Zimbabwe, Department of Agricultural Economics and Extension, Food Security Research Project.

Massell, B. F., and R.W.M. Johnson. (1968). "Economics of Smallholder Farming in Rhodesia: A Cross-Section Analysis of Two Areas." *Food Research Institute Studies* 8(Supplement): 1-74.

Masters, William. (1989). "The Policy Analysis Matrix in Zimbabwe: A Methodological Introduction." Working Paper AEE 6/89. Harare: University of Zimbabwe, Department of Agricultural Economics and Extension.

_____. (1990a). "The Value of Foreign Exchange in Zimbabwe: Concepts and Estimates." Working Paper AEE 2/90. Harare: University of Zimbabwe, Department of Agricultural Economics and Extension.

_____. (1990b). "Dynamic Comparative Advantage of Sorghum and Millets in Zimbabwe." Unpublished consultant's report. Bulawayo: SADCC/ICRISAT.

_____. (1991). "Trade Policy and Agriculture: Measuring the Real Exchange Rate in Zimbabwe." *Quarterly Journal of International Agriculture* 30(1): 21-36.

_____. (1993). "The Scope and Sequence of Grain Market Reform in Zimbabwe." *Food Research Institute Studies* 22(3): 227-251.

Masters, William, and Ernst-August Nuppenau. (1993). "Regional versus Panterritorial Pricing for Maize in Zimbabwe." *World Development* 21(10): 1647-1658.

Meterlerkamp, H.R.R. (1987). "Review of Crop Research Relevant to the Semi-Arid Areas of Zimbabwe." In Agritex and R&SS (1987), *Cropping in the Semi-Arid Areas of Zimbabwe*. Proceedings of a workshop held in Harare, 24-28 August 1987. Harare: GTZ.

Mharapa, L. M. (1985). "Survey of Rice Production Practices in the Masvingo and Manicaland Provinces." *Zimbabwe Agricultural Journal* 82(1): 21-27.

Ministry of Land, Agriculture, and Rural Resettlement (MLARR). (1990). *First Annual Report of Farm Management Data for Communal Area Farm Units, 1988/89 Farming Season*. Harare: MLARR, Economics and Markets Branch, Farm Management Research Section.

Mlambo, Kuphukile. (1989). "Exchange Rate Overvaluation and Agricultural Performance in Zimbabwe: 1965-85." In Godfrey Mudimu and Richard H. Bernsten, eds., *Household and National Food Security in Southern Africa*. Proceedings of the Fourth Annual Conference on Food Security Research in Southern Africa, 31 October-3 November 1988. Harare: University of Zimbabwe, Department of Agricultural Economics and Extension, Food Security Research Project.

Morris, Michael L. (1988). "Comparative Advantage and Policy Incentives for Wheat in Zimbabwe." Economics Working Paper 88/02. Mexico, D.F.: CIMMYT.

Mosley, Paul. (1983). *The Settler Economies: Studies in the Economic History of Kenya and Southern Rhodesia 1900-1963*. Cambridge: Cambridge University Press.

Moyana, Henry V. (1984). *The Political Economy of Land in Zimbabwe*. Gweru: Mambo Press.

Moyo, N. P., R. J. Davies, G.C.Z. Mhone, and L. Pakkiri. (1984). "The Informal Sector in Zimbabwe." Harare: University of Zimbabwe, Department of Economics.

Moyo, Sam, et al. (1989). "Medium and Long-Term Prospects for Economic Development and Employment in Zimbabwe: Agriculture." Harare: Zimbabwe Institute of Development Studies (ZIDS).

Mudenge, S.I.G. (1988). *A Political History of Munhumutapa, c. 1400-1902.* Harare: Zimbabwe Publishing House.

Muir-Leresche, Kay. (1984). "Crop Price and Wage Policy in the Light of Zimbabwe's Development Goals." Unpublished Ph.D. dissertation. Harare: University of Zimbabwe, Department of Land Management.

Muir-Leresche, Kay, and Malcolm J. Blackie. (1988). "Maize Marketing in Eastern and Southern Africa: Increasing the Efficiency of Parastatal Systems." Working Paper AEE 7/88. Harare: University of Zimbabwe, Department of Agricultural Economics and Extension.

Muir-Leresche, Kay, and Tobias Takavarasha. (1989). "Panterritorial and Pan-seasonal Pricing for Maize in Zimbabwe." In G. D. Mudimu and R. H. Bernsten, eds., *Household and National Food Security in Southern Africa.* Proceedings of the Fourth Annual Conference on Food Security Research in Southern Africa, 31 October-3 November 1988. Harare: University of Zimbabwe, Department of Agricultural Economics and Extension, Food Security Research Project.

Mullett, Graham C. (1983). "Land Values and Rural Valuations in Zimbabwe: Part I." Harare: Estate Agents Council.

National Steering Committee for Food and Nutrition. (1990). "The Nutrition Situation: Current Strategies and Plans." In T. S. Jayne, J. B. Wyckoff and M. Rukuni, eds., *Integrating Food, Nutrition and Agricultural Policy in Zimbabwe.* Proceedings of a workshop on Food and Nutrition Policy, 16-18 July 1990. Harare: University of Zimbabwe, Department of Agricultural Economics and Extension, Food Security Research Project.

O'Driscoll, Aidan, and Tobias Takavarasha. (1988). "Crop Price Policy Analysis." Working Paper AEE 5/88. Harare: University of Zimbabwe, Department of Agricultural Economics and Extension.

Palmer, Robin. (1990). "Land Reform in Zimbabwe, 1980-1990." *African Affairs* 89(355): 163-182.

Pinckney, Thomas C. (1990). "The Design of Storage, Trade and Price Policies under Production Instability: Preliminary Results for Maize in Zambia, Zimbabwe and Malawi." Unpublished paper. Williamstown, MA: Williams College, Department of Economics, and Washington, DC: International Food Policy Research Institute.

Rohrbach, David D. (1988). "The Growth of Smallholder Maize Production in Zimbabwe: Causes and Implications for Food Security." Unpublished Ph.D. dissertation. Abbreviated and revised as "The Economics of Smallholder Maize Production in Zimbabwe: Implications for Food Security," MSU International Development Working Paper No. 11 (1989). East Lansing, MI: Michigan State University, Department of Agricultural Economics.

Rukuni, Mandivamba. (1986). "The Evolution of Irrigation Policy in Zimbabwe: 1900-1986." Working Paper No. AEE 4/86. Harare: University of Zimbabwe, Department of Agricultural Economics and Extension.

Rukuni, Mandivamba, and Carl K. Eicher. (1986). "The Food Security Equation in Southern Africa." In M. Rukuni and C. K. Eicher, eds., *Food Security for Southern Africa*. Harare: University of Zimbabwe, Department of Agricultural Economics and Extension, Food Security Research Project.

Rusike, Joseph. (1988). "Prospects for Agricultural Mechanization in Communal Farming Systems: A Case Study of Chiweshe Tractor Mechanization Project." Unpublished M. Phil. thesis. Harare: University of Zimbabwe, Department of Agricultural Economics and Extension.

_____. (1989). "Trader Perceptions of Constraints to Expanding Agricultural Input Trade Among Selected SADCC Countries: Preliminary Results." In G. D. Mudimu and R. H. Bernsten, eds., *Household and National Food Security in Southern Africa*. Proceedings of the Fourth Annual Conference on Food Security Research in Southern Africa, 31 October-3 November 1988. Harare: University of Zimbabwe, Department of Agricultural Economics and Extension, Food Security Research Project.

Shumba, Enos. (1985). "On-Farm Research Priorities Resulting from a Diagnosis of the Farming Systems in Mangwende, a High-Potential Area of Zimbabwe." *Zimbabwe Agricultural Journal*, Research Report No. 5. Harare: Ministry of Lands, Agriculture and Rural Resettlement, Department of Research and Specialist Services, Farming Systems Research Unit.

Sithole, Masipula. (1988). "Zimbabwe: In Search of a Stable Democracy." In Larry Diamond, Juan J. Linz, and Seymour Martin Lipset, eds., *Democracy in Developing Countries*, vol. 2. Boulder, CO: Lynne Rienner.

Smith, R. C. (1982). "Agricultural Research in Zimbabwe." *Zimbabwe Agricultural Journal* 79(1): 29-31.

Stanning, Jayne. (1989a). "Smallholder Maize Production and Sales in Zimbabwe: Some Distributional Aspects." *Food Policy* (August): 260-267.

_____. (1989b). "Grain Retention and Consumption Behaviour among Rural Zimbabwe Households." In G. D. Mudimu and R. H. Bernsten, eds., *Household and National Food Security in Southern Africa*. Proceedings of the Fourth Annual Conference on Food Security Research in Southern Africa, 31 October-3 November 1988. Harare: University of Zimbabwe, Department of Agricultural Economics and Extension, Food Security Research Project.

Stoneman, Colin, ed. (1988). *Zimbabwe's Prospects*. London: Macmillan.

Sunga, E., et al. (1990). "Farm Extension Survey Baseline Survey Results." Unpublished paper. Harare: Zimbabwe Institute of Development Studies (ZIDS).

Takavarasha, Tobias, and Andrew Rukovo. (1991). "The Structure and Development of Incentives for Agriculture in Zimbabwe." Unpublished paper. Kiel, Germany: Kiel Institute of World Economics.

Tattersfield, J.R. (1982). "The Role of Research in Increasing Food Crop Potential in Zimbabwe." *Zimbabwe Science News* 16(1): 6-10.

Torrance, J. D. (1981). *Climate Handbook of Zimbabwe*. Harare: Department of Meteorological Services.

Transport Operators Association. (1990). "Current Problems in Road Transport in Zimbabwe." Harare: Transport Operators Association.

Truscott, Kate. (1985). "Socioeconomic Factors Related to Food Production and Consumption: A Case Study of Twelve Households in Wedza Communal Land." Harare: Ministry of Lands, Agriculture and Rural Development, Agritex Monitoring and Evaluation Unit.

United Nations Development Program. (1987). "Development of the Fertilizer Industry in Zimbabwe." Harare: United Nations Development Program.

Vincent, V., and R. G. Thomas. (1961). "An Agricultural Survey of Southern Rhodesia. Part I: The Agroecological Survey." Salisbury: The Government Printer.

Weiner, Dan, Sam Moyo, Barry Munslow, and Phil O'Keefe. (1985). "Land Use and Agricultural Productivity in Zimbabwe." *Journal of Modern African Studies* 23(2): 251-285.

Weinmann, H. (1972). *Agricultural Research and Development in Southern Rhodesia under the Rule of the British South Africa Company, 1890-1923.* Department of Agriculture Occasional Paper No. 4. Salisbury: University of Rhodesia.

_____. (1975). *Agricultural Research and Development in Southern Rhodesia, 1924-50.* Series in Science No. 2. Salisbury: University of Rhodesia.

Weinrich, A.K.H. (1975). *African Farmers in Rhodesia: Old and New Peasant Communities in Karangaland.* New York: Oxford University Press.

Wells, Peter. (1988). "Irrigation." In M. van Hoffen, ed., *Commercial Agriculture in Zimbabwe 1987/88.* Harare: Modern Farming Publications.

Whitlow, R. (1988). "Land Degradation in Zimbabwe: A Geographical Study." Harare: Natural Resources Board.

Wiebelt, Manfred. (1990). "The Sectoral Incidence of Protection in Zimbabwe." Kiel, Germany: Kiel Institute of World Economics.

World Bank. (1987). *Zimbabwe: An Industrial Sector Memorandum.* Industrial Development and Finance Division, Eastern and Southern Africa Region. Washington, DC: World Bank.

Wright, Neil, and Tobias Takavarasha. (1989). "The Evolution of Agricultural Pricing Policies in Zimbabwe: 1970s and 1980s." Working Paper AEE 4/89. Harare: University of Zimbabwe, Department of Agricultural Economics and Extension.

Yudelman, Montague. (1964). *Africans on the Land.* Cambridge, MA: Harvard University Press.

Zimbabwe Electricity Supply Authority (ZESA). (1988). *Annual Report.* Harare: ZESA.

Index

About the Author

WILLIAM A. MASTERS is an Assistant Professor in the Department of Agricultural Economics at Purdue University. He has worked extensively in Zimbabwe on agricultural policy issues.